*Use everything in your life
to transform yourself into loving,
so the transformation
of the world into loving
can take place.*

John-Roger

Transcendental LEADERSHIP

—— WE BRING LOVE ——

Robert D. Waterman, EdD

BALBOA.PRESS
A DIVISION OF HAY HOUSE

Copyright © 2021 Robert D. Waterman, EdD.

All rights reserved. No part of this book may be used or reproduced by any means, graphic, electronic, or mechanical, including photocopying, recording, taping or by any information storage retrieval system without the written permission of the author except in the case of brief quotations embodied in critical articles and reviews.

Balboa Press books may be ordered through booksellers or by contacting:

Balboa Press
A Division of Hay House
1663 Liberty Drive
Bloomington, IN 47403
www.balboapress.com
844-682-1282

Because of the dynamic nature of the Internet, any web addresses or links contained in this book may have changed since publication and may no longer be valid. The views expressed in this work are solely those of the author and do not necessarily reflect the views of the publisher, and the publisher hereby disclaims any responsibility for them.

The author of this book does not dispense medical advice or prescribe the use of any technique as a form of treatment for physical, emotional, or medical problems without the advice of a physician, either directly or indirectly. The intent of the author is only to offer information of a general nature to help you in your quest for emotional and spiritual well-being. In the event you use any of the information in this book for yourself, which is your constitutional right, the author and the publisher assume no responsibility for your actions.

Print information available on the last page.

ISBN: 978-1-9822-6701-8 (sc)
ISBN: 978-1-9822-6703-2 (hc)
ISBN: 978-1-9822-6702-5 (e)

Library of Congress Control Number: 2021907263

Balboa Press rev. date: 05/10/2021

CONTENTS

Gratitude xi
Preface xiii
Introduction xv

Chapter 1   Science 1
Chapter 2   Love 29
Chapter 3   Soul 51
Chapter 4   Cosmology 77
Chapter 5   Presence 101
Chapter 6   Reflexivity 125
Chapter 7   House 145
Chapter 8   Politics 175
Chapter 9   Sanctuary 205
Chapter 10 Synchronous 227
Chapter 11 Bring 255

Glossary 267
Bibliography 273

GRATITUDE

My gratitude to John Browning, MS, for his transcription, editorial support and being my perennial cheerleader, and to Susan Fey, Jessica Flanagan, Daniel Petersen, and Laurie da Silveira for transcription. Thank you to Joanie Clingan, PhD, for the conversation that inspired this project and for the transcription and editorial support of her staff at Prana, and to Thomas R. Ward, PhD, Director of the NCCR Molecular Systems Engineering Department of Chemistry at University of Basel, Switzerland, for encouraging me into presenting spirituality and science to a group of scientists. My gratitude to the audiences for the original material which came from my webinar in Transcendental Leadership, the I Am Soul, Master of My House retreat in Switzerland, the presentation for the Transcendent Leadership Program at Prana, MSIA, and the presentation at the University of Basel. Special thanks to my wife Karey Thorne, MA, who is my sounding board for almost everything. My infinite gratitude to the transcendent resources whose numinous presence provided the depth of understanding and inspiration for these insights. Finally, great appreciation to Reese Taylor, MA, who brought her talents to the final editing and continuity of the text.

A deep love and gratitude always to my teachers John-Roger, DSS, and Neva Dell Hunter, DDiv, who guided my spiritual travels into the inner worlds, and my understanding of the continuity of the journey of the Soul, Soul transcendence and the true gift of karma.

PREFACE

The shadow that obscures the higher vision of humanity is pan-national. The shadow is a collective force that recruits and coordinates the psyche of like-minded leaders forming a coalition of fear that infuses cultures in a philosophy of eternal conflict and domination as a means of preserving civic order, that is controlled by a dominating elite that always claims that it serves the greater good while guiding policies and actions that protect the elite and produces a world of haves and have-nots. This is a force that communicates sub-rosa through the collective of humanity. Through these devious and insidious means our leaders inadvertently sell out to the dark interests of corporate control and the dark agendas of nations and their leaders that are more interested in power, dominance and profit than cultivating a civilization that fosters the well-being of all.

It is out of our fear and sense of lack that we give ourselves over to such ways of framing our minds and obscuring our perception. Beware of the leader, whether religious or political, who promises you safety, prosperity or salvation that does not exhibit a strong character rooted in eternal love and anchored in Soul as the influencing force of his or her mind, attitudes and actions above all other concerns.

Our challenge appears very much like an extinction event. As in all such events the deeper impulse of the Soul to thrive and transform itself into loving is an eternal force and is unstoppable in the long run. As a collective consciousness of life, we have so far prevailed. Will we continue to prevail? In the long game we are at a turning point. Though ominous, these times embody a great opportunity for humanity to change the narrative. To do so we need to rise above the inversion layer of shadows into transcendent realms and resource what is needed. Prophecy portends a "new day and new dawn." We are that promise. We are the people of prophecy. The mantle of Transcendental Leadership resides within us.

Some say we live in a prophetic time of transformation and change. We live in a time that invites a vision for humanity and leadership based on integrity and spiritual awakening. We create in the world according to our understanding of ourselves and our purpose in life. Whatever the case, I believe it is a time of opportunity and that the challenges of these times call humanity to a new level of evolution.

Remember. As we incarnate into the human condition, the most essential and most forgotten element of life for each of us is that we are the ones that *bring love*. In our first breath, we encounter an overwhelming challenge to identify with the world in which we find ourselves and forget the world of love from whence we came. From our first breath on, we are negotiating our identity. In order to center into and hold our Presence as Transcendental Leaders, remembering who we are in truth (the ones that *bring love*) is essential.

To this end, I invite you to participate in an adventure of Self and the possible blessings that we are yet to fulfill. I encourage you to engage in an exploration of Self that is continuous and reveals the truth of life without fear, inspired by Soul and guided by love. Consider perhaps that the promise of a "new day and new dawn" refers simply to a change of heart. Transcendental Leadership occurs when we connect to our visionary nature, awaken to an integral perspective, and apply our greater virtue and spiritual depth in response to the challenges and callings of life.

INTRODUCTION

At first the concept of Transcendental Leadership may seem a bit abstract. So, let us consider the word, its ramifications, and implications. The dictionary is always a good place to start.

Transcendental:

- *Relating to the spiritual or nonphysical realm: the transcendental importance of each person's Soul.*
- *A priori and necessary to experience.*
- *In mathematics a number that does not have a rational root or is not capable of being produced by a mathematical operation.*

Consider the implication of that which is transcendental cannot be controlled or produced rationally and is the inherent value of each Soul, and precedes, yet is the essence of experience. Does this seem a bit lofty? Consider that love, gratitude, respect, kindness, inspiration, and visionary practices cannot be controlled, and are implicit to each Soul, and a priori yet known through experience. Some might say that jealousy, hate, fear, violence, and shame fit the same construct; however, these do not rise above or provide resolution to conflict, divisiveness, polarization and division, which are implicit to our Ego. Our Ego is a transactional construct based on managing life as mirrored through environmental, survival, social, and prestige needs. In Transcendental Leadership, our Soul overlights and permeates our Ego, and our material life becomes congruent with the expression of our Soul. We are able to grasp choices in terms of long range good for all rather than short range gains for the few. From the transcendental perspective, we will consider the consequences of our choices for at least seven generations.

In the polity of the United States and the world as well, we experience increasingly entrenched polarization and tribalism which creates a barrier to the guidance of our higher virtues. In our human endeavors, whether we are dealing with the civil affairs of social need and political power, environmental health and extractive wealth, or scientific discovery and its right use, the belief in our ability to find solutions from the same transactional level as the issue dooms us to repeat iterations of the same dilemmas. As exhilarating as righteousness may be, it does not transcend the fray; it does not reverse the downward spiral that dissipates love and leaves us in fear. Transformational Leadership moves us to realign our expression with a higher order. Transcendental Leadership portends a change in reality in which we change the context that supports negative expression in a way that it either no longer exists or cannot thrive.

In the transcendental approach to leadership, our identity derives from our sense of Soul and we live in a context of a love-based cosmology, in contrast to a fear-based cosmology. Our process becomes an eternal connection to the higher dimension of ourselves. Our Ego in and of itself is a management system for surviving in the material world and is insufficient, in and of itself, to rise above its conditioning and strategies for surviving and commitment to thriving in those conditions. At some point, we reach an impasse that directs us to deeper and higher constructs of how we know ourselves. In this quest, we find a depth of love and transcendent inspiration that is of a higher dimension of consciousness. Our sense of connectedness to a transcendental realm enables us to think, love, and envision holistic resolutions to the traps of duality and materialistic reflective definitions of self.

From the transcendent qualities of human consciousness, our connection to unconditional love and kinship with all life and substance is evident. As a consequence, we can find solutions that are systemically healthy and generative. Even in science we are no longer limited by the enigma of quantum vs. material science because we become the agency of fourth and fifth-dimensional physics. The evolution of our humanity and our endeavor to create and maintain civilization has been a problematic, hard-won adventure. When we look at the full length of our trajectory, we are on the eve of a make-or-break opportunity. Is this world a good place for all of us or just for a few? Do we choose love or fear as the basis of our policies? Both have power. Fear-based choice employs the power of domination. Love-based choice initiates the power of love.

The transcendental perspective of leadership is not against the amazing developments of humanity. In the nature of transcendence, all creation is incorporated into an expanding perspective and increasing complexity that can perceive the true causality of numinous realities and use the practical ways of science and governance to develop methods and technologies that are conduits of the cosmic energy of the whole.

Our scientific and social actions must no longer fight the physics of love that forms the matrix of life and is the impulse of evolution. When we reach into the transcendent realms of self, our Soul appears. We realize that conflict, global warming, the haves and have nots which now inspire polarization, tribal politics and war, and the dystopian specter of environmental disasters are fertile fields for Transcendental Leaders that recognize that these situations are symptomatic of our reluctance to embrace a higher order of human nature as embodied by Jesus, Buddha, Mohammed, Lao Tso, Krishna, Quetzalcoatl, Dekanahwida and others. Facing the pure radiant form of the Soul takes great courage.

My understanding of leadership evolved through actions that deepened my sense of self and the ways that the richness and power of the human Soul impacts society. Of the many styles of leadership, there are examples of men and women who reach into a higher visionary perspective for the solutions to the challenges that confront them. Inspired and charismatic leaders have arisen to show the way. The politically astute inheritors capture their legacy or go underground to preserve the inner flame awaiting a more opportunistic time. In our ability to know the truth, the power, and mystery of love, we must each reach into our full capacity and take responsibility as Transcendental Leaders. As Transcendental Leaders, we open into the higher realms of love for guidance and vision and ultimately inherit the ability to translate transcendence into practicality, into common human good.

At the height of my activity in the Civil Rights Movement of the 1960s, I met a blind preacher in Georgia who lived fearlessly and was highly respected and inclusive of the racial divide of his community. He had respect from his black and white constituencies. In our meetings, he would light us up with his Presence. *This Little Light of Mine*, a popular song in the Civil Rights Movement, was his favorite. In him, in his humility, enthusiasm, and love, I experienced a depth of Soul. His leadership was transcendent and out of that came everything else. I saw this same quality in Dr. Martin Luther King. Non-violent direct action was the result of a transcendental awakening, developed by Gandhi and also applied by King. This realization became the lens through which I re-evaluated myself and my actions to make a better world. When motivated as Transcendental Leaders, we may become fatigued from time to time, but not disillusioned.

My activism translated into its source, the human Soul. My studies then focused on social change and awakening to the potential of Soul. I was curious about how some are so easily swayed by the powerful and the charismatic while others have the strength of character to stay true to their higher angels. I was attending the University of California at Santa Barbara in the so-called awakening of the 1960s. Exposed to many experiments and debates, I had two main educational drives: to awaken spiritually and to transform society. The decade of the sixties gave me my foundation. I met spiritual teachers who initiated me into the transcendence of the Soul and the transformative action of Karma.

Nations have spiritual destinies. I was intrigued by the Founders of the American Dream. Most of them held a transcendent perspective as participants in transcendentalism, spiritism, Rosicrucianism, and Masonic studies. America's destiny was guided and founded on the principle of Transcendental Leadership. Though highly compromised by the overlay of greed, entitlement, and power that perpetuated indigenous genocide and the preservation of a slave economy, our destiny called us to establish the higher ideals of freedom, justice, love and opportunity. Our hope is in the awakening of the Transcendental Leader within each of us in significant visionary ways and the more modest ways of kindness, gratitude, respect, and love.

Ralph Waldo Emerson's 1837 address to the Phi Beta Kappa Society at Cambridge was called the *American Scholar:*

> *A nation of men [and women] will for the first time exist, because each believes himself [herself] inspired by the Divine Soul which also inspires all men [and women].*

Emerson admonished the gathered students to leave their small ways and the blind policies of the established tradition of the times and to take up the cause. We will explore more about Emerson later.

In terms of politics, each Soul must awaken and vote or the beguiling and powerful will dominate and the nation will ultimately fall. As Transcendental Leaders, we must each take into ourselves the anointing given by Emerson to the American Scholar. From my perspective it is in the DNA of the United States in particular and in the nations of the world in general to fulfill their destined higher virtue.

As Emerson challenged the American Scholar, each Nation has a higher calling that is persistent and emergent. Though for a time dominated by our lesser virtues, this calling will emerge as our Soul becomes our source. In a national atmosphere of "true believers" and science deniers contrasted to those telling truth to power, the extremes are too hypnotized by the exhilaration and false redemption of self-righteousness to rise to the more excellent vision of Transcendental Leadership. Even with Marianne Williamson and others challenging us with her *politics of love*, the fascination with polarization, conflict and domination is great.

Many years before the vision of Emerson and the American Transcendentalists, in the formation of the United States, Benjamin Franklin and others moderated an educational forum between the Iroquois, or rather the Haudenosaunee, (pronounced "hoo-dee-noh-SHAW-nee") confederation and the gathering league of the 13 colonies. The Haudenosaunee Confederation is perhaps one of the oldest democracies in the world. It was founded on the vision of Dekanahwida. As the story goes, he inspired Hiawatha to establish the Confederation, symbolized with a white pine (called the Tree of Peace) with roots reaching in the four directions and an eagle perched on top. The roots spread in the four directions so that everyone could find their way to the great tree of peace. The tree reached up as a bridge between heaven and earth spreading its branches as a refuge and the eagle perched atop the tree as the protector and messenger to the transcendental sky worlds. The needles of the pine represented arrows which when bound together can't be broken. All policies of the council were measured by their impact on the descendants of the seventh generation.

On the Great Seal of the United States the Old-World transcendental teachings are symbolized as the pyramid and the all-seeing eye and on the obverse by the indigenous transcendent teaching seen as the Eagle holding the arrows and olive branch. In 1988 the U.S. Senate paid tribute to the influence of the constitution and principles of the Haudenosaunee Confederation on the democratic governing of the 13 colonies and formulation of the U.S. Constitution. Essentially the vision of Dakanawida translated into the symbols, principles, and constitution of the United States of America. The transcendent vision that founded America as a nation is based on a comingling of the higher vision of the *old-world* visionaries and *indigenous* wisdom. The common threads are that loyalty to one's Soul, respect for one another, and gratitude for all of life are the keys to peace and the transformation of the world. These threads are providing our guidance.

Out of this history from the 13 colonies and indigenous nations came the philosophical reflection and spiritual practices that formed the foundation of Southwestern College in Santa Fe, New Mexico. Southwestern College is a graduate school for the study of counseling, art therapy, and visionary practice based on a curriculum of spiritual foundation that I founded with others in 1976, the 200th anniversary of the founding of the United States of America. The mission statement of the college is *transforming consciousness through education*. Our experience with the evolution of the college and its many challenges further developed and shaped my understanding and appreciation of Transcendental Leadership.

When we each look deeper, we see that we each have a life that fosters re-centering ourselves in the higher virtues of love, kindness, respect, sustainability, reverence, gratitude, and care for the seventh generation, thereby piercing the internal barriers of fear that block transcendental awareness. As a world humanity, we face a crisis in character which threatens our visionary hopes. With the risk of repeating, as in the introduction to this writing reflects, the call to Transcendental Leadership is imperative.

A new world will not arise from an old conversation.
A solely material, mechanistic and rationalistic analysis of the world as it is,
is an inadequate translator into what can be.
The intelligence of the heart is as necessary for transformation
as is the intelligence of the brain.

Marianne Williamson

CHAPTER ONE

Science

...

I had the opportunity to speak to a group of scientists in Switzerland on the topic of spirituality in science. My background is in the social sciences and spiritual education. I view what I do with my research into consciousness and its application to personal and social transformation as equivalent to the rigor of material science. I was mildly intimidated at first by the invitation. I was not sure how this audience would respond or if the metaphors familiar to me in the American social and spiritual science world would translates gracefully into an unfamiliar mind set. Perhaps my caution was unfounded because of the influence of Carl Jung in the formation of my approach to the Soul and the science of psychology. Jung does not represent the span of my endeavor to discover and communicate the depth of the human mystery and enterprise as spiritual science but represents an apt beginning, or mind set, for this forum and my journey with the gathered participants into the world of spirituality in science.

I was aware that we do our work in our own silos, so to speak, and even within each branch of science there are many silos. (A silo is an agriculture storage tower for grain and is used as a metaphor for organizations that communicate vertically and keep to themselves with little or no horizontal communication with other silos.) It's like getting into our little silos to work and staying in a different silo from most people represented in the meeting room for some time. In my silo the laboratory is inside, it's internal and so I spend a lot of time inside. I discovered that some of the terminology from the material science/quantum physics silo was well suited for articulating the internal experiences of my spiritual science silo.

Working in our own silo is very isolating and leads us to believe that the limits of our cosmology describe the whole of reality. We bracket our focus so we can concentrate on something manageable. On the downside we eliminate significant variables that consequently remain unseen. Though I was nervous at first, as I spoke to the gathered scientists, my sense was that we shared from a deeper level based on our love for discovery, we shared a common resonance and that we could connect on a visionary level, transcend our narrative habits and share meaningfully with each other. As it turned out, I was right. My talk was very well received. Having said that, we began our discussion of spirituality in science with just two silos and the premise that those who seek a more scientific approach to spirit and those who seek a more spiritual approach to science will join to lead the way. As well, we shared a vision that the dialogue between spirituality and science is at the heart of the emerging call for Transcendental Leadership.

For the physical scientist, the focus is on the material because that can be measured. The physical scientists put a bracket around the physical world and that is what they study using physical instruments to make those measurements. For the spiritual scientist, they focus through their faculties of awareness into the inner worlds of psychic and spiritual reality. Spiritual scientists' awareness is the measure and their calculus is metaphoric and analogic. Interestingly, both are motivated, to some degree, by their transcendental faculties. To excel, both are visionary. The spiritual scientist needs a *scientific attitude* to test their subjectivity and the physical scientist needs a *transcendental attitude* to inspire research. Increasingly with the advent of quantum physics, the two realms have shared realities.

To set the tone of our inquiry, consider this statement made by Albert Einstein.

Anyone who is seriously involved in the pursuit of science becomes convinced that a spirit is manifest in the laws of the universe, a spirit vastly superior to man and one in the face of which we with our own modest powers must feel humble.

I am humbled and I would like to suggest in the beginning and maybe at the end that in every research we do and everything we explore, that we are discovering ourselves. In some way our activity reflects the actualization of our spiritual journey for both the physical and spiritual scientist. We know that the electromagnetic physical world is measurable and that the psychic/spiritual energy of the so-called invisible world is measured through awareness, experience and results. We, as physical and spiritual beings, are central to the evolutionary arc. To a large degree, the bias of the physical scientist is that our consciousness is an epigenetic phenomenon of our biological evolutions. The inclination of the spiritual scientist is that our biology is an epigenetic phenomenon of our consciousness.

Transcendent Self

My first big persuasive introduction to my inner reality is important to this discussion because it oriented me to a particular way of looking at life, spiritually and scientifically. When I was nineteen, I was in a sensory deprivation experiment sponsored by the U.S. military. I was placed in a small cubicle without light or sound for three days. It was my first serious exposure to the scientific method. They gave us tests that reflected our concepts, beliefs, and attitudes. The tests measured our stereotypes and whether or not the disorientation of sensory deprivation could influence those beliefs. They gave us the test before and after the deprivation and periodically they verbally exposed us to stereotypical information during the test period. They were trying to find out if the sensory deprivation made us more susceptible to belief change. They also noted how much the sensory deprivation influenced our cognitive and emotional states. Did we lose it? Did we come apart? They were looking for answers about how people were brainwashed in the Korean War. As it turned out, rather than being disoriented and more susceptible to suggestions the experience put me more together and awakened in me a deeper and more tangible understanding of my spiritual nature.

In the experiment, we were matched in a test and control group. The test group entered the cubicle and the control group lived their normal daily routine. I was in the test group, which meant that I spent three days and nights in a small room without any light or sound. The room was kept at normal body temperature. The idea was to lose awareness of our bodily boundaries, among other things. The absence of physical light and sound deconstructed the normal operation of our lives. All of us are accustomed to our visual world of reflective light, relating to other people, sound, light, and with the physical body as the center of our sensory reality. Our thoughts and beliefs, as well as, what we make up and decide, are in relationship to our bodies. For example, who am I? What do I look like? How do I appear? What gender am I? All of these questions are reflective of being in a physical body. When we start deconstructing these relationships, we begin to loosen the matrix of our mind, in a sense. When that happens, something that is deeper within us can emerge if we are open to the experience. If we are too survival and fear-based, that emergence can be very frightening, and we will "freak out" or grasp, even embrace, whatever contact is extended to us from external sources.

In my test group there were four people and I was the only one who stayed for the three day duration of the experiment. The others either couldn't take being alone for that long or they couldn't handle the scattering of their consciousness. One person suffered from severe muscle cramps from being in a confined space for a lengthy period. After about a day or so, I lost track of time and my physical boundaries. Early on, I experienced a brief episode of every shrill sound I had ever heard going through my nervous system. The only disturbing part of the experience for me was due to the auditory release of every discordant or shrill sound I remembered, mostly fire engines and air raid sirens. And then it was really quiet. In that quiet, in that stillness, the only thing I could do was be present with myself.

After the first day, I found myself in another dimension in which perceived light radiated out of objects and forms instead of being reflected off of them. The colors were incredible, far brighter and more vibrant and impressive than the colors of the physical dimension. And there were several realms of that inner reality in which forms were different, but they all had a quality of radiant light. Then every once in a while, I had an experience in which I would fly out of body over my home neighborhood. I was nineteen and I was homesick, so I'd fly home and check things out and then come back. That went on frequently and it was pretty clear that it wasn't a dream because it was just like flying home except, different. As we will discover, I left the world of electromagnetic reality and entered the realm of dark energy and matter. Since I had used art to process many of my adolescent issues, I used art as well to process the symbolic and metaphoric content of my highly enlivened inner experiences. Later we will learn that I brought the *science of correspondence* to the more conventional aspect of this research design.

After this experiment was completed and with the impact on me internalized, I completed my military duty and returned to the university. The research experience made tangible the accounts of spiritual worlds and out of body experiences that I had read about and been fascinated by in the Bible. Since a new dimension of reality was now open to me, when I returned to the University, I spent half of my time with academic studies and the other half with spiritual studies. I wanted to know more about my experience. One of the things I discovered was that some of the metaphors, descriptions, and discoveries in quantum physics, through the science of correspondence, gave insights into the spiritual world and vice versa. The metaphors and analogies of the spiritual world clarified the physics.

Alexander

Eben Alexander is a renowned neurosurgeon and a scientist. He was a well-known neurobiologist and neurosurgeon. He was committed to the perspective that our consciousness is an epiphenomenon of the brain, meaning that consciousness is caused by the brain. Then came his transformation in 2008. He became ill with a very severe case of meningitis that placed him in a coma. It took his brain function down to zero. There was no way his brain could produce consciousness. He was barely alive, physically. In his coma, he had an incredible experience of the inner worlds. His description of his experience was far more impressive than the experiences I had during my sensory deprivation and yet was related. He went to different realms and levels of consciousness. Objects and structures illuminated from within. His internal travel started in a very dense area and went to a lighter more glorious place. He heard music upon which he could travel from one level to the next. He found that if he paid attention to the Sound, it would provide a way to transport him to these different levels. His experience took him into a central place of consciousness that seemed to radiate a tremendously powerful energy of love.

When he came back into his body, he healed all of the damage from his illness. This is not uncommon in NDE (near death experience) cases. I understand that whatever that consciousness is, it will heal or revive the physical body. When he came back, when his consciousness came back to the physical body, his body began to heal. His body healed to the same intellect and level of functioning he had before his illness with the addition of an incredible understanding of the nature of reality and a powerful sense of love. He got his health back completely and had a spectacular recall of his experience throughout the process.

He didn't return to neurosurgery. He changed his profession to teaching about his experience, researching near death experiences and creating ways to help people access other dimensions of themselves as a means to greater health, well being and liberation. It was quite an experience for me to be able to hear about his adventure and subsequent conversion and be able to relate to it. And, yes, he concluded that the brain was an epiphenomenon of consciousness.

Traction

There's a fascinating thing about what happens to the physical body when exposed to higher dimensions of energy. My experience is that when I'm in my physical body, as my awareness opens to the deeper dimensions of self, each frequency level has a sensation of energy permeating my body along with an expanded awareness. When the transcendent experience is out of body, there is a distinctive visual and felt sense. On returning to my body, there is a corresponding felt sense. By focusing I can enter different places within these particular dimensions.

Jim Beachler, a neurocosmologist at the University of West Virginia, points to our neural-net as the crossover of psi-energy and the physical body as the place to focus scientific research. His perspective is that we need tangible traction to measure adequate scientific research. His theory is that when somebody comes back from a near death experience, NDE, or in a deep state of meditation such as samadhi, it rewrites the neural network. Beachler also observed that collectively there is an increased occurrence of such experiences suggesting an evolutionary process or progression.

Implicate Order

David Bohm is a foundational thinker in Quantum Physics. His theory of the implicate order and explicate order corresponds to the spiritual and physical relationship we have been describing. The explicate physical order unfolds from the dimensional implicate order. Things that are physical matter unfold from this background of energy. In his model, all cause is non-local, meaning that the cause occurs in a higher order implicate reality. Anything that happens physically, even us being in this moment of reading my writing has a synchronicity, a confluence of non-local causes, that began with our interest and imagination of meeting just now. Imagination is a dimension of the implicate order. Inspiration is an even deeper dimension. Our Presence in the physical, local, space, unfolded from our non-local imagination and intent. Therefore, the brain is an epiphenomenon of consciousness. From this perspective, we have agency in unfolding from the implicate order.

When we go back and review the Copenhagen double split experiment, they found that light was wave or particle depending upon how we "looked" at it. It started the whole idea of the observer effect. Since then we have been puzzling over all of the ways the observer impacts the observed. At the subatomic level in quantum physics, it's pretty easy to see that observation has an impact. But then out here in the physical world of our lives we might ask what do you mean...I observe something and wonder if I can make a truck show up out of seemingly nothing or something? Well that's the wrong question because in the complexity of our consciousness and the complexity of our group relationships, the observer aspect is a bit more complex. Then we might ask, why does a prolonged political demonstration change a government? My explanation is that at some point, there is a critical mass and enough observation effect is created to shift the consciousness.

The implication of Beachler's and Anderson's perspective is that when we have an awakening or activation of the deeper dimensions of ourselves, which changes our neural network, it changes how we are physically. It changes how we look at things. So it's going to have a different impact on what we are doing in our research. Beachler points out that this issue is further compounded because our perception is programed to see the physical world as three dimensional when in actuality, it is four dimensional. We are excluding variables that, when measured, would more clearly reflect the four dimensions of the physical reality. There are many subtle forces at play which include mass, magnetism, gravity, bioelectrical fields, and even attitudes. From a transcendent perspective the wave/particle phenomenon becomes...both wave and particle. How do we know that the quantum isn't observing us and deciding whether to manifest as a wave or particle? Perhaps the universe is watching us and deciding how to appear?

Science of Correspondence

The primary mode of discovery for spiritual scientists is direct experience translated through the language of metaphor and analogy. The primary mode of discovery for the material scientist is to translate the observation through mathematics. For the trained material scientist, the observer effect can be a nuisance. For the trained spiritual scientist, the observer effect is the point. When we are having a conversation, it is in the context of observing each other. Our dialogue produces understanding, truth, and transformation that is the result of our underlying intention. The spiritual scientist operates in this form of dialogue with research. The more the material scientist attempts to compensate through objectivity, the research increasingly responds as an object. I suggest that the material scientist's skepticism regarding experience comes from an issue of trust in their own sensibility. We recall the wise words of Socrates:

> *People make themselves appear ridiculous when they are trying to know obscure things before they know themselves.*

Scientific correspondence works through *pattern matching*. Pattern matching is when we focus on a symbol or image and imagine a place or sound with specific intent creating a resonant response that brings our consciousness and that specific transcendent pattern together. The following are examples of some of the ways *pattern matching* function in the science of correspondence. We may visualize ourselves in a place and join the place in our subtle body. Mantras can serve to track our awareness into the sound current. We can engage and activate various centers of consciousness by joining those frequencies through pattern matching. We can also access and recall information of transcendent resources from events in our lives.

Kazanis

In his book *The Reintegration of Science and Spirituality*, Kazanis demonstrates in a convincing and detailed way the correspondence between material and spiritual science, subtle energy and dark energy, and the complementary endeavor of our metaphorical and rational nature. In this section I will extrapolate from his in-depth discussion as it supports the purpose of this writing. If you like this discussion, you will enjoy reflecting on Kazanis' deep dive as a biophysicist and spiritual practitioner into the nature of reality and scientific discovery.

We are reminded that the great minds of science were visionary and had a knowing sense of themselves; some were even mystics. Kazanis makes this simple observation encouraging a complementary spiritual science alongside our highly effective material science.

> *This may give insight into why Western Science techniques have been so successful in exploring the physical universe. The best suggestion might be that scientific thought can be based on precise connections utilized naturally by the human mind. So for example, when we utilize precise logical connections we develop our Western science. But since the human mind can think and connect in other ways as well, such as analogically or metaphorically, it would therefore seem reasonable that*

> *precise analogical* connections could also be developed into a science. The determinant factor for creating a science may not be dependent upon the *type* of mental connection, but rather the *precision* of the mental connection. Poor logic obviously leads to an inaccurate conclusion, as would a bad analogy. (Kazanis,99)

The larger portion of the energy and matter of our physical universe is (so-called) dark. The reason it is called dark matter and energy is that it has no electrical charge so there is no apparent light in the physical sense of light. Things in the physical world have an electrical charge, and as a result we have chemistry and atomic building blocks that make structural forms. Electromagnetic energy knits together and holds this reality whereas dark matter and energy have a different physics. It does have physics. I call it Spiritual Physics. With my experience in sensory deprivation and many years of working with applications of consciousness, it's clear to me that dark matter is somehow similar to the darkness that was lit up in my experience in the sensory deprivation cubicle. It is another dimension that is tangible to our internal sensory awareness in a corresponding way as the material world is tangible to our physical senses. Dark matter has a different physics in which light comes out of things that seem to be material but clearly are not physical. Perhaps it is a different kind of photon. The use of the term "dark" should not be conflated with the religious or superstitious use of dark meaning something sinister or devoid of holiness. The opposite is true. When we speak of dark matter and energy, we refer to the spiritual dimension out of which the physical dimension unfolds: "Darkness was over the surface of the deep, and the Spirit of God was hovering over the waters. And God said, Let there be light and there was light." (Genesis 1:2)

According to Kazanis, Dark energy constitutes 68% of the density of the universe and dark matter 26.3% of the density, making normal physical matter and energy composition under 5% of the density of the universe. Interestingly, this is similar to the ratios of physical energy to subtle energy (consciousness) within the human construction. When we model consciousness composed of physical, imaginative, emotional, mental, archetypal, and soul dimensions, we can see an analogous pattern of the seen to the unseen. Our physical body is less than 5% of our consciousness. With dark matter and energy, there is a gravitational attraction, therefore subtle and physical energies and forms have a common coherence. In spiritual terms, this coherence is unconditional love. In this sense, conditional love analogously integrates polarities and resolves charges from forming limitations and barriers. As dark matter and energy interpenetrate the planets of the universe, subtle energy interpenetrates the physical body, so, by analogy, they are the same.

Energy Lense

Our physical senses are due to the property of electrical charge and the myriad ways those charges shape and combine to form tangible realities into a form we can grasp for study. Subtle energy and dark matter lack such a charge thus they are able to pass through physical electrically charged matter just as subtle energy can pass through physical matter. Consider too that dark energy and matter and subtle energy make up the implicate order as theorized by Bohm. Bohm's theory states that physical reality and the explicate order unfolds from the implicate order. By developing our capacity to experience, we sense subtle energy through the instrument of our physical, emotional, and mental bodies. In the realm of dreams, we are in a reality in which subtle forms are solid; thus our five senses extend into perceptual realms beyond those prescribed by an electrical charge. Dreams and extrasensory awareness are perceptual but not electrical.

We are looking at the universe through a lens of comingling fields of visible and invisible energy in which waveforms collapse into structural forms on various dimensions. Rupert Sheldrakes' theory of the morphogenetic field as form-making transfers information through morphic resonance. Much like the relationship of the implicate and explicate order, morphic resonance theorizes that biological organization occurs through the information transmitted through resonance in the morphic field. This theory of resonance also sheds light on metaphors as the mathematics of the mystic and the efficacy of the Science of Correspondence. Species communicate through vibrational resonances. When one in the species learns they all learn. Through resonance then, we are continually communicating with each other and with ourselves and the whole. Correspondingly, when we learn we add knowledge and understanding to the collective of humanity.

Ervin Laszlo invites us into the Akashic Field (perhaps another perspective on dark energy and matter). The observed universe is embedded into a secondary field (Akashic Field) that is a continuous memory of the transactions of reality that existed before there was form. The universe is an expression of this energy into higher density and expansive complexity. Our material and spiritual science is a discovery of the Akasha and its consequences. In this regard, intellectual and experiential knowledge are different, yet complementary. Material and spiritual science posit a pre-universe from which our universe is a manifestation. The blueprint of the physical universe is the Akasha.

Summary

Thus far, we have explored the relationship between material and spiritual scientific endeavors through correspondence. Emanuel Swedenborg's mystical discoveries demonstrate the application of the Science of Correspondence. Metaphor, analogy, and symbol are the mathematics of Spiritual Science, coding the experimental equations, transactions, and geometries in the laboratory of subtle realities of Akasha. They have an objective connection, which is not necessarily logical. The Akasha is living energy. For example, the individual mandala is an actual correspondence with the whole. In Bohm's theory the implicate and explicate order are contained and guided by the unified movement of the whole or holomovement. Bohm's model corresponds to the theories of dark matter and energy, Akasha and the morphic field.

George Washington Carver

My favorite example of a spiritual scientist and a Transcendental Leader is the life and work of George Washington Carver. By looking at his life and the things that he did, we can perhaps get an insight into how it would be to live as a fully integrated spiritual and material scientist and Transcendental Leader. He's not as commonly known these days but in the late 1800s and early 1900s, Carver was very well known.

Awakening

Carver was a black man living in Alabama for most of his career. He was born in the Southern part of the United States before slavery had ended and unfortunately his parents died when he was young. He held an exceptional consciousness. Early on, he sought out any education he could get, which is a major accomplishment in itself considering the life-constraints for black citizens in the South at that time. When he was still a young person, he was meditating in the loft of a barn and had an experience in which it seemed like God overlighted him, permeating his being. This Presence came and stayed with him. It introduced him to the spiritual aspect of life, the fourth or fifth dimensional part, and anchored awareness of God into his physical body and permeated his mind and emotions with it. That's exciting enough, but what he did with it was even more impressive.

By looking more carefully at the dynamics of his life and his psychology, we can pick up clues about how we might access a more powerful sensitivity regarding who we are in relationship to the universe in which we live, the natural flow of things and how we unfold and tap into the secrets that we are trying to find in our research. As a young boy, Carver discovered his ability to attune to nature. He was fully aware of his consciousness of love and God; he experienced God as an all-inclusive higher consciousness, permeating all things. He became sensitive to those plants that held a specific remedy or application for the benefit of humanity.

Development

He pursued his education with a singularity of purpose, hard work and humility. By doing laundry, he finally worked his way through university and graduate school. He took up a position at Tuskegee Institute in Alabama, which was the first black college in the United States. He was tasked with setting up their agricultural research department.

As Carver gained technical, scientific and academic training, he seamlessly incorporated his spiritual understanding into his growing breadth of knowledge and consciousness. I'll give an example. As an outreach to farmers in the area, he would go around and teach improved crop methods. As a result, their crops grew better and had better yields. The farming improvements that he taught worked so well that they produced too many peanuts. The farmers were going broke because they couldn't sell their harvest. He asked God if there was something else the peanut could do besides just being something that we eat? Through his rapport with higher consciousness and nature, he went out into the fields and talked to the peanut. Through a higher dimension, he was shown the purpose and uses for which the peanut was created. (Plants and everything in creation come with some gift or purpose or something to fulfill.) He went on to create all kinds of applications for the peanut. He synthesized plastics, fabrics, lotions, and many other things from the peanut, by listening to what the peanut said about what it was meant to do. Then, he would take that information back to the laboratory and, with his chemistry, translate the metaphor into laboratory experiments. He was a biochemist and he synthesized in the laboratory the products that fulfilled the purpose of the peanut developing over 300 products including flour, paste, insulation, paper, wall board, wood stains, soap, shaving cream and skin lotion, and he also experimented with medicinal remedies. At that time, he was credited with saving the agricultural economy of the South. He also developed hundreds of products from sweet potatoes and soybeans. He made many other discoveries by talking to plants and taking what they revealed into the laboratory. When we find the resonant frequency matching us to the plant, we experience a synchronous communication through which love and information shares. I do recommend that as scientists, we talk to our research. In nature there's a purposefulness to everything.

Application

Carver would always carry a flower with him. He said this was his way of tuning into God. The flower was his way of focusing his mind, tuning in, and accessing the field of wisdom from which he gained knowledge and insight about the essence, inner purpose and material value of plants and elements in the natural world. In other words, when Bohm was talking about the implicate order and how waveforms collapse and, by observation, become a physical form, he was talking about agency. By agency, I mean that by our Presence we are an instrument of creation. Through our witness we give awareness to the whole. It's a compelling version of the observer effect. Bohm's view was that perhaps as we are observing the photon through an experiment, maybe the photon was also observing us and also making a decision about whether to be a particle or a wave. The research was a dialogue, an intimate relationship. When we look at the example of Carver, we can see a demonstration that it was very much that kind of conversation. Carver's observation and his consciousness of the whole and nature in the particular case to which he held his focus was symbiotic. The conversation occurred through his love and his focus of intent. From our discussion of Bohm's take on the observer effect consider that in Carver's conversation with the plants, they were choosing how to manifest to Carver as well.

I don't know if Carver heard from nature in words or gained input by impressions when he focused on nature. I know in my experience, it's more a visual conversation. Also, my area of focus is people, whereas Carver is famous for talking to plants, though he was not limited with people either. This sort of communication is on a different level and somehow we can enter into the field of the whole, and there is a synchronous or simultaneous "thinking" going on. We might not even notice that we are having a conversation in this higher consciousness except at that particular time, we felt very good when we finished with the conversation.

First Pillar of Carver's Ability

There were three pillars to Carver's ability. The first one was *love*. Kazanis also believed that dark energy/matter was an expression of the love that permeates everything. In my experience the ground frequency of the universe is unconditional love, which is different than conditional love. It's interesting in this world of reflecting light that we have conditional love held in a field of unconditional love. Love has to be unconditional because if it weren't the entire system of creation wouldn't exist as a coherent collaborative whole. The universal energy that was so infused in Carver's being was love.

The love in Carver had a purity that he called God. He understood that when we love anything enough, it's going to give us its secrets. This is true for people as well as plants. He even gave an example of a criminal stating that if you love him or her enough, that person will reveal their secrets. Of course being in the therapeutic world, this demonstrates itself all the time because we are teaching our practitioners to be present in unconditional love. In this Presence of love there is no projection on the client (or plant) and the truth simply reveals itself. Just like when we talk with a friend in unconditional love, we talk about things that we would not share with others. In a sense, we cross that frontier between the third and fourth dimensions of consciousness when we talk with our friend in unconditional love. As a scientist, when we speak to our experiment with unconditional love, it will tell us its secrets.

Second Pillar of Carver's Ability

The second of Carver's pillars was *expectancy*, and what he meant by that was awe and wonder. In his expectancy he would notice or look at "something" and through that "something" he saw a window from the spiritual worlds come into the physical world. The spirit was love. That love would emerge through the person or thing and he would see the truth, light and radiance of the person, plant or form. In a sense, he was looking at people and things in the physical world the same way I was looking at things and objects through an altered radiant world in my sensory deprivation experience. Ensconced in that inner world, I saw light radiate from objects. In effect, I experienced the same kind of awe as Carver. He would look at people in the physical world through spirit and see light. For him the dimensions of awe and wonder were simultaneous. He called that *expectancy*.

Third Pillar of Carver's Ability

The third pillar of Carver's ability was *humility*. This pillar may be a tough one for some of us because we get into our fear, defensiveness, self-importance, and entitlement, which cuts us off from higher consciousness. In humility, Carver was relaxed when he engaged his experiment, whether it was out in nature where he meditated every day or in his laboratory where he was working with chemistry. Whether conversing with nature or in the laboratory, he exhibited a countenance of humility, reverence, and deep respect for the holiness of life. His Presence was always an agency of the Divine. He had that kind of humility in which he held himself as equal to everything, meaning equal to the humblest humanity in his life and living very humbly in all aspects. Whether he was meeting with dignitaries, his students, or talking to flowers, he held this humility. But he was also equal to the spirit of love that was in everything; that was his understanding of God.

Synthetic

For George Washington Carver, his take on creation was that God gave us four domains: *animal, vegetable, mineral* and *synthetic*. Whether nature causes the creation or God causes the creation or whoever or whatever, isn't essential here. The important thing is that we are given a view of creation by whatever the intelligence, or whatever law was guiding creation. Creation distributed into these four domains. We are aware of the *animal, vegetable* and *mineral* domains. The one we are less aware of is the fourth domain that he called *Synthetic*.

Carver believed that God gave the *synthetic* domain as the leading edge of discovery and innovation. That is where we land in this exploration of spirituality in science. A chemist colleague of mine, Dr. Thomas Ward, told me about his current work of exploring how to synthesize prostheses as a cell inclusion that changes basic carbon into food. Prosthesis in this case is an artificial organelle inside the cell that changes the chemical production within the cell. It's a synthesizing process. Synthesizing is an extrapolation from nature into a new or novel form or process. This is the synthesis that Carver was talking about from his place of enlightenment. The evolving fourth domain is synthesizing something out of nature that nature hasn't yet created.

In a very real way, each of us as a spiritual scientist has agency of creation. We are agents of the higher intelligence to which Einstein referred. An expression of our agency is to discover the essence of nature, and out of that collegial relationship with God/nature, we create new things as a natural process. Organisms for billions of years have been running into challenges, obstacles and extinction events, always looking for another way of doing things and synthesizing the next step. What makes this different now is that we are modifying our evolution in two ways: one is by synthesis, and the other is by transcendent experiences that change our neural network. We synthesize by extrapolating the specific purposeful vector of creation and applying that to practical issues. We change our neural network when we activate or awaken to the higher dimensions of our consciousness. Evolution of the material self is a vehicle to the expression of evolution. The neural network exhibits purpose by responding to our change in consciousness. Changes in the neural network can make corresponding changes in our genetics such as in the functional expression of epigenetics. From my perspective, the spiritual leaders of the new age are awakened scientists that manage to discover their deeper relationship to the whole while doing practical experimental work.

Relational Science

Carver believed that communication through rapport created by unconditional love would reveal the truth whether it is between individuals or nature.

Jilted Lover

An example of communicating through unconditional love, in the pattern of Carver, occurred for me when a colleague and I were in our doctorate programs together. We would often have dinner together and exchange war stories of character-building experiences. Usually the stories were about girlfriends that dumped us. The character-building experience I was talking about that night was the play between conditional and unconditional love. I was talking about a woman I was engaged to a few years earlier that dumped me. It hurt deeply. That's the way conditional love is. I was telling my graduate school colleague about my war story. We were also studying at a mystery school where we were doing a kind of energy therapy in which we became more aware of the energy fields of the body and various levels of consciousness that reflect in layers around the body, and how beliefs code energy. These layers, which also interpenetrate the body, are known as the imaginative, emotional, mental, archetypal, and Soul, which we will explain more about later. Beliefs, judgements and trauma code structures in the geometry of the energy field around the body, shaping awareness, perception, well-being and health.

As I began to tell my story of my fiancé rejecting me, I looked out about eight inches in front of my heart and another ten inches to my left side. My story was of a time when my fiancé rejected me. Evidently, she felt dominated by my projections and objectification of her as a means to balance my insufficiencies. When I touched that traumatic memory with my attention, there was an explosive feeling inside my body and an ecstatic state welled up through me and took me into an altered consciousness of love and joy. That was quite impactful. That's the same kind of love we are talking about with Carver. In my training in the mystery school my sense of self as the unbound loving of my Soul and my ability to hold in that alignment created a contrast to the self-pity inscribed by the belief and judgment that I made when my fiancé left. The contrasting frequencies and self-forgiveness rapidly deconstructed the strong hold of my belief of rejection and thus I experienced an explosive release of the trauma. The strong negative hold of my judgment rapidly released into the joy of my Soul. Now when I think of that person, love wells up and the pain and anger are long ago dissolved.

It may seem odd that I offer this example in a presentation of spirituality in science but consider my saga as a metaphor for our relationship as scientists to our experimental work. We are married to our work are we not?

Energy Self

There is a personal energy field around us in which all our beliefs are rotating like satellites around our bodies. Our beliefs, judgments, and attitudes are made of codes that shape the healthy function of the field and the denser corresponding body elements. These beliefs, judgments, and attitudes are formed by our choices as we respond to life challenges and take positions in the field relative to the meaning and intent of our choices. Like dark energy and matter the beliefs form a gravitational effect in the field of our consciousness, yet invisible, or dark, to the physical eye. The energetic matter of our beliefs goes into the unconscious mind and we are looking at life through it and it is our perception informing us about life.

Have you ever watched someone's eye movement when they are thinking? You can tell where their memory is held in the geography of the field by where their eyes point. There is a lot of research on eye movement and how we access our memory. Brainspotting, as a trauma technique, is an application of this phenomenon. I notice that when I access inspirational thought my eyes go up and for sad memories my eyes go down. Often we can tell where a belief is established in our surrounding field by our hand gestures while we are talking. Notice the next time you are animated about what you are talking about. The space around your body is the location of the personal unconscious. In terms of physics, beliefs have magnetic effects but not electrical effects. Our nervous system is electrical. We sense the belief in the movement of our awareness (electrical) and the belief (magnetic). Consider, as scientist, that belief structures in our consciousness interact inductively with our research.

Observer Effect

Our beliefs reside in an atmospheric filter between us and life, shaping and coloring our perception. When we consider that our personality, as a "galaxy" of energy that is shaped and guided by our character, beliefs, emotions and thoughts, we can imagine the potential impact on our research and queries into the nature of life are vast. Our communication with life in general and our research focus specifically is intimate and complex. Consequently, the implications of the observer effect are profound. We are not separate from the so-called object of our study. We must at least entertain the supposition that science is relational. Relational Science does not preclude our current methods of research. However, at a minimum we can consider that as we bracket reality for the purpose of study, that we keep in mind the whole context in which the specific phenomenon of our bracketed study exists. As in the example given by Carver, perhaps when love is the context, our specific research will unfold its secrets and reveal the truth. As scientists, the *eye of unconditional love* will see the truth, while, on the other hand, when we see our science through projection and domination, we become the jilted lover.

Wrap Up

There are some practical things we can do without taking the whole leap. We don't have to get meningitis to be enlightened. That's good news. We can meditate. There are simple ways to do this. We can take a little timeout in the midst of our work to remember who we are, and love ourselves, love our research and experiments. We can talk to our experiments with the expectancy that we will receive answers in some way. Our experiment may not respond in conventional ways. It may come in a dream like Kekulé in his discovery of the carbon ring. Someone may say something that triggers us, but I guarantee that if we start talking to our research and expect an answer, in some way or another we will get an answer and things will move forward a little more easily and quickly.

Another thing to practice is respect for our colleagues. I know when I get together with Dr. Ward, my chemist genius colleague, a great thing happens between us. It's like we become one consciousness. The silo that I work in and the silo that he works in join. It's like my IQ goes up. I loved talking to him before creating this chapter because my IQ went up a few notches so I could think in bigger terms. Beachler described the coherent nature of the brain when it goes into unity; our brain and mind come into unity, into a resonant state when the action of our research and the truth of our research are aligned. Outstanding science is ethical and true to nature. It is free of narratives that lock us in our silos; we can think outside the box/silo. We can identify good science because it has a coherent resonance in the brain. When we are doing our scientific work, whether as a spiritual or material scientist, we start to feel good, peaceful or excited inside; then we know we are on the right track. Coherence is love. When our work is true, the confirmation comes in our resonant feelings.

We started with our silos chasing our ambitions, and that seemed rather stark. Silos are isolated workspaces. In our silos, we aren't talking with each other, but I think there is a plan, a plot to it. Don't worry too much about it because there is an evolutionary process involved. Each silo is working on a specific issue or problem that needs to be solved. At some point, as we respond to our evolution, all the silos are going to come together and reveal the whole picture. So enjoy your work and have expectancy about the evolution. Be humble, love your colleagues, love your work, talk to your experiments, and expect an answer. Love is the organizer and will bring us all together when the time is right.

...We are on the cusp of a new scientific revolution that will again be led by physics and consciousness that perceives and interprets the world as scientific and natural, a fact that is obvious to many scientists and academics, but also on the cusp of a new evolutionary leap....(Jim Beichler)

Question and Answer

Colleague One: Just today I read that the brain function between a man and a woman are very different and I think that men use seven times more of the gray matter than women and women use ten times more of the white matter. Do you know of any difference, for example from near death experiences between the two sexes?

Robert: That's an incredible question. As I access more of my inner reality, my sense of male and female disappear. When the neural net changes, it affects our genetics and our biology. There's an evolution, just as we notice that we realize that there's a different expression. Also, as a cultural evolution, a lot of people are experiencing genders that flow together. They have a fluid sense of gender.

As far as any near death experiences that I've looked into, everybody is so moved by their experience in the transcendental dimension that when they revive their bodies their life is radically changed. I haven't heard of any near death experiences that change anyone's gender or gender identity. Still, I've heard a lot about near death experiences changing a person's attitude towards their gender and offering greater ease and creativity conversing between the two genders, breaking down the entitlement, the dominance, misogyny and all of those politics. One thing that disappears is gender politics with near death experiences. I find that exciting.

Colleague Two: In the society where probably spiritual scientists are a little bit in the minority, how do you cope with a lot of rejection of your beliefs by the scientific community?

Robert: Did you get that?

Colleague Two: Yes. I mean the rejection that people get from others who don't believe there's a connection between spirituality and science.

Robert: We are controlled by how people see us, by criticism. Depending on which silo we work in, we share divergent cosmologies. We could be working in a silo where we are the one person who believes that the brain is an epigenetic phenomenon of consciousness, and everybody else thinks the converse. All of these people may be very ambitious and excited about their intellects and their mental power, but we might be in an intellectually deadly situation if we are that person, because the silo syndrome promotes an identification that what one believes is right even to the point of becoming a religion and purporting that a consciousness-inclusive mindset may be considered apostate.

I've been exploring the relationship of spirit and science for a long time. I just love the attitude in this room. It's pretty good by comparison. Most scientists here are the curious kind that at least see me as some kind of strange phenomena that arouses their curiosity. That's not very mean, but there's an odd thing that happens: when we live in our Ego, we are usually fear-based and we're trying to protect the Ego. That's how we define ourselves, and we interpret ourselves by what reflects us. As we deepen inside, we start accessing our Soul and our Soul works very differently than our Ego. Soul is an agency of unconditional love. There's a different way to source how we feel and how we experience ourselves. There is a psychologically healthy process in our Soul arising from the well of unconditional love.

We move to the basis of organizing our reality as an expression of unconditional love. The more we migrate into this, the more resilient we are. When someone attacks us, we respond more like when someone pushes their fist into a bucket of water, the water distorts to the shape of the fist. When the fist is removed, the water returns to its equilibrium and you can't see that the fist was forcing a shape into the water. I've tried this. I pushed my fist in as hard as I could and when I pulled it out, the water went back just like it was. Criticism and judgement of you is a different frequency. Criticism and judgement may hit you, but the only way it can affect you is if you decide to take it personally. When you take it personally your consciousness holds the shape of the fist (so to speak). You choose conditional or unconditional love. Love may feel the push of the attack and then returns to the shape of love when the attack subsides. We're back to one of Carver's points about expectancy in which we are always looking at people in terms of the loving that is their essence.

Another way to deal with critical energy is by being present in a loving way. There is something about being present with what is without projecting a bunch of stuff on it that gives us a highly astute awareness. We need to meet people with this expectancy. When you take something personally, you polarize and start fighting with them, and usually you will lose. But if you choose to start getting interested in where they are coming from, what they have to say, and what is the contribution of their viewpoint even though it is initially said with hostility, it changes the polarization. A rapport begins that evolves through dialogue into a sense of unity. These are a few reminders in case you run into criticism and the urge to polarize.

Colleague Three: I just wanted to ask a question from the perspective of an artist and a musician. So as a musician, I've experienced a state of high consciousness from having interactive performances and sessions with other musicians that I love to interact in that sense and as a universal language. I wanted to ask, do you work with a lot of creative people, artists? Do you see it as another side of science, and is it calculable with your experience with music or art, and do you do any research with that? I want to ask if you work with a lot of creative people and artists and if their experience has informed you in any way?

Robert: Oh yeah, I work with a lot of creative people. It's incredible to see what is going on with them. Before this presentation, a jazz ensemble played as an event opener. As the audience listened and they allowed the music to affect them, they began to relax, to let go, integrate, balance their day and become more receptive. That's a very powerful way to heal. We go from there to some kinds of music that resonate with deeper levels of consciousness. Just as we spoke of subtle energies in terms of radiant light in contrast to reflective light and electromagnetic energy, we also have radiant music. Just as the mystic hears celestial sounds, one day we will have instruments that can respond to those higher frequencies. In the spiritual physics sense, music creates the universe from an eternal source. It's what mystics call the sound current. There are meditations called Surat Shabda Yoga (attending to the inner sound). They go to the sound current. I talked a little bit about this referring to Alexander's NDE (near death experience). He heard music. He described it as music, and by tuning to it, he could ride up to the higher levels. That's internal and radiant. When we play certain music here in the physical world, it resonates with the inner sound. The highs you are describing come when the inner and outer frequencies of the music resonate.

You remind me of a client I had a couple of months ago who was a trumpet player. He was having a lot of emotional issues, so I asked him if in his trumpet playing if he had a God note? And if you talk to a trumpet player, they probably have a God note, and maybe others do too. He said he did. I told him to meditate on that note. Why don't you imagine hearing that God note in your head and just hold to it and ride it out? I can appreciate your experience as a musician and yes, this is good.

We can also work with sound tones. It is a kind of music application in which we wear earphones. One side is slightly out of phase with the other. What it does is it resonates with the brain by listening to the tone in both ears. Sometimes classical music will do that. It creates that brain coherence I was talking about and integration with the heart, which then, in that state, it's easy to access higher dimensions of consciousness.

That reminds me. I was talking to Dr. Ward about researchers and how you can tell if they are having this coherent brain experience. I said if they are doing their research and start whistling or singing then they probably are on the right track because they are reflecting their inner experience of brain coherence.

Colleague Four: I have been in research a few years now and I need to admit that I have never done meditation, pure meditation, myself. Something I have observed is when I am in the office and I'm trying hard to get the best ideas I can get, I never succeed. But if I go to sleep, take a siesta, go jogging or swimming or whatever, my brain pops up with the greatest idea for that specific project. This has happened a few times already. I was wondering why we have the best ideas when we are actually trying hard not to think about our work?

Robert: If I understood you correctly, you're struggling with your work, and you go away, and you go to sleep, or you meditate, and then the idea comes. See that is the natural process I am talking about. I don't know if they have them here, but the image I get is when I was little, stores in America had these tubes, they were suction tubes, and they would insert a small cartridge, and they would send it up, and the cashier would send it back with change. Some banks still use it for their car service. I see it as a metaphor for how we get answers from higher consciousness. The struggling part is building energy, the physical Chi and energy, and building energy up on your question. It feels like tension and frustration because it is, and then you just let it go, and you do something else or meditate, or you go to sleep. Then your question goes up, out, and somebody, or the universe, is listening. Something's listening and when you're receptive and humble, you get the answer downloaded. It's a natural thing.

Meditation

Let's close our eyes and take a deep breath, settling into your space. Be aware of your body in your space, and you, as your space in your body, take another deep breath then let go.

Imagine yourself in your favorite place in nature. Sense the sights and sounds of this place. Depending on the location, listen to the surf, wind through the leaves, songs of birds or the hum of insects, the stillness of the desert night, or verdancy of the forest. Some of you may find yourselves high on a mountain top.

Now continuing, become more present in all of your senses, in your place in nature. Sense into the earth; look up at the sky and feel the flow of energy between heaven and earth — breathe this flow of life for a while.

Now bring your focus into the center of your head, focusing there on the point of light. See the light expand until it gently encompasses the space of your head — breathe your Presence into this ball of light.

Imagine now that you are in a laboratory. Your laboratory takes on the characteristics of your area of research, whether chemistry, physics, biology, or a space of healing and spiritual discovery. Invite your image to become stronger and embrace your sense of actually being there. Fill your laboratory with great love and reverence.

Now move your awareness to the location of your research. Be creative. Reach out and touch your work. Feel the love and respect connect through your touch. Ask, for what purpose is your Divine expression into this world intended to serve? Open your heart and allow your imagination to flow into the reality for which you seek discovery and understanding. Then, let it go. Travel with it. Relax your body in your breathing.

Listen with ears of tolerance.
See through eyes of compassion.
Speak with the language of love.

Rumi

CHAPTER TWO

Love

...

Love is one of those things we know the most...and the least about. We keep learning new things about love so it must be infinite. It must be at the ground of everything or otherwise we would somehow manage to understand all of it. The truth is in finding a way to allow love to envelop us because love is the ground of being. Love is the initial impulse that propels everything. Love is the energy that holds everything. Love is the energy that resolves everything. The way I understand the will of God is that *love will have its way.*

Imagination

One way I like to look at love is as the "mycelium" of the universe, of creation. Do you know what mycelium is? It's a fungus that in nature networks into everywhere. We were at a place outside of Santa Fe, New Mexico, and a lady was telling us about mycelium that spreads for miles along the high desert surface. She cautioned us to walk gently on the desert because it breaks that fragile layer of mycelium that is a thin network across the surface. It's one of the biggest organisms on the planet and a single individual mycelium network can spread for great distances. It's quite fascinating. Mushrooms are the fruit of microscopic networks of Mycelium.

The mycelium of a single mycorrhiza can extend and connect multiple plants of different species. They form a hybrid underground system called a "common mycorrhizal network." This network allows plants to communicate as they transport sugar supplies to one another when they are needed. (Hamilton)

In the new *Star Trek* series, they found out that the whole universe and all of the dimensions interlink with "mycelium." On Star Trek they discovered a way to use the interconnecting mycelium to travel through its network into all places, dimensions and parallel realities. By connecting to the consciousness of the mycelium, the Star Ship Discovery instantly traveled to any place in the galaxy. While watching this saga, it occurred to me that the mycelium web would be a great metaphor for the universal field of Love that is the fabric of creation and that the construct of Star Trek would be a great exercise in the scientific use of imagination as a means of discovering and understanding frontier realities and beyond.

An original mission of Star Trek through the decades has been to provide a forum for visionary imagination and to reflect on the social, psychological, ethical and scientific issues of the day in new ways. In the original series the theme *was to go where no one has gone before.* Much like Jules Verne in the time of oil lamps and sailing ships imagined atomic powered submarines and electric lights, we are inspired to envision places in consciousness that we have never gone before. As practiced by Einstein in his transcendent capacity to go where no scientist had gone before, Star Trek is an imaginal mind experiment. Einstein constructed experiments in his mind's eye and watched them play out, as his visionary spirit sought a unifying theory of everything.

Imagining a vibrant web of life interconnecting all the dimensions of the universe is a powerful metaphor that stirs our visionary consciousness to reach beyond the familiar boundaries and universes in which we habitually think, feel and love. We live in a time in which we are called to the possibility of a "new day and a new dawn." In the tradition of transcendentalist Ralph

Waldo Emerson, we are the students who *will build a nation for the first time based on the wisdom of the Soul*. The Transcendental Leader is called to be a traveler in consciousness and then to proceed on foot *where no one has gone before* and is also called to inspire others to do the same.

Mycelium Love

What I call mycelium love is a metaphor, because love is a living organism that interconnects everything. It is the love that holds and inspires everything. Mycelium in physical life is a fungus. It is an excellent metaphor for universal love because it spreads everywhere as one organism. It is living. It is sentient, and networks everything. Bees tend to their health by drinking the nectar of mycelium because it empowers their immune system and apparently it does the same thing for humans. The colonies of bees that drink mycelium nectar become completely immune to things that are killing other bee colonies. What a beautiful vision as an evolutionary bridge, in these chaotic times, to drink the nectar of mycelium love...drink the living waters and thirst no more.

Mycelium imagery gives us a frequency pattern for a universal communication and travel network. It is similar to the Great Tree of the indigenous shamans of South America. In a visionary state the Great Tree appears to them as an internal awareness and they use the Great Tree to travel the universe metaphorically and actually do so in their subtle bodies. We can develop an image of this network as well. By imagining the matrix of mycelium love and relaxing into that frequency, we allow it to invite us as we make ourselves available to it. We can start to feel it in the cells of our body. Through our cells, we become connected or consciously linked to mycelium love. In order for our cells to connect to this frequency within us we attune to the frequency corresponding to the metaphor. Through the mycelium love network, we are globally aware and connected in a physical and metaphysical way.

The mycelium metaphor for the universal fabric of love implies an eternity, a continual unfolding Akasha...implicate order...dark matter and energy. It may be that it's so unconditional, that the more we discover about it, the more there is to discover. Our activity of waking up to love may mean actually increasing the love field into not only the planet and hearts of all people but also the universe...the ultimate observer effect.

One of the things that I always like to emphasize about divine love (or unconditional love) is that it supports everything unconditionally, so everything you say or do, create or attach yourself to, believe in or change is supported by divine love. Our good, bad and ugly qualities and deeds are all supported in this field of love, unconditionally, however, they are delegated to realms suitable to each field. This is true for every being, even rocks and stuff that we may not like. Rocks are sentient too, they're just very slow. Rocks think in terms of millions and millions of years rather than something fast like a tree budding. Rocks have a long-range plan, we might say a glacial plan, so we know that with this field of loving we can even have an experience of rocks, big boulders, mountains or glaciers as love.

Imagine what it is like to place our consciousness into a connected field of loving and literally travel anywhere. Imagine that we are traveling into the lifecycle of a glacier, the building of snow and the compression and purification of it. Consider that ancientness is suspended as more glacier builds, and then follow that and eventually, well...maybe the planet heats up, and pieces fall off, and it starts to melt, and then someday that glacier won't exist anymore as a physical form, but it lived as an experience in this field of love. It leaves a trace in that field of love and is remembered in the water.

In the numinous field there is the Akasha or the Akashic record, which is the record of life inside of creation. As Soul, we travel through the levels of consciousness into the realm of Soul, which exist in a place transcendent to the realms of manifest creation. It follows that in our capacity to be vulnerable to the loving nature of our own Soul, we transcend into the higher realms of Soul. As the prodigal sons and daughters, we return home. Only that which we fulfill and complete in love enters our Soul.

We are the Answer

When we can accept our affinity for stepping into Soul consciousness, we cooperate with our life here on earth. We can bilocate our awareness and be in the transcendent field of love and then access wisdom and the resources of love while doing battle on earth. In our transcendental awareness, we can access an infinite supply of energy that is all giving, energy that doesn't begin or end. Our incarnated life is bookended by an alpha and omega energy that holds us so we can live in grace, honoring the laws and physics of the created worlds and realms of the earth.

Our inner world reflects back to us from the mirror of life so love can see what love is doing or needs to do another way. We come to know how love is making reality through its holographic reflection. In the perception of our world, we are the code makers that conditions love while also being a conduit of love that resolves the codes. As soon as we incarnate, we metaphorically become two lovers trying to find each other. One part searches life looking for our Soul. The other part is our Soul looking for experience. We are always approaching ourselves any way we can, trying to find ourselves and it's important to remember that we can't avoid this search. As humans, we are bound to the search. When we look outward for our lover, we encounter experience. When we look inward for our lover, we find resolution. We long for our own doppelganger, our Soul mate. We can't avoid the search because that is the setup. We are the prodigal sons and daughters actualizing our Soul urges through the experience of life on earth and then turning inward resolving our life on earth by returning home to the source of love that is the "all parent" that gave us life.

God's will is what gives us life and motivation and arranges things. From my perspective God's will is that *love will have its way*. The nature of love is to always find its way because love is the ground of being. Love finds the way to itself and finds the way to its home. The more conscious we make ourselves of love, the easier we navigate life because we can see more of the twists and turns of life. Hopefully, we hear this little guideline of *love will have its way* often repeated, not only in the teachings we receive, but inside of ourselves in terms of the admonition for each breath, each moment, each thing we do, inviting us to use everything to transform into loving because that is the shortcut to a life of love. Love goes directly to the nature of how we create and how we draw from creation. Our creation holds the wisdom that we are looking for. Whatever has been used in old dysfunctional patterns, such as againstness, trauma, and life challenges, is part of a process of creating love. Love is a key to our broader purpose. As our evolution persists through the mythology of avatars (waiting for promised world teachers to save us), we realize that we are the ones we have been waiting for. We are the promise. We are the agency of God knowing itself.

The Dance of Love

Through our trials and tribulations, there is purification. Once we realize that trials and tribulations are supported by unconditional loving, then our place is to engage challenges as they are, not make up stuff about what they should or shouldn't be. The dance of love and life are trying to resolve something very precious for us. Sometimes it takes us into a new consciousness. Sometimes love removes identifications that are false-self beliefs, such as: all the things that are beliefs we acquired through the politics of identity, all the nuances of our importance from doing good or ill given to us by the world, the entire sense of self based on conditional loving and everything about ourselves that we have not yet transformed into loving. This is really tough because we are fond of the conditional side of loving which is a natural artifact of the ways we make sense out of things. By trusting that we can look at our conditions and situations and realize that the current experience is guiding us to more in-depth discovery. In each action, there is a deeper purpose that leads to resolution, to understanding, to wisdom, to discovery, and to loving in everything. You see, that's the way we learn how unconditional love reflects back within ourselves. Through the reflection of unconditional love, we awaken to the true nature of ourselves.

Through the various encounters and expressions of daily life, we learn the physics of reflective love and inspirational love. Reflective love is the way love comes back to us through distortions of our idea of things, other peoples' opinions of things and the milieu in which we are living. Inspirational love rises from the Soul in response to a problem-solving process. Our dance of love is the dance of these two aspects of love. From our dance, we create a consciousness that enables us to hold more loving as a direct Presence. Loving is not philosophical or conditional. It is not controlling. Loving just is. As a Presence, loving becomes a power. Loving is everywhere present in the one thing, that is all consciousness. By coming into the reflectiveness of duality, we are enabled for our journey on this planet, and perhaps throughout the galaxies. Duality makes love conditional, creating a contrast between love and its opposites like greed, lack, fear, hate, domination, etc. Through contrast and the measure of unconditional love we build on a sense of self that is transcendent to duality enabling us to build resilience, reflective wisdom, resolution of duality, and peace in the midst of chaos. We magnetize to love, which attracts more love to us and creates a force field that stimulates, resonates and pulls loving forward within anything and everyone we contact. In this way we become agents of the one love that is the purpose and matrix of all that is.

When our priority is to keep building up the magnetic pattern of love, we need to do so with great finesse so that we can work with love for love's sake rather than for any disadvantage, or control, winning or losing, or projections of how anything should be. Leave the zero-sum games to the zeroes. We touch life with vigilance so that when we see our Presence awakening into conversation, we can seize the moment as love. We seize the moment guided by and trusting the indicators that reveal patterns and trajectories of our relationship to whatever occurs in a given moment. We observe and remain present with what is and see what we notice. There is going to be a clue about how to proceed, so we seize that one, even if we have to stop in the middle of something to allow inspiration and give love to our speech. The love that is here is communicating through the mycelium network and is always collaborating with itself. Love is unconditional and awaits our invitation. We might think of unconditional love like there are love spies in every element of living, and they are waiting to assist us because they know the secret of how to work with any situation. The love spies are embedded, always vigilant and ready to assist us. With a silent, gentle turn of our heart the love spies become our consorts and speak to the truth of the moment.

When we are looking at life through the lens of karma, the illusion can all seem very real. We can live through the experience of karma and resolve consequences of our actions, or we can follow the guidance to use everything to transform ourselves into loving. Love provides the resolution of karma. We can either live out karma until we are so diminished that all that is left is loving which often happens in death or we can wake up to loving which is essentially a second birth. Love is the eternal destination of everything and loving is driving the process. As we wake up more and more to the Soul-self, the loving self, we find grace to show us the way. Through grace this transcendental pattern shows us the truth of what we are doing, and through this truth, love coagulates inside of us as a new consciousness.

Lack

When we are resolving areas of lack, love gives us an edge. When we try to fix our sense of lack, we may be missing the point. Think of lack as an empty receptacle in the sense that an empty glass lacks a liquid filling it. Consider that the real purpose for lack is making places ready to be filled with love. Our attitude makes the lack seem negative, but lack is really for receiving. Choice is about filling these spaces with love or aspects of our lives that we love. We can fill lack with judgment, being a victim, remorse, or even anger, or we can fill lack with love. When we push against our sense of lack, it creates a focus that attracts more lack. We see that lack has its own perfection in the way we choose. Since we are beggars with our lack, why not beg for love. The challenge of a reflective reality is that we generally expect love to come from someone else. We miss the reality that filling up with love can arise within us and flow from our transcendence.

We have all the rights and privileges of the beloved, including humility and the ability to see through the Eyes of Soul. I like to suggest to people that their feelings are information, not identity. Identifying with feelings makes a form and then unconditional love supports the form. Such an identity cascades a simple choice into a complete reversal of incarnational truth creating an apparent concern. Remember, feelings are information, not identity. Having said that, once we see this habit, we can apply our well-developed ability to identify with information to our advantage. As we awaken to transcendence, we experience loving, joy, wisdom, understanding, and strength of Spirit. When transcendental realities of self permeate our felt sense, it is important to take those realities personally. Identify with those positive feelings. Remember, a feeling is information, not an identity except for the feeling that is the transcendental love. Awareness of transcendental love and the feelings arising from it, we take personally. When we identify with love, we can take responsibility for our existence. By so doing we realize and come to know the ancient adage that: *I am the Truth, the Light and the Way.*

We Seed the Christ

Our center is a light column, a vortex of living love, anchoring our transcendence into the fertile earth. This is the core of our Presence. We are a bridge between heaven and earth. The results in our life are the consequences of seeds we planted through our actions and attitudes. Our transcendent Presence is the authority that manifests from each seed in our ground of being. When we look at everything in our lives as something that grew from a seed that we planted, we can reverse engineer that view and look at the code of our intent to help us to grow in our mastery of how to create in this world. This is the way to bring love forward and the way to live more abundantly with well-being for all.

Our unconscious serves as a womb for creation, a tranquil place held in our Presence. We weave the constituencies of what we want to create into a seed and place it deep within the belly of our Soul. It operates as a secret within the mycelium love network held in silence. We enfold the essential elements from our lived experience, contoured by ancient wisdom and held in the archives of our Soul. In this way, we edit the ways history repeats itself, while adapting to the reality of the present and consulting the scenarios of the future.

When we have the essential image for our seed, we take our ingredients, and with great care, we focus our intent, rechecking everything for impurities like self-judgment, inadequacies, lack, fear, aggression, dominance, or entitlements. The love center of our Soul powers our inner nature. As Transcendental Leaders, we work to strip all distortions from our nurturing and creative field in everything we create. By so doing, we are able to network with the highest frequencies that formulate reality. There is no "againstness" in these frequencies. Any unfinished business that we acquired along the way, we use to fashion the seed and resolve all potential unintended consequences, and it thus becomes transformed. In this way, when we plant the seed, with great care we can release and surrender to higher consciousness, to the transcendent firmament from which all things sprout into the sky and the spirit of earth. In this way, we serve a broader mission of the incarnation of the body of Christ. Our first cause then is to seed the one thing that makes all else possible. We seed Christ, the agency of love.

I Am Soul Authority

In the structure of consciousness that we live in as human beings, we have an inherent authority. Whether we choose to use it well is another thing. This authority is called I Am, and in our geometry, I Am resides energetically in the alignment of our body center line above our head. This authority makes so whatever we claim in the name of I Am. We often use this authority in careless ways, for example: I Am unworthy, shameful, worthless, etc. Soul is our true self and the spiritual force from which we inhabit our Egoic self. When, with strong intent, we claim that I Am Soul, we open a flow of consciousness through our vibratory centers, that gives us measure in our house of self regarding what is us and ours in contrast to what is them and theirs. I am using "house" as a metaphor for the personality we build through our life experience which has many rooms built from different aspects of our life and self. This authority empowers our choices to make of life and ourselves what we may. Through I Am Soul master of my house we incorporate elements into our sense of self, into our house. All of us will experience living in our house (Egoic self) in different ways.

The following is a student's experience:

I had this beautiful awareness the other day with my inner teacher. It was like pouring out a thousand percent loving and gratitude for who I am through all of me. It was not as an ego thing, but just that every part of me that I've held back from myself, that would radiate more loving and be able to actualize and heal more. The challenge is that last little piece where we really let go and embrace I Am. It's that last small piece. That is the practice.

It's the hidden piece. I saw hearts coming down, like streaming hearts coming all the way down through every little part of my being. I know it can be part of my body as a receptacle and conduit. That is the part we leave out. That last little piece is to claim it "This I Am" and then go with the consequence of that declaration. I get how that changes our awareness from identifying with information to being us.

We have a tendency to identify ourselves through our feelings and that can be used to our advantage through transcendent frequencies. Because we are always looking outward, trying to make ourselves into what we see reflecting back from the mirror of life, our identification with feelings is inferred, so we have a feeling and tendency to identify with our feelings. Imagine that someone says something negative about us and then we feel depressed. We say inside, "I am depressed." We identify with the depression and we use our I Am Authority to incorporate depression, the negative reflection, into our self-concept. We become that feeling in our identity. It makes the depression identity a law inside. Unconditional love supports our choice. We may make a negative choice, which we can also change through a countermanding choice of self forgiveness. In the long game, we are building up a skill of using our feelings as information instead of identity.

As we build up the skill of using our feelings as information, we become more conscious of the process. We are waking up to the fullness of ourselves. Consequently, we can then go to our transcendent connection, to loving, which also comes with a feeling, and we then identify with that transcendent frequency and make it so through our I Am Soul authority. It's a very cool process.

By utilizing our I Am Soul authority, we are dis-identifying from information in which we assigned a room in our metaphorical house to outer authority as well as evicting those miss-information folks who claimed false residence in our house through outer authority. We then identify with the new transcendentally referred tenants and give them a room to live in. This is a sorting process, a purification process.

Spiritual Bypass

Ego is our consciousness as personality and is based on our physical and emotional life as reflected by survival, safety, security and self-esteem. At a high level of Ego, we can fall into an "over-identification" with the idea of archetypal transcendence. This is an illusion that appears as the true self but is actually a reflection, not true transcendence. True transcendence is a knowing without over-identification. True transcendence satisfies all our needs from Soul. Issues of life, Ego, and outer authority become practical matters rather than existential issues in true transcendence. Spiritual bypass is denial of the real challenges and needs of our Ego through creating and identifying with a fantasy projection of transcendence.

When we identify with our Ego, we want to be important. When we Identify with our Soul, we are equal to everything and know that we are loved completely in every way. When we identify with Soul, we no longer need to make survival choices on the basis of lack and fear, even though survival may confront us as a practical concern. As Ego personalities we build our sense of self from the reflection life gives us. Our Souls evolve by awakening within the reflective relationship. Illusion acts like a reflective curtain that obscures the truth. Love enables us to resolve the conflicts, judgments and polarizations of life. Our love sees through the illusion.

The cosmic mirror is a spiritual membrane that reflects and holds the totality of the created universe. Essentially when we use the term *cosmic mirror,* we are saying that life mirrors us and causes us to reflect on situations and circumstances in our life so we can re-evaluate and make changes. As we grow internally through experience, we make wiser choices. As we're waking up to the levels of our emotions, mind and unconscious, we move nearer to the cosmic mirror and there the reflection back is rather grand. The reflection is the limit of our unconscious mind before we enter the purity of our Soul. The Soul itself is not reflective so the Ego serves an evolutionary purpose as a reflected consciousness. Looking in the mirror as Ego we see a reflection of our Soul that we mistake for the full radiance of our Soul. Like Narcissus the ego falls in love with its reflection. The Soul is transcendental and when we reach past the reflective levels of life, we see directly through the constructions of life from the transcendence of the Soul. The true home of Soul is beyond this mirror.

The highest level of deception is when we believe we have arrived at our source, when in fact we are looking at an illusion of the true self. Some people wake up at a high level and upon seeing their radiance reflected in the cosmic mirror, they assume they have arrived at the highest divine place. That is a deception, even a seduction because as beautiful as it is...it just reflects. It is still a reflection, like an archetype to identify with instead of the essence of the Soul. We can, if we identify with the archetype, be stuck in a high reflection of the Ego. When people are exploring, many times they run into the archetype of the divine this or that, or the warrior, or some other archetype. Archetypes are powers. They are like gods, but they are not God, of course, in the greater sense. If we identify with these archetypal powers, they can take us over. That takeover can be very exhilarating but it is not the same as merging with the wholeness of love. Falling for the reflective light of the Ego is a foe to the Soul and is the ultimate bypass. Our ultimate challenge is coming face to face with truth because truth challenges all the false ways that we have identified with ourselves.

Similarly, our families of origin are like archetypes or a collection of archetypes. A similar issue might be a family message that said we were no good and, perhaps we identified with that message and decided that we were no good. That's the no-good archetype. We might say that believing the archetype is a process of over identification. When we identify with our feelings as us and then keep building on that identification, then we become too consumed by that identity. Often people will get into such a victim consciousness that they become over identified with being a victim. Watch out for believing these identities.

On the other hand, transcendent love is so unconditional that over identifying with it isn't an issue. Transcendent love is so soft, intimate, loving and complete, that it makes all illusions irrelevant. Even in our misidentification, transcendent loving is present. As we remember that we are love we once again identify with loving diffusing our misidentification. We just go into transcendent love. We easily identify with transcendent love because it's our essence. The identification moves out through us, it does not take us over...it overlights. We become secure and powerful in our individuality in a way that resolves the self-importance of which Ego is so prone. Through inclusion transcendent love does not exclude anything else that might have an existence in our reality. The authority of transcendence is that *love will have its way*, so our authority lies in how we choose and act in the context of our life in congruence with that admonition.

As Is

Transcendent love is a total acceptance of oneself *as is* and what is going on *as is*, which includes those parts of ourselves that we are unhappy with or judge. The higher perspective is that: it's all loving. A test for this is that the reality of the thing (the dysfunctional part of us or the orphan or whatever) becomes totally clear. From a higher perspective there isn't confusion and our judgements no longer define us or obscure our clarity. Transcendent love exists as a higher perspective, loving us *as is*. We need to be careful with this, because as soon as we love *as is*, then we have to remember that so far that's a mental concept and we have to go one step further into the sweetness and into the intimacy of transcendent love. An example is when Mr. Rogers says to the little guy, or girl, "you're fine just the way you are." Mr. Rogers is a definitive example of living out and demonstrating how we live from transcendent love. With him it's not a concept. For many of us this can be difficult: we might say, "You're wonderful just the way you are." You may wonder what is the way we are? If we need to ask then we need to recognize that we already have a judgment that is shaping our reality and distorting our perception in a way that makes us highly resistant to being seen and loved unconditionally.

How can we look at what's going on outside of ourselves, with the planet, or with the world as it is, and see it from the perspective of inner connectedness? From my point of view, we need to know that if we can't experience our connectedness in this moment, life will find a way to connect with us. We need to trust our life which is on the path of mycelium love. Trusting our lives is inevitable in the long game, so why not trust our lives in 10 minutes instead of 10 million years. Trusting our lives is ultimately unavoidable. Once we start playing around with trust in the interconnectedness of mycelium love within ourselves, it become us. When we awaken to love, we won't get distracted from ourselves. Sometimes the problem is that we look at the news or see a terrible event and get distracted from ourselves, and then we get frightened and identify with fear. The true conspiracy theory is that *love will have its way.* We can trust our lives.

Every time we practice appreciating received information as information only and extracting our self-identity from fear and then turn inward to our deeper self, we create a different perception. From this new perspective, our reality of an event is that the world is already working with its transformation. At the transcendent level, in our Presence, everything is inside of us. We may not be tracking all of our transformation, but transformation is tracking us. We just have to get the sense of it, how to navigate and finesse it. If we can play with these small effects in the intimacy with ourselves and not get distracted by the largeness of transformation, the formidable Presence of whatever we are looking at or contending with will diminish.

When we are present, we open a simple communication with ourselves: God bless me, I love me. In Presence we have an invitation to build awareness as our metaphorical default setting. With this enhanced awareness there is no need for a pause, love is present communication...it just is. There's no distance. There's no separation. It may be hard for our minds to get this concept. We may think...I'm talking and I think my mind can't understand it. Is that true? So, we practice. We do spiritual practices. We strengthen our spiritual muscles. Then our default setting is to come home to transcendence, and into the heart of God. Our humanity computer has a default setting. That default setting means that no matter what is going on, we are automatically going to God. We make transcendent love our default setting. Whatever the game, when we get lost, we look for the default button. Press it to connect with God. George Washington Carver always kept a flower to remind him of his default setting.

These concepts involve remembering our lives. Perhaps we remember playing on the beach when we were a three-year-old. Joy and warmth permeated every cell of our body. This memory is a button that when we press it the energy of that event floods through our body. Whatever our button is, it is "thou art holy" rather than "holier than thou." The presence that comes from that memory is entirely complete in itself. One of the consequences of experiencing Presence in our lives is that we become completely satisfied inside and our lives become more graceful. That's a symptom of practicing the process of connecting within. In this connection we find our satisfaction inside and there's more grace in our lives. Fulfillment and satisfaction reside inside.

The peace prayer is a good mantra for our breathing: "I love you, God Bless You, peace be still." We keep breathing in and mixing that frequency with our metabolism, with our emotion, with our thoughts and folding it all into our attitude. This is a way to get into the moment of creation, into God's moment, which is our now. It's unavoidable when we practice. Every moment is an opportunity to practice; it is a constant thing. Once we get that, we are in life differently. We are part of connectedness, part of alignment, part of inspiration, and we become a vehicle for the actuality of wholeness. When we are in our connectivity, our Transcendental Leadership, we become guides along the way...arrows pointing out the path. We become way showers.

Look to the Fringe

There is an old adage that if you want to know what is really going on or what is next, look to the fringes. Or, according to Rudolf Steiner, *our Soul approaches us from the horizon.* Expanding this viewpoint to the cosmos, we look out into the starry night sky and often sense the Presence of our soul. We can wonder if the cosmos is looking back at us. Cosmic and solar rays constantly hit the earth. Periodically, these rays cause unusual disturbances that affect the magnetic field of the planet. The magnetic field keeps the poles, gravity and the atmosphere stable. In 2019 an energetic pulse allegedly hit the planet, but the solar arrays didn't catch it. The scientists don't really know what happened. A Spiritual perspective of this event proposed that the loving on our planet was sufficient to attract this energy as a force to change the dimension that we are in. The event moved us into amplification of an evolving loving dimension. Complementing this alleged shift of the consciousness of the planet, the North pole is migrating from Canada toward Siberia. We are able to track the movement but as to why, that remains a mystery. Taking liberty with our speculation, we can imagine that the migrating pole is seeking a new alignment and is a physical reflection of the evolving dimension that we live in.

Emotions, subtle energies and magnetic fields have an epigenetic impact on our genes. Consider that forces may exist to adjust the electromagnetic context of our way of living. The theory correlates the change in the electromagnetic field with an increased saturation of loving. We are speculating on the source of the saturation of loving and its correlation to the shifting of earth's magnetic poles. In this discussion, we are inviting you to consider that energy fields, regardless of type or dimension, compose the matrix in which our consciousness and organism resides. Is the reciprocity between our consciousness and the consciousness of the earth affecting changes at a genetic level? Our genetics are sensitive to the physical, electromagnetic, environmental and consciousness changes as the electromagnetic environment becomes more receptive or compatible with the consciousness dimension of love causing a greater feeling of accommodation. On the other hand, if we resist, we become viscerally angry and fearful.

The theory that cosmic forces are conspiring to shift the consciousness of the planet and activate our genetics in ways that cause a greater consciousness of love onto the planet earth is a lot to take in. Can we test this theory of electromagnetic and love field shifts with our personal experience? From my perspective, any test will be subjective. My sense is that in 2019, a new epoch began, a new page turned, making new things possible. A greater affiliation between what's going on in the cosmos and what we're doing here on earth was introduced. I don't know if this affiliation is true or not, but as a metaphor, it fits. In some ways this shift reflects the discussion on epigenetic relationship of the brain and consciousness. Consider that we are in an evolutionary shift that is due to a dynamic relationship of the fields of the cosmos, consciousness, electromagnetics and our biology. We don't have to believe a shift in consciousness is occurring at every level of reality. We just need to trust, be present with what is and see what we notice. We need to be vigilant and correctly respond to the signs of the times. When we live in a dialogue with creation, we ride the currents of transformation, conscious of the essential choices that show us the way.

While the poles are shifting there have also been recent cosmic energy bursts hitting earth since 2019 which have temporarily disrupted communication on earth. As an analogy, consider it almost like a kind of water balloon that came at the earth and disrupted the whole magnetic sphere around the planet, and then it bounced back. It happened a couple of times, perhaps like an earthquake. Imagine, a great deity out there throwing a water balloon at us, perhaps a love balloon. The speculation on the event was that the encounter moved us into a love dimension. Well, that is the way we reset ourselves as well. Perhaps it was our collective creation project that "threw the balloon." The plot to the movie *Interstellar* posited that our "dire need" was actually creating a wormhole to open up and bring us the answer. At the level of Transcendental Leadership, we are creating a future loop to bring the solution through, say a library wall passing from father to daughter (as portrayed in the movie *Interstellar*). In a sense, our visionary practices are a future creating a future causality. The more we center, the more the circumference speaks...*love will have its way*. Look to the fringe.

Meditation

Once again become aware of your Presence in your space.

There may be other things going on, but they're on the periphery, so just stay with the awareness of yourself in your space.

Bring forward some of the ways that you identify these deeper dimensions in yourself. As you breathe in and out, also breathe in and out through your heart. There's a coupling between your heart and your lungs so when you breathe in and out and breathe into your heart you take everything you breathe in and it turns into love when you breathe it out.

As you attune to this love, start breathing in. Add to the love and breathe out. This is a purification process. Then bring forward in your awareness and your centeredness. Say, "I am transcendent loving. I am transcendent love that accesses through love, eternal love." And so, let that move in and out. From a biblical perspective, we may see angels ascending and descending. That is the loving within your own center, your own Soul cell ascending and descending.

Step into your heart. That is the Divine Matrix, the mycelium of creation. Mycelium, the love mycelium that interweaves with everything and that interconnectedness with everything, starts to awaken in your cells and you feel it.

It enlivens your sense of existence. And within that context, you step into the breathing of love through you, the eternal love, the living water that you drink and no longer thirst, and you engage that feeling, that frequency, and you take it personally – "ah… this I am. I am this."

Once you identify with it, the "I am this love" takes its office as your authority and starts flowing out through you, rearranging and cleaning up and tidying up so that every reflective aspect of your life resonates with I am love. Say again, "This I am," this frequency of transcended love.

In that place, you are in this universe in this life, and maybe you have a wish for yourself and so you very carefully craft that wish and check it out for any lacks or limitations or ideas of victimization or a judgment about yourself. You massage it so that your wishes are already present in the seed so that in the seed the blessings already are. So you're constructing that, and then you compress it so that it is just the essence with all of these beautiful things, whether they're trips across the planet or they are automobiles or great relationships.

Ask, "What is the essence of all of those things so I can make the seed instead of having to reach out for them?" You have become a magnet that just pulls them into creations today. So, then they're already complete in the seed just like a tree is complete in the seed. When you have this perfected as best you can, you also put into it "for the highest good" because you know that once you release this inside, it's going to be part of the whole. It's going to tell everything about you and about what you want. In that, you want the highest vibration. You want it from a grade level of love. The love level is unconditional, so it will, given permission reorganize any bit of the coding that wouldn't turn out well. So say "code this for the highest good." You know that is so as you take this authority inside of you. "This I am. I am this transcendent love. I am the Soul." Take that authority and you make it so and then you just drop it into the eternal place of love within you and release it.

See it go into the vastness. As it goes into the expanse, it also goes out into a greater expanse.

In your stillness and in your Presence just allow that pulsation to increase the movement of energy as it coagulates within you as a stronger seed. By using the love this way, you become more loved this way.

The blessing of this transcendent love wakes up consciously into your senses, into your mind, into your heart, into your awareness, and into your perception.

Love will show you the way. It's the compass. Through this, give yourself permission to travel out on that and whatever way you are relating to this energy and be receptive to being shown the possibility and the truth of yourself.

Knowing that the Presence, knowing that living love is the essence of our existence, we take responsibility for our own blessing and claim this relationship. This I am. I look into this eternal energy. This is who I am. We then turn out into the world, and we see the levels of life reflect back to us in a meaningful and ordinary and miraculous way but yet, shining through all of that, then, we also see the loving reflect back through the elements of life. Throughout the cells, through the sinews, through the atoms of life, it reflects back also. So, the ordinary world we are looking out into of reflected light also has a radiant light.

In this awakening awareness, we become conscious collaborators with the many subtle ways that love as the will of God is having its way.

Increasingly we stand up in our self and in that way, we become a conscious party to this great process of life on this planet. And so, we've heard this - be in the world and not of the world. And this is the essence of that statement. We are the essence of that statement. May we be in the world and not of it in every way in every moment and every breath.

Bless us.

*When you know that you are eternal
you can play your true role in time.
When you know you are divine
you can become completely human.
When you know you are one with God
you are free to become absolutely yourself.*

Mother Meera

CHAPTER THREE

Soul

...

The chaos in the world appears as a great design or as a sinister plot. Virtue is a calling. We want to increasingly respond to challenges from the virtue of higher consciousness. The quantum view sees chaos as implying a higher order. Carl Jung joined these two viewpoints as synchronicity. The negative and positive of life are strange twins, both are indexed to love. Our visionary evolution developed as an adaptive response to life challenges, convergent conflicts, and extinction events. *In our visionary capacity, we see from the higher order in which synchronicity becomes conscious causality.* Synchronous creativity is the way of the Soul. Each moment is a synchronous creation in which every element of the universe responds to every other element as a whole movement. We choose our reality with each breath we take. We play a part by creating, promoting or allowing it at some time, place or dimension. Transcendental Leadership involves awakening to Soul and the embodiment of visionary consciousness and the highest virtue which is love. When we choose love each moment for ourselves we choose love for all people...for the universe.

Love Seeded the Soul

Before the beginning of creation, love was pure Presence and creation was a potential. Then love moved upon itself creating a reflective awareness of itself seeding the twin Soul of creation and individuation: our journey began. Our Soul gains experience through the impetus of love, the resolution of life through love, and through the sentience of the Soul. The so-called "fall" described in the Bible was just a choice for experience, to know one's self, for love to know itself. Reflection causes love to see itself. Love creates novel forms by adjusting perceived reality to make the visualized come to pass, whether in form or a state of consciousness based on the reflection of living in this world. Serial revision stochastically discovers the most adaptive way, evolving the form, creating a baseline, so we have a measure of continuity from which we can prosper on earth. We create our form in a way that is self-similar which replicates our evolving Ego and also the nature of our Soul. However, the trajectory of love is not bound by the similar. We also seek novelty. Conditional love changes to form-making to preserve what is made. Unconditional love is always making good trouble when we become set in our ways. *Love will have its way.*

Fundamentally life is a mirror, always reflecting back to us that which is inside of us, and that which is inside of us reflects back that which is in the world. For the inner levels that we are aware of, the reflection gives us course corrections. For the levels we are not yet aware of, the reflection gives us new information, revelation and insight. In this sense, we are driving through life looking in the rear view mirror, yet always moving forward. Where we have been is where we are going. We always have a choice. To clear up the mirror, we deal with those beliefs, attitudes, orientations, and identifications that we accumulated from our pursuit of who we thought we were and what we thought we were exploring. In the process, we strive to mediate our sense of wholeness and lack of wholeness. This view changes when we awaken to the transcendent realms beyond the reflective realms.

Spiritual Vision

As we open our spiritual vision in the inner worlds, we see light radiating from each form. In the physical world, we see by reflected light. When we look for spiritual vision on the physical level, we can also see the light radiating from each form and discern creations that have inner light and those that do not, as well we can see creations that have dimmed light. As the inner light dims, the form or object loses its coherence and the light fades and the form grows obscure and crumbles. If there is no radiant light, whether past, future or transcendent, there is no coherency.

The consort of spiritual vision is sound. Celestial melodies code or program with sound, forming particular shapes and configurations. Sound awakens the light and also refreshes and refurbishes the light when it dims. Love is the wholeness and the vibrancy of light and sound. We can code reality with our minds and that creation is limited to the realm of the mind. When reality is light coded with sound on the carrier of love, creation is limitless. From this perspective, we can say that the *beginning word* was a love song and the coherent synchronous movement of the universe is the work of creation serenading itself. When we consider the mirror of life, we are also contemplating the reverberation of sound and the effects of harmonious and dissonant patterns of sound and their impact on life and evolution.

Synchronous Causality

Polarization is inherent in form because in the duality each action has an equal and opposite reaction. Each day is a play of good and evil dancing toward the horizon. The polarization divides our will between expansion and preservation. The need for survival and the preservation of our creation often dominates our life path. Love must then work through the reflective artifacts of our distractions, refractive obsessions, creative projects and conquests. Refractive artifacts preserve and exaggerate their importance. In the electromagnetic world of creation, our measure of love becomes obscured. When distorted, love becomes a conditional ethical measure and elaborates itself until at some point that distortion becomes unsustainable. Then conditioned love needs our visionary consciousness to reach into new realms, refocusing our perception into new ways of reality that resolve the duality. Synchronous causality spontaneously changes the issue by rearranging the patterns of reality and by changing consciousness. Love is the master mediator, the master synergy. Synergy always moves fragmentation toward integration and wholeness. Synergy always has more power than the greatest of fragments or any sum of fragments.

Our capacity to reflect fosters self-awareness. When we awaken to the Soul, we are able to look back at ourselves through Soul. Our Soul has perspective from our center and circumference of our perceived reality…we are present within the mirror of life. From the circumference of perceived reality, we are transcendent to the mirror and look at ourselves from beyond the mirror. Love is our "organ" of vision. Consider this carefully. Synchronous vision is simultaneous. We look out into the mirror and while seeing the love reflected back, we also see all that would normally be seen by us in our reflected reality. Simultaneously, we are beyond the mirror looking into life and seeing ourselves from inside of everything. This is love as perception. Love is original and transcendent to the mirroring of the reflective worlds. When love looks back at itself from love, the love-to-love look is simultaneous, distortions are dispelled, projections are resolved, and virtues are actualized, even while all of the elements of creation are evolving, and our lives are actualizing.

Measure of Love

Gratitude and kindness are great purifiers. We welcome the reflections of love, to convert the reversals such as shame, blame, jealousy, envy, guilt, hate, and entitlement. Each reversal has a light/shadow of love. Gratitude and kindness resonate with the Love/shadow and amplify it, thus reversing the reversals. Soul collaborates this way through synchronous love. We resolve the good/evil dance through a higher love that has and needs no reflection (thus no reward) because it sees everything from inside of everything.

As we serve as a bridge between heaven and earth, primal love flows through our center into creation. The forms that we create, the beliefs we authorize, and the archetypes we constellate, refract and code the primal flow of energy through us and energy reflects from the mirrored circumference of life and of our creation. The mirror reads our codes and collaborates to form our perceptions of reality.

The light of the Soul refracts through the many prisms of thoughts, feelings and archetypes. On the inner levels each thing radiates light, as it is configured by constructive will. The same is true in the physical world of reflected light, though the radiance is obscured by the reflection and the habit of surface vision. Perception is a selective endeavor depending on our consciousness and our pattern of beliefs. Consequently, the mirroring of life becomes much more complex as we open our spiritual eyes and awaken to Soul. For us to understand what we see, we must respect the subtlety and finesse of thought. When we react, our thoughts are dominated by illusion. When we reflect, we refer what we are seeing to our center. Our center resides in higher love as an apt measure to sort out the truth.

As we meet the external challenges of our life, we are also on an inner journey. We journey inward through the layer that is the near past, and then into the realm that is the timeless past, then into the realm of archetypes that provide the design, and then into the transcendent world of Souls where we see everything as collaboration and synchronicity. From the visionary perch of Soul, we encompass the whole of creation and realize our actual responsibility of leadership. Through the eyes of the Soul, we look out at the world through our physical world eyes and also back at ourselves through our transcendent eyes. Some problems lead us to higher consciousness and others reflect imprisoned love. Our mission then is to liberate love trapped in everyday issues. We triage these issues of the world so that we can find the one question that is the fulcrum from which we can move the universe, or the lynchpin that releases the entire pattern and all the layers are then resolved and we see clearly.

The Road Less Traveled

We explore to reveal a higher reality. Whatever the temporary limitations of thought, courage and imagination are our essential nature propels us forward. There is an ancient prayer that says *the blessings already are*. We often think of this in terms of something to receive that relates to our situation or circumstance. I suggest that it is not something "other." It is us. We are the blessing that we are to receive. Our challenges are meant to bring us to that understanding. We are the ones that we are looking for. We are the promise. Though we may not yet know this, the leader we follow is us in our transcendent form.

In order to "travel to where we have never been before," we need to rise above the mirror to a transcendent perspective. From this perspective, that which was considered the cause is now the effect of a transcendent cause. From the transcendent perspective, causality is synchronous. Therefore, our world is as we perceive it because *we exist*. As an example, future possibilities can lobby for manifested localities that will result in their existence. Spiritual seeing and hearing guides the way past the horizon of time onto the road less traveled and into the far country.

We Arrive, Perhaps

Our leadership evolves from many small changes that constellate into one large Presence. This does not mean we obsess over each little thing. Instead, when we are present with each little thing a pattern reveals itself, one that shows the implication to the whole. It is our love that makes a house a home. We can shelter in place, or we can turn the dimension toward love and be home. The consecration of a house as a home comes from our Soul and is delivered through whatever ritual we devise. In our nature, we access a place that lives within the perfect fabric or the wholeness of everything. There is a shift in perspective in the small response as we experience the whole. In the still small voice within, we hear *the word* that made everything. This is not the word of speech, rather the resonate sound of the currents that make creation. It is the word that said *let there be light*. When we open our hearts to eternal love and illuminate the small place within the center of our heads, we enter a large area and transcendence appears.

At first, such intimacy with transcendence may seem overwhelming. Seemingly there is a universe in every cell of our bodies. Even when our hearts are full and all lacks are resolved, we long to go home. With the simple caress of a breeze and the sound of wind through the leaves, we transcend our minds and enter intimacy with wholeness, with all that is. This can be challenging at first. Just as our existence promotes a resolution, we become part of the energy that is working in, around and through everything to progressively orchestrate itself into more complex systems. We find ourselves as an individual awareness in a universe that is expanding. Where are we going and to what end do we wander? Our true nature is to develop, to move into new relationships with others and with ourselves. Our destiny is not in the shallow or superficial. We look at the seasons and the cycles of the moon and there's always a developing process. The process always involves an inclusive change. Our attention is on the season at hand, even while it changes from autumn to winter, to spring and summer. Each season participates in renewal. We know that it's really just a continuation...like breathing...it's a cycle.

Rationalizing the Prophet

From the level of calling humanity to a new evolution, problems aren't the issue. The issues are there to assist in moving us to a new level of consciousness. We begin to recast our perception of problems to clarify what is inside of us and to contribute something, to understand something, and to act in a way that, through our cooperation, we find results. In this way, we bring whatever we give to ourselves. We are the prodigal sons and daughters that brought humanity to the universe. Before that, it was just a garden.

One of my teachers once said that when we engage with love and service in whatever we do, consciousness will lift. Consciousness is the relational element of whatever's going on that is the Transcendental Leader. When we lead with love our actions have practical effects: a better form of living, a kinder institution, a more effective way to do something, that's the transformational part. The transcendent part just operates in the simplicity of how we respond. We engage loving through our attitude of service. What is the primary service? It's how we look at and respond to everything.

When we see an issue in somebody's life, the first step is to ask for the Presence of love. If that is too ambiguous or controversial, then the issue is with us. Being in the Presence of Love is Transcendental Leadership. The next step in the Presence of transcendence is to observe and to see what occurs. Wholeness is always present and moving in a particular way. We take our lead from Presence, and watch what the wholeness does. We participate in how this process affects us because our feelings and responses to it are all information. If we're identified with the outcome, we can't get the information. If we are identified with our transcendent self, then our response is another form of cyclic breathing, like the seasons or the leaves turning and the snow falling and spring coming and the grass sprouting. It's like breathing in and out. We are inseparable from the transcendent rhythm that is the ordinariness of spirit...the manifestation of the transcendent in the ordinary.

Love Will Have Its Way

I grew up hearing a lot about God's will, and it still can confound me or confound whatever part of me that gets confounded. Dogma is based on belief. The word I heard was that "God's will" was synonymous with the dogma of the church, a belief as to what God's will is rather that what it really is. The purpose of dogma is to control the beliefs of the flock, prescribe behavior, preserve group cohesion and maintain one's authoritative hierarchy. In this way "God's will" is merely the politics of authority. I was able to resolve my dilemma with dogma when I realized that God's will is simply: *love will have its way*. Everything that's going on is an expression of love finding its way. That can seem pretty peculiar because some pretty strange things are happening, and some are just awful.

Are we an instrument of the scientific endeavors of God to experience creation or are we an instrument of our scientific discovery of God? This question is similar to the question discussed earlier: is consciousness an epiphenomenon of the brain or is the brain an epiphenomenon of consciousness? Perhaps our agency works both ways. We learn about (God) love as love (God) learns about us through us. Whatever the case, through our knowing that *love will have its way*, we learn, research and discover through participation, through what David Bohm might call the holomovement of love. If God's will is *love will have its way*, how does it do that?

Belief in God is not necessary for the Transcendental Leader. Embodying the experience of transcendent and present love (mycelium love) is necessary. Personal access and awareness is the only way I know to explore the existence of the ways and means of the unifying, intelligent, loving energy that is in the background of all that *is*. In other words, we know God (love) by embodying God (love). When we develop precision in our thought and feeling this becomes a scientific endeavor. Peneus Parkhurst Quimby, the American Transcendentalist healer, equated what he called the Inner Christ with science. He is an example of the precision of thought and feeling to which I am referring. Quimby's understanding of the Christ (the love inherent to our Soul) was not based on belief. It was based on direct knowing and direct experience through his person. He developed his healing protocols based on his relationship to the Christ (love) within and the functional nature of beliefs.

Quimby's scientific protocols were *Presence, reflection, comprehension, silence* and *love*. In *Presence* we are conscious in the connected subtle and physical levels of energy, which enables us to join each other, while also reflecting to each other one another's inner worlds. During *reflection*, he spoke with his client in a way that physical speech was permeated by the spiritual dialogue, serving as a conduit and mediator of the Christ (living love). Within this context, Quimby explained to his client how beliefs can distort and block the healing expression of the Inner Christ (love) resulting in what he called dis-ease. During *comprehension*, he then explored with his client the beliefs and patterns, held by them, that distorted the way love manifested through them. This enabled his client to reconcile their beliefs with their core essence of love through a conscious experience, or through having *comprehension* of the truth. Quimby would then sit with them in *silence*. *Silence* is a condition past the chatter of the mind, desires of emotion, politics of speech and the magnetism of the world which permits *love to have its way*.

Use Everything

In terms of Transcendental Leadership, we find ourselves in the present confronting (engaging) any given situation or circumstance as it appears. At the same time, from a higher level, we open to an awareness of the total scheme of things. We ask the question: is a more significant strategic movement using the current scene, which seems dark, to fulfill a higher purpose which is light and love? Our reference is that all actions initiate and resolve in loving: *love will have its way.* We align with that reference. In the tactical moment, we may see none of the loving. Only the abuse is evident. We have many options. In our Presence, we will notice from the reflected field or the internal intuitive field some action, even if it's only a holding action. In this situation, we are called upon to have no opinion or bias for the transcendent to lead. The right action can come in the blink of an eye. This concept is challenging. We are also meeting our own karma in each situation, so that too is in the calculation of the highest good. We can ask: how is my karma coloring the perception of now? We may first have to resolve our karmic relationships before we allow ourselves the clarity of Presence. Perhaps the case is that resolving our karma is our contribution. The easiest way to follow God's will as *love will have its way* is to *use everything to transform ourselves into loving.*

Shifting Narratives

When I consider shifting my narratives, I am always reminded of Emerson's incredible prophetic vision about America. In his vision, he saw the American Scholar as one who could reach past conventional thought and tradition into the realm of the Soul and from that resource build a new nation. He was a very inspiring visionary. I take it as a strategic plan, something we aspire to. As far as I know, this vision is not an emphasis in High School civics class when segments of the population feel left out of the "American Dream." Our society can easily revert to tribalism as one group divides against another. An example of this in our recent history was the split instigated from the slogan of "Make America Great Again," which was a "dog-whistle" for make America white and male again and a con to promote the wealth, aggrandizement and power of a single person. For those who believe they have been forgotten and neglected...the inspiration of the high vision falls short and distorts into tribalism, into a strategy of fear. Energy follows thought. We must always invite the awakening of the Soul so that the higher vision can be accomplished. America is a higher vision that we continually strive to fulfill.

We have a narrative that we live by. Narratives subtly weave the common perception into a story of reality that then becomes our reality. We must always re-evaluate our narratives and measure each phrase to the wisdom of our hearts. Hearts resonate to the unified love that in its secret way moves life as a unit, as a wholeness. According to physicist David Bohm, the only limit is the movement of the whole. That may not seem like a limitation but consider that the whole will manage anything that jeopardizes the fabric of the whole. That is the highest good. Our genius is in cooperating with the whole. We get the vision when we step above the narrative of the day. Even science has a narrative that shapes discovery. Now and then someone, less socialized, sees something more significant, and the world is no longer the center of the universe but a planet rotating around a sun that is also not the center of the universe.

The center of the universe started with a sound: a bang, or sound that translates to "let there be light," and an event, "and there was light." This is synchronous creation. Then, the light went everywhere. There is the speed of light, and faster yet is the speed of love which, as Jonathan Livingston Seagull was told (from the 1970 film *Jonathan Livingston Seagull*), "the fastest speed is being there." Yet for some who remain in a psychological netherworld, their earth is still the center of the solar system, and for some the world is flat. Lest we fall to the arrogance of our enlightenment, we must remember the universe makes a place for them, an abode, a refuge of their own in which they can learn to love and we can learn to love them. When we are frightened, we apportion to ourselves a sized reality in which we can feel safe. To maintain cohesion for these realities, we write narratives to live by. If there is grace here, it is because we unwittingly write these narratives in the sand that one day the wind will blow elsewhere and when that wind blows these sands of time, we adjust to the shifting narrative. When the wind of Spirit blows the timeless sands of eternity, we have a change of epoch, a new day and a new dawn.

For What Purpose

Great scientists have always stepped out of the narrative and had visions that offered keys to their work. When my favorite scientist George

Washington Carver was young, he had a blissful transcendental experience that opened his heart and visionary eye, as discussed in Chapter One. Against all odds, he became a biochemist and made many discoveries that were credited with saving the economy of the South. It's ironic since he was black and born of slaves that he would create an economic benefit that for his time saved the economy of the South. He began his discoveries by reverently and humbly talking to plants. In other words, he asked God to reveal the purpose for which a plant existed. He would get an answer. He took that information into his laboratory and developed the chemistry and the application for agriculture, for better ways to raise crops, and to use the harvest to make products. This quality of Transcendental Leadership is inherent in us, and as well, we see examples of it in the world which we resonate with inside, and it reminds us of ourselves.

We can join in the milieu of humanity, bask in our belonging, mimicking the phrases, responses and styles that match the contours of the day, or we can admit that beneath our daily participation, we are asking for love in a profound and essential way. Consider being our own scientist like Carver, looking at ourselves and asking the God inside of us, for what purpose was I made? For what purpose was my nation made? For what purpose were the challenges and opportunities on earth made? The most profound answer is always to be more loving, to fulfill and transform our life into loving, to have joy, and to live more abundantly. This is not a new directive. Throughout the millennia, it resurfaces every time the current game folds. When we evoke purpose rather than a singular accomplishment for our Ego, it is a celebration of the Soul. When we are looking for our Soul, we can project onto that endeavor and what that's supposed to look like. Perhaps the Soul is what's left when everything else is destroyed. Pray it does not come to that.

If It Doesn't Kill Us

As we reach into the high country of Soul, there is an initiation in which everything that is not Soul is stripped away. That may seem harsh, but consider that perhaps this is not a singular event, but one that happens through the trials and tribulations of life. Do we commandeer each small thing for self-importance or for love? We have common sense guidance in the form of "if it doesn't kill you it will make you stronger," and "if it can be shaken, it is not you." We seem to pursue harsh rationalizations for life, while longing for principles of grace as if under the spell of an adverse lover. The false stuff won't last if it is not loving. Life will strip it from us. That being true, perhaps we could skip the illusion of greed, lust, and domination and get to the love part. Even our lacks are of great value because they become receptacles into which we can receive, and the traumas and the issues become opportunities to awaken to something more significant. Life only tears apart that which we believed in that was less than ourselves, less than love. This realization asks us reverently to find a way of working together...for the highest good. Let's find a way of working together.

Go Fish

As a helpful perspective, consider the beginning of our consciousness. We sense that we began because we are here and we have an ontology. We recapitulate the alleged beginning with each conception and birth of a child, an ontology that is intrinsic to each of us. Our sense of beginning we will call the *First Cause*. This is similar to the term *El Shaddai,* which when sung is like an eternal serenade of the incarnation of our eternity.

For what purpose did we come out into creation? One of the ways this sorts out, from my perspective, is that intrinsic to our consciousness is a universal urge for the whole to have an individualized experience of itself through us...as us. That is the essence of what and why we do anything. Whatever this wholeness is, *it is*. And how does it know itself? Evidently, there is an engram in our origin that we strive to individuate. In the process we become egotistic and that keeps disappointing us. Then that disappointed egoism becomes a revelation of loving because that's the only thing that will ever give us a sense of fullness or fulfillment.

In our individuation, we tend to see the smallness of ourselves, which starts to change when we realize that when we look out into life, life is looking back at us and that, more powerfully, we are that life looking back at us. This changes our perspective, and we can sense the ancient memory that there is an aspect of us that came into individuation, and there is another aspect that stayed with the wholeness. In stories like the prodigal son and daughter, one person remains in the refuge, in the holiness, in the inner place, and then the other person goes out and ventures. The one that came back is the one that brings all the experience, so that one is favored, or that's just the way we tell it. Perhaps the one that stayed is our Soul mate and looking for him or her in the world is futile, yet that quest led us on our journey of discovery. The venturer is one part of the wholeness and the other part is represented by the aspect of self that holds holiness and both parts are necessary.

There's something to say for looking out at the star-filled night and having the sense that it reminds us of something. We say it reminds us of something transcendent and we assume that it is beyond us. Perhaps it also reminds us of the original element of our self and the part of us that stayed with the wholeness. When we look at it that way, it activates something inside of us that reconnects, that reminds us of the one on the individual journey and the one that is the interconnected network of consciousness that holds and provides context for the journey. We are the fish <u>and</u> the sea. We are swimming, and then we become aware that there's a fish swimming through us and we recognize that's us also, and so the ocean begins to realize, oh, I'm also the fish, and I'm also the fish that's swimming through me in an ocean that is also me. In the intimacy of living, we remember that the purpose for which we came was simply to bring love.

Try Choosing Back

Fundamentally, we have to choose. When we choose, it is essential to support ourselves. Whether we make a good choice or a bad choice, it is valuable. When selecting, it is imperative that we love ourselves regardless of what we say or do. Mostly that is what parents are left with. We can love our children regardless of what they say or do, even if we don't like what they do, or are just completely baffled by it. A key here is our relationship to our choices. This is where transcendent skill comes in. In choosing, sometimes it is a rational choice, sometimes we're taking a chance, and sometimes it is idiotic, but it is the best we have, and that is the best. When we're pretty much asleep and identified with our emotions, choosing can be reactive and symptomatic of a broad range of unconscious issues. Whatever else we do, our perseverance will sustain us and eventually false identification and unconscious issues will sort themselves out as we awaken.

When we attend to our transcendent nature, our visionary consciousness is more readily available. We can give ourselves quality advice and clarify our choices. Basic advice is to remember to love ourselves no matter how well our decisions go. The clarity of being able to see all the elements that come from being present is another form of advice. The more we practice being present, the more skillful we become at sorting through all of our regrets for the past, our worry about the future, our trying to lobby for our lacks, advocate for our limitations or hedging our bets. Being present affects our perception giving us a lot more clarity in terms of internal trust and conviction and also in seeing what's really going on. Our capacity to choose becomes very precise in this way…through practicing with Presence.

Choosing is really a process of learning how to make distinctions and form preferences. We think it's about the content or what we're choosing, but it's really about us developing courage and the trust to choose. Our transcendent love is the measure of choice. Rather than asking, is it good or bad according to certain standards, we use the resonance of transcendent love as the measure. Does it resonate? Does it match my virtue? As the saying goes, *to thine own self be true.* We check our priorities to see if our relationship with God is first, then our Soul, then our Presence and then others. The most significant application of choice is to *use everything to transform ourselves into loving,* even if it takes a few weeks to get around to that level of loving, after we kick and scream or blow things up.

Choice has an exciting relationship to higher consciousness. Birth into this world is an expression of being chosen. When we are born and wake up here, we need to choose back in the form of accepting our life and accepting the higher consciousness that chose us. However, whatever our concept, we are from a primordial essence and are selected by it. The way we activate this is to choose back. When we have a feeling that physical life is all there is or that "God" doesn't want us or love us, try choosing back. Maybe we just forgot to say yes. Choosing back is remembering that we came to bring love.

Rescue Paradox

We often meet conflicts in our lives that confound us. Usually, this occurs when someone or a situation has such a pull on us that we become invested and enmeshed, and our well-being becomes wrapped up in saving someone or transforming a human condition. When our well-being depends on rescuing the other, we know that we have an unresolved insufficiency within us that we are attempting to resolve by the rescue. On the other hand, when we are secure in our loving, we may seamlessly reach out to assist another. Our circumstances have their own integrity so our first response whether we intervene or not is respect for the individual and their karma. Respect initiates a love response. We are able to act or not act based on the real need of the situation and not from our own unresolved issues.

Our challenge is in terms of accepting and respecting our gifts and being aware of how we participate with our gifts, while not forgetting who we are. How do we remember ourselves as we enter into this challenge? When we try to do something and it doesn't work and then we feel bad, a failure or whatever because it didn't work the way we thought it should, that's a symptom of basing our value, our worth and our identity on the outcome. That's not helpful or productive at all.

If the outcome creates more consternation for us, then we've identified with it personally and made our value the issue instead of helping the other person or helping ourselves for that matter. We are acting out of our own need to fill or resolve an internal issue rather than our altruism. Consider that we need to let it all be what it is. Our challenge is the rescue paradox: how do we stay loyal to our Soul during a situation that challenges us so strongly that we abandon ourselves for the sake of acting on a perceived crisis or to receive a perceived reward?

Often, our behavior is one thing and who we are is another. A further aspect of the paradox is that the same behavior may be a response that comes from our well-being or our lack. It may be that we have been caught in the dilemma of rescuing based on our compensatory need forever. When we are enmeshed, it's helpful to consult our nervous system. It is likely to say let's get out of here, at least temporarily, so let's go meditate. And, we do that, and it helps. We'll then want to do more of that. Our only agreement may be to serve as a witness while our loved one goes through self-destruction. When they fulfill that, we just take them in our arms and say I love you and we join them in the resolution not in the tragedy. Hopefully, they listen before too much destruction occurs. Issues are invitations. We want to act, so we make the situation all about fixing the problem, and it's not about fixing the issue. We ask: can we love this person enough to respect their karma? Can we love ourselves enough to love this person and respect them while they go through their karma? There is nothing to fix. The process is working.

Juggling Nonsense

Let's say there is a conflict with a family member. The thing is that nothing we can find in our history as a mother, father, sister or brother makes the situation with our relative happen, so we don't make ourselves out to be a bad person. We definitely played a part in the conflict's creation in that we are all co-creators in some way, but the cause in the specific situation is the impulse driving the person in conflict. We did come into this incarnation with them and we do have a role. We get to be the loving one who is there for them when they or their circumstance allows for us to reach out in a way that serves. Or, maybe we are in service to the dysfunction. With that, we do what we can. Our response doesn't eliminate any behavior; it just eliminates where we are coming from. We're involved in a behavior because it is necessary, but not to reconcile our own lacks. When we use a situation to transform ourselves into loving, we are in service to healing regardless of our negative or positive role.

If we insist on interpreting the case or situation as proof of our lack, we are stuck because we are attached to our distortion. All that says is that we have to do more to reconcile our distortions. If our response turns out badly, it means that we judged ourselves. Every evidence of the situation indicates we are lacking. If only? If only? That is the way the mind is holding us. That's the way we have a grasp of the mind. We have constructed a cosmology in which the bad things are our fault and to redeem ourselves we must rescue, like that's the floating log we are holding onto when we are headed toward the waterfall and just because we can reach out and grab a branch and save ourselves, we are not going to let go of the log even as the roar of the waterfall grows louder, because that is what we know. At the heart of this scenario is our disapproval of how God is doing it or how the universe is set up, which is amazing when we have no idea what that is or means, even though, we insist that our interpretation is absolutely correct and may be the transformation. In other words when we don't know that we don't know, we are stuck in a phantom pride. We are oblivious to the truth and the grace of what appears to be a disaster. We don't know that we need to surrender our entanglement in the situation one hundred percent. When we are present with what is, we are surrendering one hundred percent. That's what being present is. This is a hard dance because to act and to not know at the same time is frightening. It can be like juggling nonsense.

There is a great mystery here that we're studying. How do we create external change by changing ourselves internally? It is not a matter of finding fault and blaming ourselves. That's a misunderstanding, our great lie. That's some kind of Ego distortion. We are relating to an alchemical process that is internal to us. We are working with a change inside ourselves. We can be entertained by our circumstances, but the real work is inside. The work is not in terms of fixing ourselves; it is in finding out how to bring loving into places it hasn't been before, into areas that we may have rules that say love can't be here. Those are the places where we start. Then we might think, if we can't fix those places, we must not have enough love. See, that's just absurd. Loving solves problems by changing consciousness not by making ourselves or others do something that we think is healthy, even though the making may have a role to play.

Some pretty amazing changes happen in people's relationships when they change themselves, when they give up judgment, when they give up harshness inside, and they give up blame. Consider that all people are our loved ones going through some tough stuff. Respect their karma and anybody else involved and their relationship to it. That is the foundation. All else is recreational, even if we tie them up, throw them in a closet, or whatever, though extreme, maybe those are right actions. Whatever, you do or think stay present with what is, see what you notice, act, and trust that *love will have its way*, that is the only way to juggle nonsense.

The Constant Gardener

In some ways, the meaning of Christ is a perennial question, because as we awaken to it, Christ increasingly permeates our consciousness. Then Christ is not a definition. It is a discovery. Often, I will talk about all the things that mean Christ before I use that word. There's a consciousness that's the seat of our being and it is interconnected with everything. It's interwoven with divine love and divine wisdom that is everything, and so the process of that divine love and divine wisdom going from the general to the particular manifesting as us is a process of Christ.

Whether we use the term Christ or not, if we trace any mystical lineage or lineage of spiritual awakening, there's a point at which we reach into Christ. On this planet, Christ is the agency of being one with everything and one with loving and living that wholeness manifesting out into life from loving. That is Christ regardless of what any group may be calling it. All the lineages lead to Christ and that's what I mean by Christ in the context of Soul.

Various groups and individuals project their limitations or elaborations onto Christ. The most common use is to demonize and push against or use a concept of Christ to demonize and separate us from others. With all the various and conflicting viewpoints, it is left to each of us to find our way to Christ and the ways we understand that according to how we are put together. Our heart knows and we need not put too much focus on what others say or how authoritative a belief system claims to be. It is how it arises within us. Christ is not someone who is coming to us from outside, especially not as a particular denomination. When we perceive

Christ as coming from the outside it is because it is also arising inside of us. We have been seeded internally with Christ from the beginning. Jesus of the Bible, who was an awakened Christ, said that he would come as a thief in the night and that the place we would find him was within. We have to consult the place of truth to know, and that place begins with our inner teacher who resides within. In this sense, you could say that Christ is the center of the truth that we came from and our inner teacher is a form of that truth. Many teachings share a concept of and name for an inner teaching or teacher.

There is an office of Christ for the planet, which is a world archetype and corresponding with that archetype each individual having an inner Christ. Awakening to the inner Christ is the way that living love manifests itself on this planet. We are an agency of Christ. We can call on the Christ within us as a form of the Cosmic Christ, and that's a kind of authority or action that we can access. As we awaken to Christ, our DNA responds, often it can even change our neural net and depending on our situation or circumstance, in our Presence, can modify the environment.

There is a debate in science about whether our consciousness is an epiphenomenon of our biology or our biology is an epiphenomenon of our consciousness. From the perspective of Christ, our biological evolution has been a developmental evolution preparing our body to be able to accommodate Christ. As Christ has prepared us through the millennia, now Christ is our comforter. There is no limitation to this process of accommodating Christ. From this expansive perspective, our physical body is an epiphenomenon of consciousness, whether it arises from within our evolving body or arises from reaching in transcendentally to mold our body. In a sense, as humanity, we have been a constant gardener on this earth, harvesting successive incarnations until one day our biology matches our Soul.

Fluffy Thinking

We act like our Ego should be sufficient to make life grand and we make up a lot of stuff supporting that viewpoint. Until we become

Soul conscious, our Ego-self will retain a grand vision based on inflated perspectives of self-importance based on diminishing or exaggerating who and what we think we are. From this perspective our Ego co-opts the expansive urge of the Soul and instead of transforming the Ego, the expansive urge inflates our Ego. Our response to this is often that we don't measure up to our ideal, or we exaggerate our importance.

Not to cast negative aspersion on our made-up life because that is how we develop. We make up stuff and then we check it out, or life checks it out for us. We start out in life a bit naive. Instead of dealing with the dark side, we use spiritual bypass to compensate. We escape into a spiritual study. We mask trauma with unicorns and rainbows. The monsters have to emerge from the deep...and they will. How else will they get the love and attention they need to transform? Well, the other way is for us to take the deep dive into the monster's realm and in the Presence of love anchor the light. When Soul begins to move, the hills and valleys of our made-up life are exposed.

Fluffy thinking not only refers to our tendency to respond to our life with magical thinking, but it also applies to a propensity to see life as a combative zero sum reality. In a zero sum reality there are always winners and losers...no win/win scenarios. Wherever we fall on the continuum of winning and losing, we have to believe our position is correct, whether believing we are winners or losers. Being self-assured is a beginning and doesn't go as far as peace, prosperity and Presence. Whatever game we choose, we have to deal with the way life deals and remain loyal to our Soul for our identity.

We all work at getting to know ourselves. We have our reference points, like when we have moments of peace, when we are present, or in our meditation, we feel the bliss of connection, or we have an out-of-body experience in a beautiful place, or feel one with all when watching the sunset. Those moments tell us that these places and feelings exist inside of us. Where we get into trouble is when we're not in those places, we forget that we are making up stuff and we miss the cues that tell us the truth. Consequently, we misread our reality, and believe we are doing better or worse than we are.

When we talk about Transcendental Leadership, we want to understand that those places in which we are doing better or worse than we think are to some extent always there, still connected and held in love and that our judgement about those places doesn't matter. This means that our core resilience is powerful, and that life always and unpredictably does what it does. Even though we're not conscious of it, we are witnessing ourselves, respecting ourselves and supporting ourselves. That's the piece to remember. When we feel like we blew it, or we are not with it, our body aches, or we have the flu (which is a purification process), we think that these things mean something. They do! We need to remember that we are loving and loved regardless of what happens or what we say or do. The challenges of life are symptoms of our loving of life.

There's always a play with life that is constantly moving love forward in ways we may not understand. This is where the value of being more disciplined is helpful. Feelings are not identity, they're information. We are continually getting information from an array of feelings and emotions. We may think, I don't know what it means, and I am also experiencing a lousy feeling, sickness, failure, holiness, bliss, joy, and on and on. Any of those thoughts just proves that we exist and that we are involved in life. We are getting the weather, nuances, information, and news. We are getting the intimacy of life, and sometimes it feels pretty raw, which may be proof that our lives are working just fine. Be present with your working life.

Fluffy thinking is when we make stuff up about making stuff up. We might think, "Oh my issue is because I kicked the dog when I was six-years-old, because I stole candy, I haven't meditated enough, my grammar school teacher hit me, or whatever." Such explanations may be excuses rather than causes. That's why we have to be vigilant around our interpretations. The more we become vigilant, the more we can just be present with what is... what really is and respect that. When we are vigilant and present with what is, we don't have to guess and doubt. We are clued into what's really going on and we are probably doing better than we think, so beware of fluffy thinking or making a stuffed animal out of it. There is no fluff in the simplicity, power and the eternal love of our Soul.

Meditation

Close your eyes and just become aware of your body and your space and you in your space.

Then we have a familiar perspective on our spiritual anatomy that there's a column of rotating energy that flows vertically up and down, corresponding to the spine and all the chakras and is part of breathing between heaven and earth, anchored in the earth and secured in heaven.

As you continue breathing through the central axis, from above and below into your heart, be aware of the aspect that is breathing in and out of your heart into the horizontal creation, at the same time condensing the love from above and below, and from center and the horizon into a powerful vortex of light pulsating and resonating in the heartbeat of all, activating your body of light.

Become aware of your body and then become aware of your space at the same time. The awareness and breathing is always inclusive, always adding the next level of intimacy and connection. So just become aware of your heart and be aware of your loving as you are breathing.

Your loving is breathing in and breathing out through your body, through your cells.

And also bring into your awareness this column of vortex light. You can just imagine it there. There is this interacting vortex between heaven and earth. As you also breathe, just keep hold of the energy of the earth that comes up as you breathe in and catch all the energy and the highest heaven you can imagine as you breathe in. Breathe all this into your heart, and then you hold it there in that sacredness, and then you breathe it out through every cell of your body as it flows out into your space.

Just continue in this way, in this integrated breathing, really breathing in loving from above and below in your heart, breathing it out through your body, into your cells, into your space. You may even have a sensation that your body dissolves a bit as you do this.

Now bring your attention into the center of your head and see a light that activates as you place your focus there. And as this light opens up, at the same time you continue breathing you fold yourself within this light and then expand. And as it expands, it joins the matrix of energy that you've been breathing.

Allow the very powerful ordination of this self, this individualized self, and its expression in this personality on this planet. This requires a certain recognition of responsibility and a recognition of who you are, and this is not an intellectual thing, but a trusting as you claim yourself. There is a connection and access into your wisdom of self that doesn't have to be thought up or figured out, it just is.

Continue now this process of bringing the light and love through you and around you and awakening this seat of the Soul within you. Also then look at yourself in a simple way and affirm that this life, this personality, this house is all your responsibility. State that I am Soul, Master of my House, and just say that inwardly three times and see what happens as that transcendental authority awakens to itself as it moves through the house of your personality.

Allow it to put things in order both in terms of content and the alignment and the flows and movements of the energy. So once activated, you just go with it.

I invite you to engage your being in an exploration of self that it is continuous and reveals the truth of life without fear, inspired by Soul, guided by love. Consider that perhaps we are the promise, and a new day and new dawn refers to a simple change of heart.

We talk about life, as the prophecy says, changing in the twinkling of an eye will come a new heaven and a new earth. That's instantaneous. What's capable of that?

You have begun.

Before you bring your awareness back and open your eyes, just be present for a moment and just ask for the light and love. Ask for the Presence, and just breathe into yourself in a way that invites that transcendent relationship inside to move more into your consciousness.

Let that light flow through all that you experienced and all you were given and received and extend that out to those people you love and those people you interact with every day, and through everyone that is touched by this reaching out.

These blessings that you receive come through you and then you become a focus or a lens that channels them out into the world.

As you wake up to these blessings inside, then those blessings can look back at you through life, and people get caught up in them and start feeling them.

Accept this agency that you have through your own transcendence, your own words made flesh.

Bless all that is and will be.

*I love to think of nature as an unlimited broadcasting station,
through which God speaks to us every hour,
if we will only tune in.*

George Washington Carver

CHAPTER FOUR

Cosmology
...

Ralph Waldo Emerson was part of a New England group known as the American Transcendentalists. They were prominent in the middle of the 1800s, when the Civil War was brewing. There was a great division building in the nation, while at the same time there was a concentrated expression of the transcendentalist. In some ways, we are in a similar dynamic right now. Whatever dragons weren't tamed from that period are arising these days. Lest we give dragons a bad rap, they were the zeitgeist, the spirits of the time. In Chinese lore, dragons were a primal creative force, being good or ill depending on how we lived with them.

At the same time that the reactive political forces were responding with dominating, divisive and predatory actions, the complementary zeitgeist of Transcendental Leadership called forward a higher unity, a greater awakening of the human heart as an adaptive response to division and hate. When massive division arises, it forces people to wake up to a unifying spirit. The practical response is to compromise, collaborate and make peace. The internal directive is to go deeper within and become conscious of frequencies that unify by transcending duality, or at least to bring peace within ourselves, which is in itself a useful contribution.

Soul Nation

The American Transcendentalists were responding to a spiritual impulse. Ralph Waldo Emerson, Phineas P. Quimby, Henry Thoreau, Louisa May Alcott, Walt Whitman, Emily Dickenson and others all had their ways of reaching higher within and pulling back the veil of perception revealing the role of transcendental consciousness in human affairs. Emily Dickenson had it easy. She just went out into her garden and everything she saw was transcendent. In her poetry we get that connection to life in a simple way. The smallest creature or turn of a leaf reaches into the macrocosm, and her attunement captured those connections.

Emerson made his definitive statement on Transcendental Leadership during his address on August 31, 1837 to the Phi Beta Kappa Society of Harvard College called *The American Scholar*.

> *A nation of men [and women] will for the first time exist, because each believes himself [herself] inspired by the Divine Soul which also inspires all men [and women].*

Throughout Emerson's talk, he challenged the students (and I'll just take that as all of us) to recognize and identify with a noble ideal etched in the Soul. He electrified the American Scholar as an archetype of a higher being incarnated into the fabric of this nation, and challenged us to define ourselves thus. He cautioned us about being taken into "common thought" or the "status consciousness" or "one who puts on airs" or "puts himself above" or embraces "entitlement." In our time, this caution would include endemic racism, misogyny, haves and have nots, and environmental terrorism. The Transcendental Leadership ethic is the remedy and sourcing of inspiration from Soul. It is more essential to us. The challenge is not to get caught up in the traditional elitist mentality or the againstness of tribalism, but to embrace the depth of Soul that is commonplace within us all as a transcendent resource of creativity and wisdom. We are not personalities shaped by traditional thoughts. As American Scholars and Transcendental Leaders, we embrace a more profound possibility. As Emerson's speech built upon itself, it was an admonition for students to rise up to the transcendence of a visionary consciousness. "The American Scholar" was about building a new nation for the first time, instead of copying this nation after the imperialistic, colonizing thought of the times, or some other way. Actually, we copied our nation, in part, from the indigenous Iroquois Confederation established by Dakanawida and Hiawatha centuries before, which was kind of cool. This nation (our nation) was something new, a new way of looking at nation-building, thus the trajectory of the seed planted in the actualization of our destiny, needs to mature. We are in the throes of that trajectory now and we, as a nation are having to find our way. Our founders were inspired by the Iroquois vision of democracy, ethics, respect, community, and planning for the long game, as well as, the transcendental and metaphysical wisdom of Europe and the ancient wisdoms of the East. Emerson's vision was of a nation built for the first time by those inspired by the wisdom of their Souls. Even though the actual nation may be new, the vision is ancient.

In a sense, he was addressing all of us as the American Scholar. By focusing on it that way, we take the approach of a scholar, as one who studies, one who wants to understand, one who wants to find out, one who is awed by whatever he or she is studying, one who is curious, and one who can look at something in terms of being present with what is. The root word of *Education* is *educare'*, to draw out, that is the scholar. How do we draw out the meaning from within? How do we draw out a more in-depth understanding from within things as well? Emerson is not only challenging us, but he is also proclaiming a prophecy, inspiring and awakening of the Transcendental Leader.

Emerson's vision was not a small notion of the Soul. Soul gets defined in different ways depending on our perspective. The Soul is connected transcendentally to everything higher and more profound. Our Soul Presence is key to accessing divine wisdom and collaboration. In our minds, we are convinced of our co-creative relationships with Spirit, with the ancient claim that "This I Am," "I Am This." This conviction becomes a knowing Presence even beyond belief. By having direct knowing, we transcend the speculation of our beliefs into direct knowledge. That's a pretty powerful statement.

From my perspective, Emerson's challenge is just as relevant today as it was in the late 1800s. The challenges of these times call for a Soul response (a Transcendental Leadership response) to bring a Soul-guided nation into being. Some of nation building is practical, like putting procedures and laws in place for settling disputes, creating relationships, and creating communities. Our practical action makes a place into which the greater Soul of the nation can incarnate as a result of Soul-action from each of us.

There is something in the nature of Transcendental Leadership in which we embody our Soul that is similar to nation-building. We are building an internal nation that exists because we call it forward inside of us, we stand up in it. We will bring this internal nation present in our consciousness and our frequency and consecrate it, and we will bring it present in substance by embodying the experience of it. When Emerson says "for the first time" on the planet, he is not only speaking of a consciousness, but a skill, a technique, a procedure. As we are creating a Soul-Nation, we are also bringing present our citizenship in that nation.

Ancient Voices

Throughout history, there have been many attempts to build a civilization based on Soul, but those attempts have always fallen short. The journey of civilization is more ancient than we realize, at least in official knowledge. The current cycle is about 5,000 years and there were other cycles before that. Some archeological remnants haven't found their way into the textbooks yet, even though I am not sure why. We can feel these things and make up stories about them. Pushing up from the unconscious are the struggles of humanity to civilize itself, to learn from nature and to learn how to build a life here on Earth.

Then we come to a time for us to renew our vision of a soul nation. We can respond to the call that a nation based on Soul will exist for the first time. It exists anew for the first time within us. There is an opening up inside us that says, "oh this is something I haven't done before." And we ask, "how am I going to do that?" First we have an emerging awareness of a soul-nation as an inner experience. A nation is born here inside, for the first time. Then at some point, this awareness seeps in through the culture of people and social groups influencing each others' frequencies and, as the awareness builds in the collective consciousness of the nation, more people are pulled into the awareness. More and more people become involved in the Soul nation-building experience.

Anchoring a high place of consciousness into the Earth requires a resonance that inspires people to reach up within themselves. There's a compatibility here because we might be standing on Earth, but it requires a connection to Earth that is organic and a knowledge that it is living earth. When we realize that the earth is alive, we strive to become balanced with the Earth's energy.

There are two streams of American Transcendentalism. We had the New Englanders, but then we also had the indigenous folks who were the first citizens, and they were very compatible. Though not so apparent at first glance, there is an emerging movement within various first nations to strengthen their heritage and their ways of connecting to the Earth that are harmonious and translating that into political action. This connection moves both ways. The compatibility and harmony going on right now between all people, is no longer American or European, but it becomes a nation in consciousness. The awakening of the Transcendental Leader in all of us is the harmony, salvation and transformation of the world.

Repeating Cycles

Some folks are having a hard time learning from the cause and effect of history and recognizing that the ways of domination and distortion are implicit in their lives. Elevating oneself as superior or in arrogance promotes sacrificing the other so you can live well. We haven't yet awakened to the full subtlety and consequence of this superior entitled stance. The physical evidence of our distortions fades quickly as we can see through some examples of the rise and fall of civilizations. Most of the "history" and accompanying consequences are woven into mythology. We may try to interpret history and events on the basis of material science, but the hermeneutics require that we use words, symbols, and metaphors to look beyond material science into the quantum structuring of events. This takes consciousness. We can't find physical evidence for very much on the cultural and material surface of life, except through reading the Akasha which requires seeing through our internal sense. When you look at the news and have a foreboding feeling that we have been here before, you are starting to tune into the Akasha. Trust your intuition.

There have been obvious extinction events such as meteors hitting the planet and ice ages, as well as more local ones like famine and droughts. A massive drought 75,000 to 135,000 years ago in ancient Africa is credited with facilitating a higher level of intelligence in humans. Meteors and melting ice may have covered over the artifacts of ancient civilizations in many areas of the world. Ancient cities perhaps as old as 14,000 years lying just offshore were obscured by rising seas following the ice age melt. Less known are stories of even more ancient civilizations in which extinction was caused by scientists that manipulated natural forces to extremes causing great natural calamities. We don't see the examples in which civilizations went too far and went extinct as a consequence of their own creations. We do pass on mythologies of Atlantis which used their advanced science to imbalance nature to the point of catastrophe. At best we may have shadowy images of our evolution read from the Akasha that reemerge in today's psyche alerting us to pay more attention to what we are creating.

I don't mean to create a scary image, but for some, it takes a cataclysm for them to catch on. Well some of us have caught on because we were present in those former times, so we know where this is going. We remember those larger epical examples in which we, in other times, were involved with experiments of building great civilizations, and then seeing them fall into the habit of consciousness reflecting as privilege and then people lost touch with each other, but they also lost touch with the Earth, and that disconnection very subtlety threw things out of balance. Then the enthusiasm and the vitality devolved into a diminished form.

We need to live from the energies of heaven and earth or we will starve energetically. We nourish our bodies from the fruits of the earth and nourish our ethics and our Souls from the fruits of heaven. Efficient access to blending these energies requires a centered alignment with the loving within us. When we disconnect, all we have to live on is the energy that is stored in our organism. The energy stored in our organism is quite powerful, but it will deplete if it is not replenished. We can replenish energy through remembering and reconnecting to our original birthright, our Soul. Absent our loving alignment, we will get the energy we need through destruction and domination and by taking the energy from others. This destructive approach to getting energy arises from an insatiable dark appetite of fear. To get access to this negative energy, we might pick a fight and take the other's energy. Oddly, even victims learn to use the energy of the victimizer. As people drop away from their internal connection to their transcendent resources, they build strategies of againstness in order to take what they need from others. Destructive people build walls in their psyche or fortify themselves by disconnecting from the environment, disconnecting from source, and disconnecting from the earth. When we turn toward Soul, we reconnect and restore our source of supply. Otherwise, we are co-conspirators in maintaining the predatory fabric of society.

With loss of Soul energy, we can become like vampires starving to death, so we have to live off of other people by creating a caste system, a tax system, debt system and poverty system, that requires money to flow up into the privileged class with very little money trickling back down to the lower classes. I think a few years ago half the wealth of the world was owned by seventy percent of the people. Now it's twenty-five percent. The disadvantage of this system results in masses of people feeling depleted from the hijacking of wealth and subsequent well-being. We get angry because somebody is taking our energy. Then we rise up, causing trouble and wanting to overthrow the hijacking of wealth and take back power from the privileged, take back the political and economic resources. Then we repeat the cycle, because we become what we wanted to have, and then we do the same thing. As we blame the upper five percent, remember that we would probably do the same things if we were members of the upper five percent.

Prideful Goodness

Now the call is to formulate and resolve our challenges in a different way. Through our transcendent access, (resourcing from our Soul) we can not only have the wisdom of the ages and the power of love, but we can also sort through confusion and see which approach will bring balance and produce well-being or which approach will bring false gifts and false solutions. Through the Eyes of the Soul, we are able to recognize that "fake news" isn't just lies, that "fake news" is the narrative that cultures believe to be correct when actually those beliefs are not true because they don't reflect Soul-love. These narratives might have a frequency of someone's evolution or karma that could create division and tribalism. Maintaining division makes tribal consciousness an opportunity-rich environment for violence and, at the very least, misunderstanding.

We currently hear the dog whistle (tribal) politics that say they're not like us, so it resonates with "not like us" beliefs, and within the growing fear we grab for safety and coalesce with our tribal aggression. However, we can choose our resonance. We can remain conscious. The Soul resonates with "they're like us" reality. We live in a universal human condition on this planet and probably throughout the solar system. We have to deal with the physical part of life and its practicality and the evolution of that physicality. But being a Soul living in the planetary, evolutionary reality, we feel that we are all in kinship always traveling to meet ourselves.

As humans "awakening to Soul", we have to deal with life physically and with the real question of how to survive and how to work with the spirits of the Earth. For starters we look at aspects on the ground, at the physical level. It's funny though, we will make up superstitions about our physical reality, about how it works, and some of those superstitions hold an element of truth. For example, we once believed the earth was the center of the universe, then we discovered that the earth rotated around the Sun, yet, then we discovered that we are the center of our universe and that the "sun" is inside of us. As we look a little deeper, of course, we realize that we always have our imaginations. We can make up anything as an inward adventure, like our starship (our imagination) in which we can go anywhere or make up anything, but how to apply these adventures is another question. We can take an imaginal journey as an escape, entertainment, discovery of our true self, or to discover the next best response to challenges in life. However, when we become fixed in our viewpoint about reality, we freeze our imagination and block ourselves from seeing past appearances. We make our imagination into our superstition.

There is an emotional basis for the Soul in which we have feeling, passion, and courage. We have a great time with this so there is a tendency to reference Soul to those great times and feelings as an emotion. These feelings can give us a sense of self but we need to remember that feelings pass. Our sense of self changes when it is based on feelings. We can develop attachment to the inner journey and attachment to others in a rapport of spirit. There may be some excellent qualities in these attachments, but emotion is still a reflection. Sometimes we might mentalize about Soul and have definite ideas about what we think, or we make up ideals and master plans about Soul superiority and constellated beliefs about Soul and narratives to support those beliefs. Emotions, feelings, mental constructs, beliefs and archetypes about Soul are passing. The persistence, knowing and sense of Soul is continuous.

When we move ourselves into the archetypal area, we can become inflated with a sense of ourselves as a high-level Ego. We can join the "God club" and identify with the Gods on Mount Olympus and then imagine we might be those God's. Steiner spoke of the Spirits of Asuras that play back our radiant reflection so that we believe that we have become the source rather than a servant that is one with the Source.

Rudolph Steiner gave an explanation of the evolution of Christ as resulting from resolving the play between the forces of Lucifer and Ahriman. As his description goes, Ahriman was too regimented, dominating and controlling, and Lucifer was too indulgent, loose, and too much of a party guy. These two archetypal beings assist us in learning how to avoid getting too rigid or indulgent, out of which unfolds Christ representing balance, the middle way or synthesis. Beyond the play of Lucifer and Ahriman, Steiner writes about a force called Asuras, which is a false-self Christ.

In this instance, we arrive at the Cosmic Mirror and it reflects back our radiance and our glory and we think we are God and fold that belief into our high Ego. We become the zealot. We say, "I've got the Word." We become "I am the one that's on top of the mountain," "I am the Christ," and therein lies the arrogance. A false idea of Soul comes in and we can't get through the eye of the needle, we can't get through to meet ourselves or our Soul on the other side of the mirror, so a kind of arrogance develops as individuals and often as a church. Whether Christian, Buddhist, Muslim or Wiccan we, like Narcissus, fall in love with the Soul's reflection, which is a shadow Soul. Once we do this, we feel slightly insecure, so we develop narratives, scriptures and ancestral stories that reassure us and create a secure buy-in for our tribe. We then become loyal to the rule, the dogma, the tribe instead of the inspiration and living love that Jesus brought forward...the love that we bring as incarnating Souls before we identify fully with our Ego and forget that we are love.

Observing behavior provides clues about where someone is coming from in their evolution. A dramatic act, at first may look the same whether coming from loving or coming from fear or revenge. We may restrain an aggressor. To an observer aggressive or dramatic behavior may look the same whether it is motivated by love, fear or revenge. Love wants to help aggressing people by keeping them from self-harm or hurting others. Fear wants to be safe. Revenge wants to get even and hurt the aggressor. Self-righteous people make up rules and dogma. As the high Asuras Ego, we cast ourselves in the "rightness of the light" as an imitation of transcendent love. In our mirrored image of living love, we lower our frequency in subtle ways, and we often can't tell because it's a light on light painting or reflection. Everything gets reflected back to us as an illusion of good. In this illusion of good, we think we might start noticing it's a little dimmer here and brighter over there. We create a narrative, and that narrative becomes our reality of the light. Narratives are great, the Bible is great, the Koran is great, and there are some gems in these teachings, but we have to keep in mind that these were narratives created to give coherence or identity to a movement, but none of these narratives are the source. *Transcendent Living Love* is the Consciousness of the Soul and our source.

Cynicism

We want to protect ourselves from disappointment. Through protection or rationalization from our disappointment, we can get a little cynical. If we know we are becoming cynical, we can turn it into dry humor and then it is uplifting. We can play with that. It also makes us really good at challenging the cynics we meet because we know how they think and are familiar with their particular brand of arrogance. Cynicism is also a form of identifying with victim mentality, so when we change it to dry humor, we transform our victimization into empowerment. Then we can use it to our advantage and transform our cynicism into loving. All of these quirky things we have been developing are available for our good. In loving, we know ourselves. We know we are loving and we know the tools we have at our disposal because that is part of our character that we have developed over millennia. Loving gives us the freedom to do things for each other in a way that is compatible with a trajectory of loving.

We live in an end-time and often project dystopian narratives into uncertain times. I have a funny reaction when I hear things like: "Oh, things are really screwed up, how wonderful, it must be time for the new age, or maybe it is our opportunity!" It is as if a cosmic clock went off. Things are really messed up, really close at hand. It is dark before the light. These are responses that have always motivated us and taken us to different places. Why not embrace the darkness with anticipation? Perhaps the end-time is the beginning of timeless Love.

Willingness

Qualities of Transcendental Leadership are present regardless of our activity. These qualities are intrinsic to us and always available, and come together in loving. It is not loving in which we expect a specific response because we show love. The living, transcendent love doesn't come out in the arrogance of our self-sense as Ego, but in the self-assuredness sense of positive regard and respect, appreciating something for what it is. Living love is the love that comes from simple kindness, respect, self-assuredness, and trust.

Imagine that you are repainting an old window. You are present with the task and you are scraping the paint. The window and the paint on the window have served the room well, so you thank the paint and you appreciate it. You might think I am scraping you off because you served well. You are no longer holding well. We are going to let you go on now and put new paint here. At the same time, you are not just painting the wood in a technical sense you are putting love into the wood and when you finish this windowsill, it is going to be a window of Light. It is this kind of attention to something that exemplifies loving. Perhaps you have a history of crafting wood, and all the while that history was honing you and you were learning about yourself. You can be sanding a piece of wood and be in the forest that produced the wood. The grain comes out and you see the beauty in it, you see the deep ecology of the forest the wood came from. The grain in the wood and the textures of our own bodies are harmonic patterns of the same golden ratio. We readily merge into the matrix of creation because all creation is built on the same golden ratio. The golden ratio or golden mean is a foundational teaching in the sacred geometry taught by Pythagoras and is the universal proportion of all living things from the feathered wing of a bird to the rotational orbits of planets. The ratios constructing the human body are the same as the plants and animals in nature. The ratio is 1 to 1.618034....

Through a willingness to engage our work with reverence and respect for the organic nature of everything we change, extract, construct and touch, we might also see that our place is to step back, observe and allow and to not interfere, so we avoid any preconception. If we are projecting onto our work, we might be right nine times out of ten, but on the tenth time we might need to step back and not disrupt the way the situation is occurring. This requires comfort with ourselves, not in our reflection, but in our being, in our heart, and in our sense of being connected to the whole matrix of reality. In our choice to step back, we might even find more empathy. We might realize that helping someone involves stepping out of their confined-selves and moving with a situation or person as they go through their thousand tribulations to hold the Light, not in identifying with their path or taking it on, but to be a light bearer. This requires fluidness, flexibility, and breaking down our tendency to have rigid ideas about what service is and what it isn't, what is willingness and what it isn't. You see we are not making up a code, we are learning to live with Spirit. With spirit, we step through our freshly painted window into a new world, one that is much like the old world only scraped clean and painted with love.

Born Again

Transcendental Leadership invites us to rise above our limited self-concept. Subtly, we make ourselves victims to our own spiritual quest. We often do the spiritual and psychological work with a form of spiritual bypass that expects our enlightened selves to become extraordinary and exempt from the trials and tribulations of life. We have expectations that if we are coming into a higher place, it should look a certain way. When it doesn't seem certain, we think that there must be a technique that will fix us so it will turn out the way we expect. We want a big hand to come out of the sky and fix us or whatever it is that is making life look wrong.

When our view of life and spirit does not prove to us that what we think should be is so, we can feel like we are going to die. See, one thing we may discover is that we have identified with our view, and with the feeling that we could die. We believe if we lose this, this, this and that, we will die. Well, that is a belief. Okay, that is one thing we did with it. That is pretty cool. There is a place we get to in which we can touch into our eternity. It is said that salvation occurs when we are born again. Well to be born again, we have to die again. We forget that part. Not physically, but the self we made up, the belief-self dies. Being born again may feel like dying. It is a birth process. How many ways can we die? All of them are based on belief, a belief about what life is and what it isn't. Is it the birth and death of the physical body? Is being born again a cycle of this body dying and then reincarnating into another one? Did we die by getting kicked out of heaven? Does that we are born seem like living? As it is now, we will lose the body we have become accustomed to. Okay, see where we go when we keep unpacking and asking, what did I decide to do?

In our quest to understand, our mind goes negative and we think about all the judgments that we made, like being betrayed by God, or what did I do wrong? Who knows? Sometimes we just feel awful; sometimes we throw up, and sometimes we get a rash, but let it go. Just drink some water and praise the Lord and *let love have its way*. God's will is simply that, *love will have its way*. (I repeat this premise often.) Let it have its way with you even though you may not like to look at what is going on and it feels really bad. We all go through stuff like this. This is not uncommon. I go through things like this also. I do something and I think that I don't want anyone to know I did it. That is embarrassing, but there we go. We need to really trust our process. Sometimes we make mountains out of molehills as the saying goes and other times we find that the mountains just have a few more thousand feet on them. Keep climbing. Growing mountains reach into high places. And humans can reach high places too. Perhaps we collaborate to build mountains in order to climb them...physically and metaphysically.

Full Measure

The highest key, the most significant tool is responding to life from Presence and trusting that Transcendental Leadership is intrinsic to who we are. Love inherently leads, and love is infinitely intelligent. Since we are multidimensional, we are looking for more than behavior. We may challenge bad practices in our selves or others, but then we still must be responsive to the dimensions that are causing and supporting our actions. Sometimes our reaction to behavior is a projection based on the person we are observing, and we may assess a crime where there is none. We can also be fooled by behavior. We may evaluate bad behavior as good because of our bias about the person or what they are doing. It is always a good idea to ask who or what am I serving? If it is not the Lord, not love, then reflection, evaluation, and recalibration would be in order. We may always ask for clarity so that we can draw out the greater good that continually strives to express itself, and to awaken the Soul inside of the internalized perceived gangster role that we or someone else is living.

As we unpack and distill the coding in behaviors, it may look like a win/lose situation, but in the deeper reality, in the transcendent perspective, it is a win/win situation. On the transcendent level everything (good or bad, win or lose) serves us and provides a steppingstone toward a greater good. It is the nature of life that all expression will resolve in fulfillment. It is in our nature to have emotions even though they may feel difficult. Then we have to take care of ourselves. When we take time to take care of ourselves, we move into our vulnerability and face those difficult places inside of ourselves. We are, in a sense, speaking truth to power. We need to touch inside ourselves and find our orphans, our past selves, those that continue to be held in fear and injury, or that were dismissed and not seen. It is possible to just be in our loving and give voice to those places and change the alignment, change any misunderstanding that we can't, shouldn't, or that we are not allowed. Invite your loving into those places now.

Whether the "gangsters" (the ones who bully, intimidate or deceive to have their way) are external or internal, we choose our loving and explain to them what is expected and where they missed the mark. The great thing about missing the mark is that it implies that we have another shot, that we are able and willing to retake our aim. Missing the mark has nothing to do with our value or the "gangster" as a human being. Sometimes, we need to place the gangsters in a particular environment in which they can't hurt themselves or others while they reflect or learn to reflect on their goodness. It may merely be a developmental issue where the gangsters need to catch up. Remember each Soul is sacred and valuable. We have different experience levels and each level allows for more grace, more practical skill. Our service to our developmental issues is often through tough love. We can be firm with ourselves without being hurtful or hateful. There is a practical aspect to this. By this I mean it may look practical or like it is just business, but if we have some kind of attitude, or wound, or prejudice about it, then it is not a practical matter anymore. Through a judgmental lens, we made it existential, about essence, about our human value and now our issue is vengeance instead of a practical matter and our judgement requires us to look at how we are identifying with vengeance. We must take care of all of the wounded elements of ourselves, one way or another. We need some way to reflect or counsel all aspects of ourselves in order to be sure our perception is clear and to make sure that our action meets a real need that serves everyone. For example, some companies are about maximizing profits for the shareholders, so when they cut people from the workforce, they sacrifice them for the shareholders. That may seem practical in the sense of "it is business," but we need to ask if it is really practical or is it ethically shady? Firing workers is using vampire action, glossed over as doing business or for the health of the organization. Is it really for the health of the organization? It may be. A billionaire owner of a corporation may say that he had to cut back on people, staff, and jobs for the sake of profit. His rationale may be about Ego instead of shareholders. Is that different? He may see it as needing to make profit in service to the planet or humanity since he produces sustainable products. Ego or not, it does seem to be in service to a vision. The true sustainable vision is when everybody wins.

We can look at companies cutting staff as a practical issue. When the cuts were made, we might ask, did we have to harden or soften ourselves to do it? See? That is another measure. We just have to find ways to measure where we are with our action of cutting jobs, so we can be as completely conscious as possible. Just observing and our awareness that we would ask the question tells me that we are conscious. As in Emerson's perspective of Soul in the American Scholar, we are trying to learn how to base our actions on wisdom from the Soul. We are also contending with what it is like to live from the Soul on a planet designed to distract us from our true identity as a Soul, causing us to forget that who we are is the one who came to bring love. Consider also, however, that distractions of survival, safety, shelter, power and prestige are integral to building our consciousness so that we can fulfill our Soul vision with competency, grace and remembrance.

We need to hold compassion for each person's path. We do what we can to cushion people, to help them on their way unless they are just outright predatory, and then, in that case we have to account for that. The predator often seemingly gets their reward as a million-dollar severance package. We seem to lack similar regard for the worker's severance package. What package, right? Some people's poverty may be due to their own self-defeating thoughts and behaviors. However, if your gain is based on someone else's loss, that is soul-defeating behavior.

Ultimately, the essential will is that loving is going to have its way. Evolution is the expression of love learning to have its way. That is the subliminal agenda of life. Everything that goes on is collaborating with love having its way, even apparent negativity. That is the value of cosmology. Cosmology helps us put things into perspective. Rather than using God's will to measure something or make a religion out of it, using it to pacify or control, we can ask: "How is loving working through this?" "How is this transforming into loving?" "What does love have to teach us today?" The best awareness we have is that God's will is going to work through everything; unconditionally loving everything so that the person that is doing evil gets the same support to explore choices as the person doing good. In the case of doing evil, however, there is a caveat; the immature player can only grab hold of a limited reality so they don't wreck the integrity of the whole thing. They don't get to destroy the universe. The only inevitable limit is the movement of the whole. There are folk myths in which the bad guys managed to wreck continents and planets, but not creation itself. They are limited. Bible metaphors point to the fall. All this means is that these guys were playing bad, so they had to go into a smaller playground. They lost privileges. The kids misbehaving on the playground get a timeout. They get consequences. We are never exempt from the consequence (karma), of our actions whether good or bad.

We need to be vigilant if we are prone to evoke God's will as a justification. We may not know the whole story, ever. Just trust loving, abide by it, so that internally you are in a Soul-level rapport when practical circumstances arise. For example, if we have to cut staff, it is not half-hearted or hard-hearted. It is not a measure. It just is. Loving reveals unintended consequences when we end an individual's employment for some strategic theory. We can say that the collateral damage to peoples' lives is an unintended consequence but consider collateral damage could also be selective perception. Sometimes we have set something up and just have to watch it play out to see if it really is like we thought. There are folks slaughtering each other believing that they are doing God's will. We have to really check it out and ask if God's will is at play or is it a case of human will using God's "will" as a cover?

We Are the Promise

The Soul is sacred. The Soul loves to experience. The Soul's urge to experience treats good and evil the same because that is how we build consciousness. No worries, all experience must be resolved in loving before it integrates into our Soul.

On the path inward we encounter the "dwellers on the threshold" which is our composite good and composite evil confronting us. First, we encounter the composite evil, and it severely frightens us because it looks so awful. As soon as we can be present with composite evil in loving, our loving response allows us to move past this dweller into the higher realms. What a relief, we passed the test. We remembered that we came to bring love. Then we meet the next dweller that is our composite good. This is often a greater challenge. We see ourselves and invariably we think "oh I'm so good." As soon as we do that, we fail the test. Prideful goodness is not the love that sets us free. Good actions are to remind us about who we are, not to make up for our lacks or prove we are good in the eyes of others. Good and bad are a contrast that is resolved when we use both good and bad to transform ourselves into loving.

Building our internal nation can be a very subtle alchemical process. Our work is to refine and purify the quality of our thought, our speech, and our touch. The alchemy of Soul nation building is a sacred process, performed with great care and humility. Though powerful, the alchemy is not based on obtaining power, rather through experiencing ordinary reverence with each breath we take. Inherent in our journey is that we are the light, the truth, and the way. In an arrogant version, we could believe we are entitled and superior. The arrogant version is not the true meaning. When we distort just a little bit from the true sense of Soul and spiritual authority, we can live in a holy war. For example, Christians and Muslims kill each other because they both believe they are serving God and forgetting that Jihad is always an internal battle. Holy wars come out of rules of distortion. While Muhammad might say that we are all brothers and sisters while preaching about the kinship of humanity, we could wonder why we are trying to kill each other?

We live in a hall of mirrors and each mirror reflects a distorted image of ourselves or a false passage. We can groove on these subtleties but living in a world that is a hall of mirrors is a challenge for us. We can meet the challenge inside though and simultaneously maintain our lives the best we can out in the world. The mirrors form into a unified gestalt of reality as we maintain our identity in the one light. It is a given, we are going to have some bumps and grinds. We are going to break things. We are going to make mistakes. We are going to miss the point. We are going to think something is a good idea and be surprised when it turns out not to be a good idea. It is just a process. We have to realize that any action eventually leads to love and that the compass that points to the true passage from the many false mirrored passages is the compass of Presence and focus of love.

Our shadows, our process, and our shame are precious because each one has the potential of virtue. When we attend to these elements we are like a baby. An infant is new. It doesn't know the fullness of itself yet. It just is. Shame has yet to be experienced and transformed. Love hasn't yet become guilt. But the infant is on its way because those are all feelings that can be worn and tried on so that we can become strong in areas of guilt and shame and realize "oh yeah that's not us, that's not me." We use this same discerning nature to observe that a person or group is not like us in a tribal and fearful way and to realize that anything different than loving is not like us. Our prejudice becomes discernment with love as its measure. As we learn to draw distinctions, then the value of shame is to realize that shame was a misunderstanding of love. We are not shameful, and we eventually understand that the one we judge is, in essence, the same love seeking to understand and to be understood. Discernment is about developing certain traits and behaviors, and that's what we are all here to do.

Expectation can be an attempt to control or dominate, we must be vigilant and always check out our expectations. Disappointment comes from trying to control other people in an effort to make ourselves happy. When we get disappointed about where our nation or Soul nation is right now, be careful but ask: Are we looking at it from our lack and from what we can extort, or from our love and what can we build? Are we judging our nation from the way it ought to be from some ideal? Are we judging it from not living up to our own criteria? Are we seeing the nation the way it really is or from our projections and our agendas? As a nation, we aren't entirely on home base yet so don't take it personally. Let's just be practical and keep renewing our expectations and judgements and using them to find out what works.

Cosmology helps us look at relationships between everything and develop a lens to see life through and to see connections and the way they work for us. Cosmology is a world view. When we have a map, we can stay lined up inside with Transcendent love, grounded on Earth, and respond to life in a way that we are in a position to discern, to work and transform whatever we're doing into loving. We need a cosmology that shows us the way home.

We need to realize and embrace our cosmology and then we can sit back and assess our progression and have perspective on our lives. Cosmology makes us navigators. It gives us a spherical surround that we can use to navigate like a star map. This cosmological star map helps us plot our position, determine the parameters of relationships, organize our tools and see activity more clearly. The center of that cosmology is the Soul reflecting from the periphery of life as our mirror. Cosmology provides us with a way to work with our experience.

When we look at our disappointments from a transcendent level, they become visionary. Emerson was a *Visionary* with a vision of a nation coming into existence for the first time based on the wisdom of the Soul. This is a vision, not an expectation. Remember, the need to control comes out of fear. Expectations turn our urge to control into cynicism. The promise is not external. The Soul works from love. The hope of an external savior will generally disappoint. Even Jesus admonished us to look inside. There is an anointed one and he or she is internal. Listen....We are the promise. This vision of wisdom of the Soul becomes like a kite held aloft and carried by the transcendent wind. All we have to do in our alignment is hold onto the string and trust that our visionary kite is going to keep flying us along propelled by the true wind of destiny.

Meditation

It's always easier to meditate if you close your eyes.

When we take a deep breath, what that does is it shifts our attention to our breath and that's a great cleanser, a great interchange.

When we breathe physically, and we breathe spiritually, it starts resolving. Breath mediates the frequencies in our body and the frequencies in our psyche. The frequencies of heaven and earth become a mediator as we breathe.

It's a natural process. Not to strain or force the breath, but the calming. It should be quite comfortable at the moment just to touch into that loving place inside as a real divine Presence in the physical body.

Sometimes we call this the inner teacher, the place of internal dialogue that guides, that we can reflect with, imagine with.

We come with so many attributes that help us along the way. As we light them up inside, we begin to incorporate the depth of our loving, and we enter Visionary consciousness. Not to measure ourselves through the vision but to be a way-shower. To pull us along so that in the knowing, in the Presence, in the Transcendence, we make our way on Earth.

In this day of national consternation, just focus on the leadership inside, the Transcendental Leadership inside and engage it in this great admonition. Consider the place and time and the situation that we are in and the small ways and large ways that we are part of creating a nation that for the first time is based on the wisdom of the Soul.

Consider all the like-minded, the like-hearted Souls reaching out and touching, forming a matrix of love around the planet as one.

See if there is a way to take this inside and bless ourselves with it, to let that vulnerability expand our sense of Presence in our space so it engages the fabric of the wholeness and any places of need, lack or incompletion inside, rather than judge those or fix them in this context, to just make them a vessel.

In vulnerability, these spaces can be filled with loving. The loving can convert that lack into whatever is needed to fulfill the impulse that is sitting behind that.

The blessing then is that the blessings already are and just cooperate with them.

God Bless Us.

*To the mind that is still,
the whole universe surrenders.*

Laozi

CHAPTER FIVE

Presence

• • •

Presence is different than being present. It is related of course. When we are present, we invite Presence. Presence is a dynamic way that our consciousness is nested in reality. It helps, at least helps me, to become present in a visual way, and a sensate way. When I am present, I am aware of my current location and my attention is focused clearly and precisely on what is in front and around me. From there, I move into Presence... my awareness is held in the central axis of my body and I am awakened in the dimensions above and below me. My heart is open into an awareness of the full spherical surround of the horizon. I feel alive in my sense of embodiment. I feel informed by higher consciousness while I am engaged with what is before me in that moment, interestingly, free of judgement or projection.

Presence is an overlighting that fills every cell in our bodies and awakens our consciousness. Presence anchors us as we step into our alignment, into our capacity to be grounded, and our ability to love ourselves in a way that allows us to inwardly reach up into a high connection. As we practice opening our hearts to love that is the fabric of creation and connecting up into eternal love, Presence creates a zone which unfolds and enfolds us into the intimacy of grace. An essential quality of Presence is that the past and the future are now. This eliminates anxiety, or at least reduces it because anxiety may also be what is. Usually, we are too worried about the future or we have too much regret about the past, which takes us out of the present. When we are not present, we are not fully existing embodied in the moment. In a sense, we are held in a psychic dimension of overlapping fantasies of the collective reality and in personal regret. A lack of Presence may even create striving for psychic or spiritual attainments which takes us out of the present and into false alignments with an imposter "higher" consciousness.

Mirror of the Sun

When we worry about the future, we embrace a negative attitude toward the future, and if we regret the past, we have a negative attitude toward the past. The past and future are always reflecting back to our present moment creating a vortex in which we orient our perceptions and reality. This energy vortex continually circulates, so we must have a loving attitude toward the future, regardless. A loving circulation takes us from the future into the moment, whereas when we have a negative attitude toward the future, the circulation takes us out and away from the moment and creates a null zone in our center. With a negative attitude the same null zone appears with the circulation of our past. As we practice loving our past, having a great attitude towards it, and appreciating our past, our history circulates into the present moment. In loving, we center ourselves and coalesce our past and future creating a congruent perception of self and location. Our loving and forgiveness transform all liabilities into assets. Perhaps the only sin is a wasted mistake. When we judge ourselves for a mistake, we project a negative perception of *what is* and we lose our alignment with and access to our center. Accepting mistakes, implementing an uplifting use of the mistake and self-forgiveness opens our perception to our centering love.

The way grace travels in time is through appreciating the future into the present. When we release our judgmental hold on the past and future, time moves freely in a natural way forming the present moment. When we project our regrets onto the past and our fears onto the future, we distort time, binding us into our collective and idiosyncratic narratives, justifying our existence through our story. It is really in our dynamic capacity to hold our loving that keeps us present. We are always traveling through time to now. In Presence, linear time is moving through us one now at a time, and our liberated Soul becomes the pattern for our reality.

When we negatively relate to the past and the future, we disperse the light that is in the present, and we can become depressed. When loving incorporates the past and future into the present, we create receptivity to the light, thus coagulating the light. We fill our present with light and build a creative vortex from which we relate to events. In other words, Presence creates a vortex that amplifies the light as it cycles through our space, transforming negativity into positive energy. In some way when we practice Presence, we become part of recycling negativity in the form of resolving past issues and dissolving future projections. Through Presence, we gain the capacity to take any negativity that comes our way and change it into loving. In Presence, we make ourselves available. We join with Presence instead of trying to will Presence. In Presence, we are living as a transcendent self while embodied and effectively engaging the practical world. We are always with our wholeness. We reach up and tap into our vortex of Presence and become an agency of it. In that agency, energy comes in and overlights us with the oversoul of Presence making us into a true light vortex on earth.

We can watch the light return, reflecting off of the mirror of life and coming back to us. We see events unfolding. We are in a relationship with life and with the world. We are an agent of what is unfolding. This is a form of perception. We are seeing everything that is unfolding as an episode of love actualizing itself. Any event, even if it seems negative, in essence is love trying to actualize itself, but if the event is negative it has been reversed through a violation or forgetting of self. When we perceive an event through Presence, we can see light within the darkness. Presence activates loving vibrations so that if we are watching a negative event, we can choose a response that reacts and judges or we can also see light working unseen within darkness and watch the coherency of negativity dissolve into the Presence of love. I am not saying we are at this point of ease with Presence, but we are at that point of promise!

We are not only the lighthouse in the midst of a storm, but we also enable the transformative possibility of the storm. Maybe it is a little bit like the sun burning off the fog...I'm not sure. I do know that the sun radiates and is always shining even when it is covered by clouds or is on the other side of the earth, the sun still radiates. Perhaps the sun reflects as well as radiates light. We usually think of the moon reflecting light. As we are looking at the sun, the sun is also living in the mirror of life. Perhaps like the observer effect that we spoke of in Chapter One, our observation changes the observed. In terms of Presence, our Presence chooses that which is revealed to us. The observer effect is mutual. As we look at ourselves through the Sun, the Sun looks at itself through us.

Field Conversion

Presence responds to Presence. In Presence, light opens into an issue and then creates the illusion of being sent and coming back to us, when actually the light is simultaneous. It is synchronous. In a sense, when we send light, we are sending it through a recipient to ourselves. We send light back through negativity from a dimension of love within the negativity that the negativity does not see or does not know. Negativity is a phenomenon of forgetting love. Remarkable! I'm not sure what this phenomenon becomes once we begin experimenting with it, but let's say that somebody is giving a speech and it's a negative speech, and we are in Presence and we acknowledge light through them. Our witnessing through the Presence of love makes it so. We observe and see what happens. In Presence, the light is already sent and we are no longer the sender. The love that dwells in us is the sender. Our Presence resonates Presence and awakens love in others. Love resides in every sentient being. Presence references our perception of love and the light within love. We have seen this happen in small ways. For example, somebody is upset with us and we just stay present in our loving and they shift. We may have experienced it on that scale. It appears that there is enough change in the vibration of the planet to expand this phenomenon into a more far-reaching application. The only risk is that now that we know the creativity of our Presence, we could very easily fall into wanting to use our creativity to control. We might think that a person generating negativity might just stop and shift in response to our Presence. We probably like that thought.

We might want to do that again but then we see that we have an expectation. We have an attitude. We decide to manipulate somebody else's expression. We lose our way. Loving Presence is not about manipulation or control. Presence impacts others however it does because Presence always moves in terms of what is for the highest good. These are divine computations that go on within the field of energy that we are living in. This is the kind of atmosphere in which we are allowing ourselves to breathe, with divine computations, with Presence...keep breathing.

The next section may be a bit confusing because it involves a choice we make on a transcendent level, which is different than our selection of what dinner to order at a restaurant, whether or not to react to someone, or buy corn chips at the minimart. It is a different kind of choice at a different level of choice. It is a realization that is nurtured within us. Try this on as a good metaphor: Up until now, our computer codes are binary (yes or no, 1 or 0). Resolution is implicit in the duality. As a progeny of "spooky action at a distance," scientists are developing computers that accommodate codes based on yes, no and both, quantum computing. Along a similar line, a third strand on DNA may provide memory storage. We humans have quantum capacity as well and it lights up in Presence.

Reflexive Light

Spiritual light is just what it is: non-physical light. As much as we talk about light and respond to situations in our lives with light, it is a mystery as to what it actually is. Somehow, we understand that the foundational field of existence is a mysterious fabric of Living Love that manifested from a source-field of Living Love, love giving birth (manifestation) to love. For lack of a better term, we call the agency of this Living Love the Holy Spirit, the light, Divine intelligence, the Word, or always on time, because time is a location.

We send the light in response to our concerns in the world, and depending on our temperament, that can be arrogance, taken for granted, or a sacred act. To align our activity and thoughts with the highest good, we ask for light for the highest good. The implication is that within the framework of creation is a permeating, everywhere present intelligence that can spontaneously measure the highest good of all and mediate our actions and choices providing we allow that. In so doing our attitude and intention is infused with the movement of *love having its way*. We send light to people with difficult situations or grave illnesses. We want them to be well and free of suffering, but we also want to respect their karma by understanding that their difficulty may be their path to a greater awareness. So, we send the light for the highest good, understanding that this mystery light has the intelligence to know the highest good. When we think about the concept of *no cause being local*, sending light is reflexive, not linear. As light, we are light sending itself reflexively. "Sending the light" is unfolding light from an implicate transcendent order into a locality.

There is no distance or separation for Souls. In our deep essence of love that is the seed of our Soul there is a continuous resonant frequency which manifests unity that is continually communicated. We can share the same space, providing so much intimacy that at the soul-level we can honestly know and love each other. In a way, then, we are a collective of Souls. Our individuation of the Soul continues, enhancing our sense of being one with all. Our individuation manifests as a greater awareness of our intimacy with all Souls. The more we are aware of wholeness, the more we experience Presence as a radiant, symphonic Soul. Regardless of where we park our Soul, we experience light and love everywhere, manifesting toward and through us, through the person or situation we are "sending" it to. Light Presence is synchronous, sending is both there and here. It is a joining, and in that joining, there is an amplification of that which is needed. This could be a strange feeling for our Basic Self. The Basic Self is our body and instinctual intelligence, which encompasses the belief systems of our self-concept and cosmology. It is the sponsor of our Ego. Synchronous awareness is a different sense of reality than what the Basic Self is accustomed to, so consider these different senses when you include yourself in wholeness. The Basic Self will surrender to wholeness through the inclusive, loving sensations that we sponsor.

When accepting the wholeness of the other, we realize that oneness, we realize the will of God (which is code for *love will have its way*). The will of God is the core driver motivating each of us, regardless of our opinion or how life seems. Whatever the agenda is for illness or issues the will of God (*love will have its way*) illuminates the purpose, the meaning, and the resolution of that which is challenging us. On a practical level, when tragedy happens, there is a sense of something being worked out in the highest way possible. There is value in not having a particular expectation about a tragedy, instead just being present joins, loves and serves for the highest good.

Presence overlights our relationship with that which is needed. It is our loyalty to Presence that makes it so. We get the idea of an image of Presence, but it is Presence allowing us to be in that energy that makes it so. We have a sense of our mind just disappearing in response to the invitation of Presence. Although our awareness may still be inadequate, our Soul is always linked to eternity. Our awareness of this may still be inadequate, however the actuality of Soul integrating with eternity extends the adequacy of self. The value of feeling inadequate is as a motivator to call upon our greater self, to help our Ego to relax and be a servant.

Once we get our eyes off the psychic and physical phenomena of what is occurring in our field of awareness and onto incubating the divine Presence, we incorporate our sense of self and body, enabling us to land our transcendence on the planet. The vibration of the Soul is active in every cell of our body. The Soul lies dormant in the Tisra Til (the esoteric organ of the pineal gland) until we activate it and it starts to move. Once the Soul moves it engages all dimensions of consciousness. When our sense of Soul moves, we can travel in all dimensions of reality and our sense of living becomes one of traveling through life as life. The trajectory of our life is a means of traveling from one state of consciousness to another.

A simple way of anchoring our transcendence on earth is to call ourselves forward into the Presence. This is an interesting statement. The statement "call ourselves forward" does not mean that we are behind ourselves physically or psychologically, rather that Presence is a slight dimensional shift in front of us or we are a small frequency shift in the past and not quite present. In terms of the *implicate order* we are unfolding into the *explicate* present as a locality. From the deep center within self and body, we geographically move forward. We out-picture the Presence, *a la* Dr. Who. (This refers to The Dr. Who from the famous BBC Sci-fi series about the Time Lord that could travel through time and come to the aid of humanity. On the outside his vehicle called a Tardis looked like a British police box and on the inside it was immense.) In the series the phrase *it (the Tardis) is bigger on the inside than on the outside,* I take as metaphor of individual human consciousness. We are all inwardly multidimensional and outwardly a small single human body. What we are looking for is the sensation of multidimensionality which includes all of time, because in that sensation, the Basic Self will relish and trust the sense of eternity and immensity so that our need for a sense of survival accommodates the infinite and thus embraces our transcendence.

I remember seeing a documentary on an unusual moth. When the moth sensed danger, it would flip its wings so that it looked like the face of a monster. We have been through a lot of danger, so we know what that feels like. When we feel a threat to our survival, we can flip into Presence and then we seem formidable to any prospective adversary. In our Presence our adversary is looking into the face of eternity. Flipping ourselves into Presence serves as an application of loving that is based on our divine construction, on the fabric of our being, the way the light body works, where and how we are positioned in reality, and how the light circulates through us and picks up our belief systems and goes out and tells the universe how to look back at us.

We think the appearance of life is static when it is actually only for the moment. When we change a belief, the light circulates through us, changing codes and that forms our reality in a new way. Our reality changes and then people change their attitude toward us. As we do this, we join with every other Soul that is doing this as well. We work this process from the inside out. Our change in vibration alters the equations of the interaction and then the new vibration reverberates through the collective. This is a revolution that comes from a dimension that negativity cannot see. It is sneaking up on the world, and we are part of having the light sneak up on the planet, stalking the world from the inside out. From this perspective, sending the light is reflexive. We originate the light action and receive it simultaneously. In Presence, all action is instantly reflexive.

Zero-Point Action

Presence is a Zero-Point in which past and present meet. Presence is also a win-win because our past and our future are the blessings of the moment instead of the curses that perpetually distract us from our truth. We can practice holding this concept at that Zero-Point so that we can graciously move our attitude to win-win when we need to. We are going to flow in and out of the Zero-Point because of the tides of reality. Presence is always there, waiting for us to join. Perhaps waiting is a prejudice of time that pulls us from our Zero-Point centering. Presence lives in no-time and all-time. The more "time" (or all time) we spend being in Presence, the more capacity we have to respond to challenges (being resilient in difficulty) and to existentially identify with Presence. Presence operates like an ombudsman mediating teaching frequencies and opening us to the realization that "Heaven is at hand."

In our desire to serve, share and teach, we can become a shapeshifter. If we preconceive how the outcome should look, or if it is an attainment we strive for, or a role we play, these frequencies also become a pattern upon which we shape our persona. When desire comes from our sense of Soul, our loving, and our service, then Presence is shaping our persona. In this way our teaching is an internal relationship that we nurture rather than being a role we play.

Presence, as well, attends to practical matters that go along with living in the world and doing business. It is an attitude. In that, there is a willingness that the light will help us sort out our Ego issues and align our Ego with higher consciousness. There is nothing to destroy or fix. You just need to get the right department in the right place. This willing attitude, inwardly, facilitates any necessary corrections. Our part is to show up and observe, just watch our attitude, realizing we are prepared and ready for what life invites us to do.

Light Hybrid

When we send the light to someone, we share a perceptual field. As such, that action is relational. From the perspective of the light returning, we are sending the light to ourselves because in Presence we are in the same consciousness, at least at the Soul level. Consequently, we will register the other's reality as information and notice impressions, feelings, images, emotions, or sensations that may feel as if they are our own. Experience helps us discern what is ours. The more we can relax into Presence, the more we will be able to determine what is ours and what is other's. It is a relaxed vigilance. When we relax and space out, we are someplace else and we can't remember, so relax and stay vigilant. In Presence...we are present.

The experience of Presence may be quite uncomfortable. Loving, as an overreaching fabric of reality, mediates the discomfort and, as we hold our Presence, may actually transform discomfort into loving. It may seem like we are looking through a hall of mirrors or through several different lenses. That is the discomfort. The Basic Self can be disturbed by this multidimensional view so we may have to remind our Basic Self to relax in its vigilance.

When we send somebody the light, we don't realize it but we are also silently and simultaneously prompting them to send us the light. That would be another way to look at this. It is subliminal. We are sending a message out: send me the light. The Soul inherently responds, while often the personality is jammed up. Feelings are information, and in this process we become more aware of the feeling/information distinction. When we are present with what is, our projections fade and we see life truthfully. In relational loving, there may well be disturbing frequencies. Our homework is to practice being with our uncomfortable feelings, not shaped or defined by them. We don't need to take them personally or identify with them, but we don't reject them either. Feelings are there to help us respond accurately to whatever is. We have a relationship, but our Ego doesn't dominate the perception. The Ego is a style.

When we are in Presence, we experience whatever is going on in that Presence. We have to remember that. We don't need to know the meaning of any discomfort; it is just information. We might have a very personal emotion, but we are not consumed or defined by it. We practice ahead of time in our imagination. In our practice we take emotion as a gift. That is just our nature. When we respond to something that we care about, it is a process whatever the emotion is. We can be vigilant without losing our center. They are just emotions which provide a range of information in the form of color and meaning. Unless we are incapable of experiencing empathy, there is always an empathetic response to someone's feelings, or our own, but never a justification, because emotion is whatever it is. Through Presence, emotion will disclose the message. In Presence love transforms negativity into light.

Presence hybridizes us, hybridizes our Ego and hybridizes our consciousness. I don't know if it changes our genetics or not, that is an inference to hybridizing. We do expand and conform to transcendent love, which hybridizes our intuitive soul and instinctual body making us more ourselves and less who we thought we were, thus our false selves become mist that evaporates, transmuting into the atmosphere.

The Soul is constant; however, the Soul incarnates into the developing body by degrees. Starting at birth, in seven-year stages, our body becomes developmentally capable of receiving and holding higher levels of consciousness. At first, an infant can't handle the frequency, so it keeps building capacity to carry higher frequencies. Presence can overlight us throughout our developmental history but at some point, it incarnates into our being when our physical frequency can hold it. As we incarnate according to the capacity of the physical body to hold our consciousness it is true for this lifetime; it has also been true for the epochs through which we have participated in the physical embodiment of our human evolution. The incarnation of the Soul into each developmental stage, epoch or phase, is the remembrance that we are the ones that bring love.

Robert D. Waterman, EdD

Organizational Presence

During a presentation on Transcendental Leadership, I had a conversation with a colleague that is very salient to the application and appreciation of Presence. That conversation follows:

Colleague: *I woke up this morning with this question that has been with me my whole life, and I had the thought well it is just Presence. Forgive me because I sort of struggle with the words and my comfort level around talking about it. I've shared with you about this in the past. I've shared in Mystery School. I've shared with John-Roger (J-R) about this. I talked to John Morton. (J-R and John Morton are spiritual teachers.) One of my life questions that I work with is this balancing of doing a deed. And much as I feel I have been drawn in my life to do, to be in a leadership role, to do community organizing and activism and to be involved in things, I have also had this really lovely experience of Presence, of trusting the perfection of all of it and being absolutely fine with all of it and that is what I worked on a lot in my life.*

I played with that question in so many ways, and so right now I am in this position of bringing forward a program in leadership and leadership with a focus of Soul leading and spirit leading. I am in an environment where there is so much openness to that and so much longing for that, and then there is also a culture that I don't think that I recognize, that it is hard even to say it because I look at what are the judgments that I have about it. My observation from an accepting place is that there is a culture that has a lot more going on than just, "Oh well let's just do that, and we will all shift into being in a kind of acceptance and loving, and it will just be grace and ease and peace and joy." Like there is something bigger than that going on, and I trust that, and I get that, but I'm finding myself again struggling about going with this question of am I supposed to be here supporting this energy that is coming forward around this wisdom of the Soul in this community that's looking for that or do I do what I need to do, and I can just go on and be happy in my beautiful little cabin in the woods? I'm just feeling conflicted.

Almost every day I go back and forth between I should do something, I'm here to do something, I'm being called, it has called me to do something, and then I think no spirit has it. I don't need to do anything. And I don't even know what my question is except that this thing just continues to dance. And I guess what it is, is that there is nothing. My understanding of spirit in my life is that it is all perfect and there is nothing. And that I've got this desire and this karma in my life that I want to do that. I want to work. I want to change. That I'm being called to demonstrate my understanding of spirit in my life and that I have this understanding that it is all perfect and there is nothing to do. Yet something seems off.

RW: Yes, our Ego wants to put that in conflict. It is all a style. You just show up, and each day you are like St. Francis. I understand one of the monks was his daily direction finder. As the story goes, each morning they would start out, they would spin the directional monk like spin the bottle (I hope that doesn't date me too much). They would spin him and whatever direction he'd be facing when he stopped, that is the direction they would go. The mission was to go out every day, but they didn't know which direction. We feel called to do something. How do we do something without obligation? You are called to do something. Well, it is how we show up that is the difference. Is it to share our fullness or is it to make up for some lack?

It may be true that karmically we have done it all and we could do anything we want. You could go sit in your cabin on the mountain karmically, but here you are and you say well I'm here. "I might as well see what else I can do, and not only that I'll see if I can do it in a way in which I don't make more karma." Of course, the key is to do it through Grace...do it through loving. See that changes. I like to call it the contrast between practicality and what is existential. It is a practical issue. When we organize a program, we make out an agenda, we put people in different roles so they do the necessary jobs. Then people show up and we do the event. It takes organizing.

We have a full range of how we are in service to loving. The first one is just to be present and observe because there is something about the physics of loving that requires a witness. And then there are other levels of service where our bodies are made to participate. What is that an instrument of? Is it an instrument of our aberrations or an instrument of our loving? Are we an instrument trying to control things because of the insufficiency we feel or to bring something about? The thing is that with our service to loving we won't have any investment in it, so with each thing we do, we'll just observe, and see if it needs tweaking, or if it is going well on its own. Of course, we are in a milieu of people who are all over the place with their loving and with all different concepts of it. We are set up in this reflecting reality, so in a sense, negativity owns the stage. We can play negativity in a positive way or play it in a negative way.

At the deepest level, negativity looks like light. Life is really an incredible mirror, and it has an intrinsic consciousness. And at the shallowest level, light can look like negativity. So, how do we relate? Does negativity make us rigid? Does it make us into a zealot? Do we stand up to something to support our viewpoint of how we think we are in the light or do we stand up for something because love moves us into it?

I'm an eight on the Enneagram and my tendency is to be present and loving, and when something is off, I'll just be a warrior. I'll challenge, but then I'm done. I don't retain an investment in it. That is just my temperament. Through awareness we get to know our own style. Life will help us learn how we are made and how to be effective. If we pay attention, as we evolve in this life, we become all the styles. For example, the story of Jesus chasing the money changers out of the temple was an important demonstration. In other times Jesus didn't do that. He did not judge, he allowed, and accepted. We always have to measure to loving what is good for the whole, and if we really opened our channel so that we could be informed by the highest good, we would be little better off. But by just dropping down a little in our frequency, we can crystallize. Inadvertently we identify with the Ego reflection of Soul and believe it is Soul, God or whatever. We become a habit-personality and use the way we are made as a measure instead of a lens or an instrument. Love is the measure, not our eccentricities. Even knowing all of this, we are still going to be human with each other.

Organizations are designed to help people work out their karma. Say you are presenting a program in an environment that was designed to help people work out their karma. You have had a lot of experience with organizations where people are working out their karma. That's just the way it is. What is the real thing you are doing? Just helping people work out their karma. A program is one way to do that because it provides a container into which you invite people to look at everything in a new way. They are moving from a "teacher groupie" to a Transcendent Leader. That really frightens some people. Some people think they are already there, so they're stuck in that belief and they may try to stick you with their belief as well.

Colleague: *That's something you said earlier that really resonated for me. I know I have spent a lot of my life thinking that if I am kind, they will be kind back, and so when I came here there was a lot of that, so I just hold in my loving then. And then I realized no, no, no some people are very attached to where they are at, and they have no interest in shifting that, and so I hold in my loving and the karma being what it is. People who want to come in and play can do that and people who want to stay in the, "I've got it all handled," will just do that. But there is some part of me that still struggles with being a part of an organization, and being a part of a family, being a part of a community that says the word loving and kindness and caring and communication and trust and all these things that we care about and their outer actions don't exactly look like that from that place of Presence. So that is fine. And from that place of leadership, I think, should I be doing more? Is there anything? And I say, no just be. There is nothing left to do.*

RW: There are a lot of ways to do that, but that comes from an inner prompting instead of a power struggle. In our political morass, people have to have their power struggle. That is the level that we have to work on. You may challenge in your organization and it is not a power struggle. It is just a challenge.

Colleague: *Well, and there is this other teaching that keeps pulling on me that I have it written in a book that I wrote thirty-some years ago and I look at it. J-R said to surround yourself with those people that bring out the best of who you are. There is that part of me that wants to stay in the woods with my dog and my husband.*

RW: Well, J-R didn't say how they should do that. He didn't say how they bring the best out of you. Maybe this is the best of who you are. "I have the judgment that the best of who I am is when I'm completely happy and at peace and there is no conflict." Is that so? You may be on the wrong planet. We are often our best in the face of conflict and great disaster. Somebody that is really in the light may do something outrageous that you know is off, but consider that they just did that because you needed that and then you respond and then you are both over it. That J-R statement is precisely what we've talked about, except that we are doing it from a basis that everybody surrounding us is bringing the best out of us, even the best karma. We are bringing the best out of them. Some of them will get it right away and some will get it in a thousand years. That is just the way Spirit works. You honor the projection of their karma, and knowing that everybody is running a risk in the leadership of the organization because you have to be in a leadership role in a negative reality. That is always playing off of the way choices are made. In the long run, it works itself out. Sometimes the run is too long and we ask, "when is enough, enough?" That may or may not be our concern.

Colleague: *It seems like maybe there is just an opportunity for me to love that part of me that wants to go be the monk on the hill and be in my bubble. I want that.*

RW: If the monk leaves because of disappointment, I would really question that. If the monk leaves because leaving is next, that is just what is next. Your monk hasn't said next yet even though it is in the wings. Someday it will say next, but it hasn't said that yet. You are still talking to yourself. You know it is there, but it is not instead of anything. Another way to look at the monk is to see it as not something over there, but here, inside. In meditation, you are invited to be the monk on the hill. The more you go be the monk on the hill, the more you expand into everything. It is a perspective. It's a viewpoint. It is the orientation you take in which you are so anchored within the depths of yourself that you are in the intimacy of everything and can operate through the intimacy of everything. The image of the monk on the hill may just be saying that you've got to go inward and see what opens up, see what blooms, see what expands out of you. It is another level of asking just what is this monk on the hill?

One of the things I used to do with the Bible before I met other metaphysical people was that I'd try to decode the message behind the words. There was a story about Jesus. He wanted to talk to the group that was gathering, so what he did before he started talking was to go up on a high place. He spoke from a high place. John was on Patmos (a Greek Island where John had a great revelation, also code for the pineal gland) and did the same thing. He went up on a rooftop, a high place, and the sky opened up. This seems like what happens when we meditate. Oh yes, of course, the monk on the hill. Then he spoke and John went traveling into the higher worlds. So, it is not questioning, it is re-evaluating the structure of reality.

We are used to going, being here and going there. There is no there, there. It is all here. It doesn't preclude being physically on a hill and being a monk. What I am saying is that there is another dimension to it. The lifetime when we were the monk on the mountain now comes into an application because you can do that inwardly and just channel the Presence of that monk on the hill. If you are creating conflict inside of yourself, you may be asking the wrong question. Or you are not asking the right question yet. Confusion is just a soft conflict. Confusion could also be a symptom of a shift in consciousness as well or your old way of solving something that didn't work. It keeps slipping, so you called it confusion because it is trying to show you a new way to look at it.

Open the Door

The meditation at the end of this chapter is a means of initiating ourselves into a greater awakening into alignment with the dimension of living Presence. We move to a doorway in the Tisra Til, a spiritual gland that resides in the same place as the pineal. When we stand before that doorway, there is an invitation to an initiation that awakens a transcendental nexus with Presence. This can be a compelling experience for us. One of the students shared that when guided to respond to the invitation and step through the doorway, she became afraid. It reminded me of when the angels appeared before the shepherds to invite them to meet Jesus. Whether that actually happened or not isn't the point. It is a metaphor. She found the meditation very inspiring and unsettling.

> *When the meditation led to the place of opening the door and walking through, I was just terrified because I would like, "oh no, go inside myself?" That was a really emotional experience, "oh my gosh, it is really right here, it's all right here," and then the invitation came to reach out and go further. My first reaction was I was terrified, yet invited by a place within myself that was unafraid.*

When we encounter the full glory of our transcendence and are confronted with the reality that it is within us, at that moment it can be overwhelming. That is incredible. When the light moves in it makes things apparent. Our Basic Self may have a remembrance of danger: like when they nailed us to a cross when we spoke out as a liberated citizen of this world about the residency of our Soul. The experience carries that kind of feeling, so when we're exposed to glory, we need to hold with that feeling because there is an adjustment going on. There is a need for a sense of safety in the Basic Self. Our Basic Self takes its job of survival and continuity very seriously.

In Presence, we can share and download the frequency of safety to our Basic Self. The best protection is being safe. That sense of safety changes the equation between us and our reflexive interaction with ourselves and our environment. As temptation shifts it improves our existential response to the alleged danger. In this case, we are not in danger. We do need to honor the response and hold it present while we adjust and that will resolve our post-traumatic response to spiritual convergence. The practical aspect of living in this world is still with us. Consider that we may have to run like hell from something. But that is something we encounter on the physical level, even perhaps at times on a psychic level, not something we encounter on the level of accessing Presence. In the transcendence of Presence, we may also be the one chasing us.

We practice Presence so that when we have an encounter with our radiant self, we embrace the transformation rather than interpreting it as an existential threat. The only threat is to our limited beliefs. We remain vigilant in case we need to move our physical body around the corner for practical reasons. It is a practical issue just to keep our bodies healthy.

On the other hand, we might be like the Tiananmen Square guy who stood in front of the tank. We may have to stand in front of the tank and admire the face of the cannon that we trust will not speak. That's all that is. It's a re-education, so embrace it. Honor the fear. We all have orphans that need loving. As we embrace the next level of initiation, we move to a higher level of organization in the inner and outer worlds. Always ask for the blessing of Presence.

Meditation

Close our eyes and shift our focus internally.

As we do that there is a frequency that also goes out. As we focus inward, our consciousness expands so that we encompass what surrounds us in the energy of what is inward. In that focusing inward, invite the awareness of the way consciousness circulates through this body, the ascending and descending energy through our center.

In breathing in and out, the heart field energy goes in and out and reflects back to our heart. And begin to touch into the full sentience of this energy. And so, we invite that forward inside of us.

Just focus for a moment into the center of your head into the Tisra Til, into the place even though this has been open for you for some time, put your intention there. And remember that you've gone into that doorway many times, that you've opened ten doors into the depth of your Soul, and just imagine there is another door. Trust whatever color appears. As you hold that focus, be present in that doorway and just stay with that. At some point, it opens and when that begins for you, just step through it into that dimension. Then allow that dimension to flow, to move out through your axial alignment and your sense of Presence, and your sense of the field of loving you are just in.

Begin to experience the field that builds up around you. You have a sense of a sound or silence. There is a subtle progression as the frequency changes. And we just ask for this Presence to the capacity of your awareness to come within you and anchor it into the earth and to enshroud you in its glory.

From this perspective look out upon the current state of the world. And look into the darkest places and in those places find yourself sending the light back. You appear in all those dark places as the center of the darkness and become the light. Is it exactly how it occurs? We don't know. It is just the closest metaphor or image we can provide. So, you may see the dark clouds parting and the light beaming through. You may see other things.

You may have heard it said once, "I am the truth, the light, and the way." Own the statement and repeat it three times. This brings us a little closer to understanding the meaning of that ancient statement.

Open every cell in your body and allow this frequency into every sinew and fiber of your being and your body.

*Be the change
you wish to see
in the world.*

Mahatma Gandhi

CHAPTER SIX

Reflexivity

I use the term reflexivity according to the ancient adage: *as within, so without and as above, so below.* That which is outside of us corresponds, collaborates and manifests in a way that reflects what is inside of us. I know we have looked at reflexivity in many different ways; what reflects back to us in life gives us information about what's unconscious inside of us. It's always good to be careful with this because we are just looking for the information. We are looking for some sense of our relationship in reflexivity to discover where we need to go inside for resolution and what to focus on in terms of what we want more of in our lives. We are loving ourselves at different levels rather than fixing ourselves based on a one level ideal. Through our awareness, we are able to repurpose and change patterns by changing our reality. Everything is a progression. When our external reality changes, consider that at some level we are inwardly colluding with those changes and vice versa.

Law of Attraction

The Law of Attraction has been a very popular concept. It says that what you want, desire, need or hope for you can manifest. For some people the Law of Attraction worked really well, I guess. There are a lot of ways to work with the Law of Attraction. I had a client that was hugely disappointed because life wasn't working out the way she had hoped. She had a good friend who was into the Law of Attraction and would judge her as a loser because she wasn't attracting what she wanted. She wanted a life partner. This set up a perfect shame scenario. What some people miss about the Law of Attraction is that it really works. What shows up is what you have been attracting. We get so focused on the part that is not working, we miss the part that is working. My client's focus was also on her shame and lack of having a partner. When she wanted to attract a partner, she did not first resolve her own sense of inadequacy and shame so those elements were incorporated into her attraction. Life gives us what we focus on and in her case she focused on wanting a partner to make her worthy, to fill her sense of lack, so she attracted lack and relationships that reinforced her unworthiness. When we want to attract something, we also attract the lack because that is what we magnetize to ourselves. How does that Bible saying go? Seek first the glory and the beloved within and all else will be added to you. When referring to scripture like the Christian Bible, I always prefer to paraphrase because chances are good that what I am repeating is someone else's paraphrasing. Consider that after the paraphrase "in the beginning," it is all up to interpretation, even that all of creation began at the so called beginning

We follow our life growing, accomplishing, and applying our understanding of the light as best we can. As a way to nurture that process, we settle into a deeper place and open a loving space in our unconscious. By doing so, the ground of our being becomes a fertile place, a place that amplifies the seeds we plant. Be careful what your seed seeds. The seed may take a while to create the perfect jewel, so hold it within the womb of the unconscious. Let it germinate there. Let it develop and keep it in that loving womb inside of you. Actually, Christ as a seed gestates within us in a very similar way and awakens and matures through the same loving process. By holding your consciousness in a sacred place, in transcendent Presence, we communicate up into the greater fabric of life, and that's a different Law of Attraction. This "Law of Attraction" goes up and attracts broader wisdom, in higher intelligence, in the intelligence of loving that is the fabric of everything and brings about the event that was portended in the seed. At some point the seed coagulates and germinates and then begins to show up in life. The life mirror is reflexive and reflects manifestation back to us. Following this process is how we will manifest heaven on earth.

The manifestation may or may not show up the way we expect, again be present with what is. We have the skill to notice from Presence when the manifestation starts to occur, then we can reach out and cooperate with it. This is a much more powerful and graceful way to manifest than expecting, demanding, dominating, or trying to will it so and being confronted and confounded with failure, distortion and unintended consequences. As part of the process, we may have beliefs, actions, karma, or elements within us that counters or resists the manifestation that we want. If so, then those things will be pushed up into awareness to be cleared, balanced or resolved. We may have to push up a hundred demons before the environment is proper for the manifestation of grace.

We may be stirring up a mess because we want heaven on earth and we have to plow up a lot of ground and transform the seeds of hell before we can plant the seeds of heaven. We may have to liberate a lot of territories to make space, therefore we can't be too critical of appearances or results. If we are looking for angels and we see demons, it may be because we must exorcize the entire planet before we get our heaven. Be patient. Let God, the universe, or whatever cooperate with us and our internal alliances with all the other awakening people that have a play in this so that we have plenty of other folks taking care of stirring things up as well.

In a more profound sense, when looking at the Law of Attraction, we too have been exploring and accessing transcendence, loving, and embodying that loving. When loving becomes our priority focus, we keep building love and that becomes the reflexive relationship that develops in our world. Life is designed to enable and assist us. Everything we do in our life is intended to develop consciousness, and that is the key. Everybody has the same potential, but it's our inner work that builds up the consciousness that creates our field of enterprise. In this discussion, the focus is always on the inner work, the building of consciousness within.

When we are working from a perspective of love, it simplifies everything because then there is a conversation between our unconscious and the unconscious of the world, and we keep working with the attraction of our loving. And in that, we trust that whatever comes is utilizing the loving in some way and love starts to sort everything else out.

Karma Thief

When we see someone in trouble or in need, we see our reflection and we typically want to reach out and help. When something comes back in a disturbing way, it may disappoint or cause an emergency. This reflection or reflexivity looks like negativity. I'm suggesting it is not necessarily as negative as it seems and that it needs sorting out. When we are using a reference point of love, we have a more significant sense that love is holding everything and love is the fabric in which everything exists. It is very easy to get into a kind of spiritual bypass or illusion that says, "well, it is all good," and on the other side that "it is all bad." But then we miss the point. There is a skill to develop. In holding our Presence and holding our center, we are strengthening our skillful means for holding in the greater field of love. With skill we can respond in a way that is genuinely for the highest good, an ultimate cosmic win-win response.

When we see somebody in need, we want to help. Our lesson is to help in a way that does not disrupt or take their karma or stop them from learning something or developing something inside their own destiny. How can we tell? For example, you see someone drowning and wonder, should I jump in and get them? Well yes, of course, it is an emergency! We can work the karma out later and perhaps saving them *is* working out the karma. We need to trust our perception and intuition in the Presence of the situation. There will be a knowing that arises about how to reach out, how to support, or how to intervene so that we are responding from the highest good rather than any need we have to rescue, or from a reactionary political view, or out of a post-traumatic trigger.

In the way of the world, it's tough to tell when we should challenge a person or event or just hold the light for them. Actually, the answer is both because if we are really present in loving and in a supportive, holding space and present with what is, we will be in the knowing and perceiving how to act and knowing what to do. It's collaborative with the highest good of the situation. The highest good is a universally reflexive intelligence. Everything is synchronously measured to living love and spontaneously part of the consequences. However, be cautious about using this as a rationalization. When we place a person or event in the light for the highest good, we act on faith. We also need to be vigilant and present so we can act responsibly to what arises next in the situation or circumstance. We are responsible to following any guidance that may be called for.

We are always refining our sensibility to the highest good. We need to be eternally vigilant. The intelligence of the highest good is self-corrective so that in our sincerity when we make a mistake, we are already heading toward the correction and our error is being calculated for an excellent alternative scenario. The Covid-19 pandemic can be seen in the metaphor of the archetypes of the Greek gods Nemesis challenging Hubris. All the ways we have been arrogant in our entitlement, health care, racial discrimination, economic equality and environmental balance are all being challenged. In the moment people are dying, losing their businesses and fear and hate are being exploited as political forces. On the other hand, people are waking up, joining forces, helping each other and creating new visions for social justice and environmental health. Learning to trust the corrective power of love takes a lot of inner work. Arrogance and entitlement will distort our ability to lead with love. We need to be humble and vigilant. We often hear "oh well, it was meant to be." The "it was meant to be" confirms our preconception or may be the expression of a spiritual bypass, whatever that might be for each of us. It may well have been meant to be, but we need to learn to check the resonance each time to see if we are cooperating with the highest good or if we are choosing a spiritual bypass and using the highest good as an excuse. The key is to respect each others' karma and be vigilant and receptive to acting in accordance with their trajectory. When we intervene, there is a potential for us to take away or diminish the experience they need to grow, learn or resolve karma. We can be tempted to be a hero, yet we could be a karma thief instead.

Inner Work

Through our inner work, we come to peace and satisfaction with life in a way that avoids being hungry for something to happen in a certain way. Trump's presidency caused me to doubt in equanimity and my trust that a new level of civility and kindness was emerging in the American culture. I thought we were much further along than we were because the picture that showed up outside was not consistent with where I thought we were inside. That was embarrassing. We always like to believe we are enlightened, right? It doesn't mean that the vision of our collaborative light lifting the world didn't have a basis or that the karmic wheel isn't turning into a new age of grace. It means that another level of awakening is necessary. When our vision is masking subtler forms of elitism and entitlement, a greater humility and vulnerability may be needed. From that perspective, perhaps, we were further along than I thought. As Transcendental Leaders, we have the depth, enlightenment, wisdom and love to surface a deeper level of shadow from our unconscious and, in doing so, be in service to the evolution of humanity. With the Biden election, I am more circumspect, yet we appear to be entering a new phase in our governance, yet requiring perhaps a subtler vigilance.

Some years ago, I had an inner experience with my spiritual teacher, which deepened my trust and strengthened my resolve. It occurred at another time when events were looking somewhat dark to me and I felt despair. I was shown an image that while events appeared on the surface as if nothing was changing, behind the scene spirit was setting in place a new day and a new dawn. To avoid interference from negativity, the scenario of the light was developing sub-rosa so that it was invisible to the negativity. Business as usual continued as appearance. Then, one day in the blink of an eye, spirit's scenario became evident. By then it was too late for negativity to interfere. Cause and effect are reflexive and as such in our transcendence cause and effect are synchronous in a way that we often don't see a direct line of cause and effect. That which is complete inwardly, manifests outwardly as an emergent phenomenon. Change unfolding from the inside out is what David Bohm, the physicist, described as no cause being local as a process of an implicate reality unfolding into an explicate tangible reality. The outer, the explicate order of life unfolds from the implicate order. Our choices create our destiny. Or as Carl Jung said: That which we don't resolve inwardly will appear in our lives as fate. I suggest that the converse is also true: that which we resolve inwardly will appear as fate. I appreciate the reminder and continue to work inwardly on becoming the change I want to see, in the timing that is true. We continue to build our Soul networks and strengthen the collective loving, while negativity seems to have its way and believes it is winning while in a deeper level of creation which the negative forces cannot see a new way is being prepared for manifestation at the right timing and at that point, it will be too late for the negativity to stop the ascendence of a positive world based on the wisdom of the Soul. How many "American Scholars" harbor within the awakening of Transcendental Leadership?

We need to be aware that disappointment stems from wanting outer change to cause inner transformation. We want to control events in our lives to resolve our internal issues. A good strategy then would be to practice disappointment as much as possible because then we discover a list of the places in which we haven't cleaned up our own lenses. We may need to reach deeper. That might be a good assignment, let's go out tomorrow and get disappointed so we can go in and look at our own lenses and ask: "What's going on in there? Is this an ancestor? Is this my DNA? Is this a belief I'm holding? Did I get this from getting kicked out of kindergarten when I was four-years-old? That really wasn't fair. It was the other guy. Am I expecting my kindergarten teacher to come up from the outside and tell me how good I am in my new age?" We need to trust the negative insertion into our experience and not be afraid to risk disappointment because it might show us the very place where we can find resolution and then we will be much more settled so that our loving can meet life in a sacred, powerful way, and that the loving is reflecting loving. Through meeting life with sacred loving, we can start sorting disappointments out in a way that any biases, misunderstandings, or beliefs that are tied into some dystopian zeitgeists become apparent and we can sense these entanglements in our field with such clarity that we can effectively respond and restore balance. We have to name the entanglements and bring loving to any distortions.

Often in our culture, well-meaning people are looking for ways to resolve crime, poverty or prejudice, and never find a solution without unintended consequences that recycle the issue. We have made some progress. That is good because we keep trying. We look for external action. Even system fixes may help for a while. Reflexivity tells us that the eventual answer will be through character changes, changes within ourselves and collaborative ventures that create the future we want to see. Collaboration is a conduit of transformation when it includes all of the stakeholders. We don't know the critical mass of collaboration necessary to reach a tipping point. Without the understanding that for all of our issues, we are the solution, we will always create answers that have within them embedded agendas. When answers don't work, it is because the sponsors of those answers are protecting something. We possess the power of reflexive change within us. We often just don't use it. We need to do our inner work and trust that the seeds we plant within will become the trees that grow and bring good fruit into the world.

Empathy

The Basic Self can go out looking for what is coming our way. It can go ahead of us and scout the way. I suppose it could pick up when the highway patrol guy is down the road when you are going 90 miles per hour if we let it. Sometimes the Basic Self searching works for me and sometimes it doesn't, but the potential is there. The adventuring of the Basic Self may take shedding the fear of getting caught in exchange for the joy of the game. Then joy of the game takes the Basic Self out of fear and lack and puts it into loving. Say we are having a karmic handball match or playing karmic Ping-Pong in the joy of the game, and both people, teams or aspects win. In fact, the winner could never succeed without the loser. You see it is always teamwork. The Patriots football team was so great because they won. But they could never have won without the other team, so I don't know why they are so proud of themselves. The gift of winning is understanding that you can win. The opponents not only helped them win, they helped them get better. As winners, even though we applaud the illusion of victory, we are inwardly building the capacity to accomplish and succeed in the face of challenge through empathy and winning. In a Soul sense we are both teams, creating experience through loving each other through the dance of taking each other's measure.

As we develop empathy, we can reach out into the Akasha and read the records. At first, it might be like reading braille. With practice, the Akashic record may appear as a streaming video. When we look at a situation in a town that is in poverty or a place where there is an industrial accident or war, or a pandemic we can start sensing how the event impacts people or at least gain an understanding of the karmic event that is going on there. Then we begin to hold the light from the perspective of the Souls as they go through tribulation. We also can know our relationship to what we see. It is a different call for each of us. When we see the starving child, we may have an urge to go there and help. A medical doctor might dedicate his/her life in service. Someone else might donate money, and another, prayer. In this sense life is a "ball game" with itself, a sporting event in which God always wins as us.

The Death Passage

Dying is a passage. Done consciously, we can join in the transition and enable passage into a higher place. In a war zone where there is a lot of collateral damage, the person who is experiencing the damage could develop trauma, or hate, or an injury that takes lifetimes for them to get over. With a broad enough empathy and a deep enough resonance with the karmic flow of that person, we can help them to resolve that right then as they die.

In the practice of Soul Transcendence, we can go back and forth to the other side before we die and we can know the way and be fearless. That is not the only way. My grandmother told me a story about her father. As he was dying, people would visit him from the other side. A light appeared to him and his deceased relatives and old friends came to him as he moved out to meet them. He told her about this. One day he apparently just walked off with his relatives. It instilled in her a trust of death and served her well as a nurse and in her own eventual graceful passage.

We have the potential to so deeply empathize with these situations that even the negative expression is part of some kind of experiential process of our evolving Soul. When we can join that empathetic potential at a deep enough level we don't get caught. We keep going. People that come from tough situations and come out of those traumas have exceptional resilience. There are people coming out of deep poverty, or war, or trauma, and they seem to transcend those limitations. This process is a form of death and rebirth. Somehow they were able to stay in touch with their soul-seed and push up through the layers of carnage and reach up towards the sky where fruit could manifest and their Souls could flourish. Often there was at least one person on the young journey that gave them unconditional love in a way that reminded them of their true identity, that they were the one that brings love. Resilience is a particular Soul development. Some Souls need more experience and care in order to reach the heights. If we could practice bringing care into the various levels as seeds become trees and trees bear fruit, it would have a different impact. One way to begin as Transcendental Leaders is by forming a resilient Soul resonance within us that awakens and energizes as we prepare to manifest a greater glory on the planet.

Visionary Future

While we are building our visionary future, we have a parallel consideration. One option is building our internal representation of what we want to create. The other is gathering the information we need to refine and clarify our desired form. Of particular interest are codes of lack, such as: "I'm insufficient, I'm unworthy or I'm great, I want to be famous, or I am entitled." We need vulnerable self-reflection to awaken our reflexive power. When we filter out the lack, blame and shame, victim/victimizer, domination and submission, and all of those other codes, the seed of the vision will coalesce on its own.

Alchemically the visionary process is a distillation and coagulation process. The result is that the seed takes on the form of a resonant jewel, which then amplifies itself and attracts supportive forces and then it is out of our hands. We release the seed into the depths of our own void so that the manifestation of the seed can find its way. Another thing we can do with shaping and manifestation of the seed is to check inside and see if every aspect of this vision resonates with transcendent loving so it will go unobstructed into the flow of God's will (love having love's way). In this way manifestation of the seed has the power of holy love and the highest level of transcendental authority. There is a feature to this incubation in which we are not telling people about it. We are not blabbing about how great we are, or about this great thing that we are doing. It is done in "secret" (discretely) so that in sorting and distilling it, not only our negativity, but also the negativity of the world can't see it. Then we look like a reasonable person walking down the street with our inadequacies like everyone else. Negativity can't tell we're cooking our vision in our internal laboratory. When the cake is baked and we release it from our oven, it is too late for interference to have an impact and our vision will come about in the world. It can't be subverted. It's food for the Gods that translates into food for everyone. The concept of "fishes and loaves" is an internal process.

In the process of creating visions, if you get impatient and reveal your hand too soon, then there's an opening for interference. People will try to talk us out of our vision. Our true purpose may be distorted or misunderstood. We have a great idea, and we have our favorite person who is pessimistic about everything we do, not only with our ideas but with us. Who needs friends like that, right? We all have them. They come around and talk us out of the greater good that we want to do. Talk to God and selected confidants and you will get better advice.

As we open our vision, a knowing comes in that informs and clarifies. Reflexivity can act very quickly. We bypass consternation because of the Presence of loving in our regard. Loving our vision will disperse the shadows and resolve limitations as we observe. A clear sense will arise that it is time to act. Not to worry, seeds like right timing when they are completed and ready. We can't hold them back. They will go into the depths and into wholeness. When we trust our impressions as an indicator that we are in a right relationship to the process of manifestation our observation and vulnerability quicken the delivery of our vision-seed. The experience of trust and observation will be one indicator. As we observe, the manifestation of the seed sprouts wings and floats in the air. Now, all we have to do is keep showing up at the station until the train comes in or blessing the farm until harvest time. We allow a greater level of consciousness to take the lead in which creation appears synchronous as this student observed:

There's an energy that really does work, at least for me. And I noticed in the meditation, when we were working with both love and the light going out and then coming back, that I was experiencing that simultaneously, as one phenomenon that was happening simultaneously, instead of something happening, and then something else happening.

Responsibility

When responsibility is a burden, it is often compensating for our inadequacies or as a justification for the false value of self. We want to keep our trait of responsibility and resolve our inadequacy. Responsibility is our ability to respond, which derives from a hierarchy of internal loyalties: loyalty to our Soul first, our well-being second and to others third. Soul is the eternal essence of our consciousness and has authority as a co-creator with the divine pattern or consciousness which is everything. When we are loyal to our soul, we can embrace the mantle of being a responsible creator. The reflexivity of responsibility will create more burdens when we use it as compensation, and it will lighten our load when responsibility is an expression of loyalty to our Soul.

Responsibility is like a muscle that we have to exercise. It takes inner work such as meditation, staying conscious, awakening, remembering, self-forgiveness, lucid dreaming, Soul travel, etc. We are also responsible for all levels of creation because we are looking back at ourselves through creation as a Soul and as the health of creation taking care of us. In this context, we could say that there is fear-based responsibility and love-based responsibility. Reflexively, love-based responsibility is sustainable.

When something bad happens, we take responsibility. In consciousness, this is not about whose fault it is. It is about being responsible for how we respond regardless of who is at fault. That seems to work out. At a deeper level, we take responsibility for everything in our creation, not in a burdensome way, rather in a reflexive way.

This is where we turn to Ho'oponopono. Ho'oponopono means resolution through living love and is a Hawaiian approach to resolving individual and group karma. According to Ho'oponopono, whatever appears in our world, we played a part in allowing, promoting or creating. In some way, we collaborated with the collective to create the particular challenge we are facing for some reason, at some time, in some dimension. For example, war is necessary for some people to move through their experience, so we hold that. We are creators of war or need the experience of being a soldier, or we are the general that spends his life as a warrior and then at the end decides to become a peacemaker because he found out that war is not the greatest way to resolve issues. We may need the same endeavor for a different reason. This is a form of collaboration and collective reflexivity. In collective reflexivity we find that responsibility then becomes synonymous with participation. In Ho'oponopono we say to those who are in strife around us or act against us and against themselves, those who are our relationships, relatives and even ancestors to please forgive us. We say, "please forgive me, I love you and I am so sorry." In this way we erase the negative information that informs karma. We ask for forgiveness as a metaphor for what is happening within us. We take responsibility so that we have the power to resolve the energy.

The most challenging responsibility is in having an inner life that is equal to everything. The greatest, most powerful transcendent glory of loving that any consciousness could have is within us and is equal to whatever drama arises in the world. If we turn our attention towards glory, it responds wherever our attention invites it. That is the highest level of responsibility. We are the kind of creatures that have the capacity to accept and to claim responsibility and then stand up in it and resolve it. We really have to be over our childish stuff, because any way that we are still bratty is going to undermine responsibility and the possible consequences. Taking responsibility doesn't mean we are justified in our injustices, what we want, or shouldn't have. That level of stuff goes away because this level of responsibility doesn't negotiate on the level of childishness. Responsibility brings forward the Soul and the power of love. Love shines right through the cosmic mirror and meets us in the moment and what is present is all there is.

When we get to a place of activation, choosing from the primal power of love provides the greatest responsibility. If we are off just a little bit, the ensuing manifestation will amplify and rapidly accelerate any slight divergence of our choice. The good news is that we can correct our divergent choice quickly when we see the error. The bad news is that if you are still complaining and don't want to take responsibility, the brat in us will multiply its own brattiness and we will believe the false center of our newly created reality. Our reflexive creativity will soon place us in the middle of a metaphorical swarm of bratty locusts. Approach divergence with great care. That's the responsibility. It's the deepest one. Truth, compassion, humility and gratitude train us for high responsibility.

When we are still caught in fear and power, we always believe that we have to win or lose. When we awaken transcendentally, win/lose becomes a game instead of an identity, we are free to play in the confidence of our loving. Some things that look like win/lose may not be, so we really have to hold our sensibility looking into the Akasha because something that might seem like a loss may not be. Sometimes a loss is a win in the broader scope of things.

In a meditation a student illuminated and stepped through the spiritual doorway located in the Pineal gland and this is what they observed:

When I went through that doorway as well, I saw that I was the universe and the universe was inside of me. It was, and I think I want to, I mean, it was just amazing. And then I had that fear come up. The meditation almost felt like it was connected to an earlier meditation and it just went to this other step and that piece about responsibility feels like the answer to that fear.

Center and Circumference

As our awareness develops, we are able to navigate the various dimensions of consciousness. The fabric of the universe is multidimensional, and we grow into a conscious awareness of these dimensions and experience the dimensions as levels of our consciousness. All the levels are right here and now, and they are also now and there, meaning that we are traveling through the levels. We are either traveling through the levels or the levels are traveling through us. As we navigate we increasingly becoming aware of our center and the circumference of each context, or place, we are in. On whatever level of consciousness, our perceptual envelope is in the center and we see the horizon of our surround as circumference. In a physical space, we are aware of our body in a room, forest or an open field. The circumference contains our reality, even when it is the horizon or the vast blue sky. Each context has a specific sensation on and in our bodies. The same holds true for any dimension or reality we are in. We can use our imaginations to navigate and be in various dimensional spaces. Different dimensional areas can also use our imaginations, feelings, sensations, symbols, and thoughts to inform us as to what the context, center or reality we are in. We use awareness to navigate or to stay stuck if we go unconscious. We can always choose.

When we are in different spaces on the physical level, each space has its specific psychic/spiritual frequencies. These frequencies are woven with emotional, mental and etheric textures. Perception is subtle. For example, when we attend groups, we will experience the physical/psychic/spiritual textures and frequencies of that place. The more we are secure in our alignment, the more each of these spaces registers information and the more clarity we get concerning which frequencies are ours and which come from some attribute of the space. We can even recall an area or event by eliciting those sensations that were present at the time.

In retrospect, when we recall the center and circumference of our experience within a group, we can sort out our frequencies from the energies that we may have picked up during our participation, clear those energies and reflect insight about the experience. Each set is receptive to the spiritual and magnetic energy circulating through that group of events. Some magnetic contexts are more conducive to the transcendent flows of energy than others. The more we are present, the more the magnetic and transcendent energies modulate for us.

Robert D. Waterman, EdD

Leading Meditation

When leading a meditation, the physics of center and circumference are very much in play. When I conduct a meditation, I am very present and speak from the imagery that appears to me. The reality is that the meditation is guiding me. Guidance shows us the best magnetic conduit for transcendental frequencies, so conducting a meditation is a collaborative venture. Naming the imagery entrains our consciousness and we create rapport and movement commensurate with the transcendent invitation of our consciousness. We collaborate to travel into those dimensions and relationships that are shown to us. On occasion when I am guiding a meditation, a participant will see the same imagery that I am speaking about. When a student made this comment, my response was that the key is that the meditation does me. That is the key.

Student observation:

I just wanted to say that there is something about the way you do meditations that is so powerful. Over the years I've become wary of people who guide meditations, but there's a way you engage it energetically that is very activating, and it works for me immediately.

The imagery provides a context and we place our sense of self into that context. There is a play of the psychic/spiritual energies through this. Consequently, our experience will fluctuate between feeling, sensation, impressions, intuition, imagery, colors, fragrances, and sounds. Synesthesia may occur in which an image actually reflects sounds, like the imagery of a waterfall is actually the sound of the waterfall. When we enter dimensional or virtual space, we don't analyze or wonder what is wrong with us or others based on these traveling impressions. Just like when we are walking through a physical environment and feeling the breeze, watching the clouds, hearing birds or smelling flowers, we don't try to control that. We just take it in through observation and appreciation. When we do that, meaning will inform us. When we transcend the mind, we often register a blank even though our self (that is in that place) has a rich and textured experience. Blanks are not problems, they are just spaces to fill in or spaces with rich content that will fill us in later.

Often a gateway or portal will appear in meditation. Sometimes this is a symbol. Usually, it is a passage from one dimension or state of consciousness to another or an entry into a specialized space in which an initiation or a sharing of specialized information can occur. Examples of this are: journeying into our inner classroom and meeting our inner teacher, or traveling through a portal in the physical heart into the sacred heart. As we establish ourselves in the dimensions of light and love, through constructing conduits or nexus through visual intention, we are able to share those energies with any location or relationship that may have a need. In these dimensions of light and love we gain trust. The meditation leads the leader.

Once we enter the altered state of meditation, we may have visual experiences of images that are sometimes similar to lucid dreaming. In the following, a student shared her experience from a guided meditation. We share energy currents with the participants. The visuals or images and sensations experienced by the participants often diverge at some point from those we see. In both cases, ours and the participant's images are a response to the same energy currents. Our guiding opens a door and assists the participant to enter and then it is up to the participant, their inner guidance and consciousness of the reality we have entered. The following student sharing illustrates our discussion on leading a meditation.

My experience of the meditation was so real. When I entered that new portal in the Soul where we had maybe never been in before, I dropped into this absolutely deliciously warm, kind of rose-colored place. And then you had us go into trouble spots or painful spots in the world and I went to Venezuela, and then I went to the current presidential administration, and in both places I had the same thing happen. Suddenly there was forgiveness because you could see the adolescence that was behind the trouble. So it was, I mean, the very horrible things happening were coming from immaturity, you know, and so it was kind of innocent, it was forgivable. And that colored my week. The week was really, really hard. I encountered a tremendous amount of pain, almost unbearable pain and had to sit in meditation to try to move the pain, both pain with my daughter and pain with the world. And then I had a client who went through something absolutely horrific and impossible to hold. So, suddenly I'm sitting with all of this pain and I went into meditation and did my best to move it and had a hard time moving it and so I asked the divine mother what I consider to be a crucial question. I started thinking, my God you think of all the people praying all over the world, all of the time, how in the world do those beings hold the pain of the world. How do they do it? And so that's what I asked her, I said how do you hold the pain of the world?

And at first, when I listened, I got quiet and listened, and the first answer that comes back was something to the effect that pain is just energy and so move and I got that. I was able to work with that a little bit, but I could feel I wasn't really getting it. And then I heard this beautiful thing that said bless it. And when I felt that blessing the pain would go, energetically how that works, it was very similar to what you had done in the meditation where you said take that love and send it into all the difficult places on earth. And then you see how that catalyzes the pain anyway. It's a very productive process. That's all I want to convey. It's catalytic.

Meditation

Direct your attention towards the Presence of the Christ. You may have to drop off a little dogma for this. The Christ is an essence of loving in mastery that resides on this planet and resides inside of humanity and is available for the deliverance of each person.

The real cross is our physical incarnation. It's really a sacrifice to the awakening of the Christ within us. So, if you want to avoid some of the carnage of your physical sacrifice, invite the awakening to the Christ within, because then you don't need so much tragedy to wake up.

Let us be present with that.

Bring that loving forward. Gather the depth of yourself and the breadth of yourself into your heart. As you look out from that place of the heart, the love just goes out. It just goes through like a wave through everything you look at, and it keeps going out through situations and circumstances in the world, and it keeps going out.

At some point it starts to return and reflect back and so you become vulnerable and so everyone is looking back at you, and the loving comes back, back through them, back to you, it comes back many fold. We receive in the reflexivity of within and without, outside and inside.

Then there's reflexivity of heaven and earth, so when you take in this light, this transcendent light, this transcendent love, embody it and send it out. There is reciprocity with the wholeness, so that's what you use with God to give God to the world. It is now also returning many folds from the transcendent reality into this embodiment. There you go, allow it. You did the work, take the amplification of the work. That's taking responsibility for the love that you are and the love that you live.

Whenever you are ready, open your eyes and be present with what is.

*A good leader can engage in a debate frankly
and thoroughly,
knowing that at the end
he and the other side must be closer,
and thus emerge stronger.
You don't have that idea when you are arrogant,
superficial, and uninformed.*

Nelson Mandela

CHAPTER SEVEN

House

• • •

Scripture is sacred writing that can then be referred to subsequent times to gain wisdom and guidance. Scripture is allegedly inspired by a higher consciousness and often regarded as a sacred representation of a transcendent holiness. When we share stories from our lives about how our challenges have transformed us into loving, we are speaking from our own scripture. Any scripture we look at, whether it's the Bible, the Bhagavad Gita, or the Popol Vuh, is a sacred story of ways we are using challenges to transform ourselves into loving.

In my early years of attending church, I often heard the terms salvation, redemption, and restoration. That sounded nice, but the dogmatic spin of the words made those qualities hard to find. Finally, I gave up on it and started to look for the deeper meaning of the words and how our images and language work with consciousness. I discovered that those words—salvation, redemption, and restoration—were about transforming ourselves into loving. Implicitly that's everybody's project. One of the first steps is realizing consciously that transforming ourselves into loving *is* our project, and once we embrace that everything goes much more gracefully. Our lives are scripture relating our sacred journey into wholeness. As a metaphor, our house evolves as our personal space in the dimensionality of the earth.

We are the "house" that Soul built. Each aspect of our life is a room in our house embodying the affirmations of I Am Soul, Master of My House. Each room in our house reflects an aspect of the Soul and each room of our house is integral in our life scripture. This embodiment is one of the most significant challenges, or rather *skillful means*, for Transcendental Leadership.

Authority

Looking at language in terms of the vibration of the word and what it resonates with reveals how words are a conduit of spirit. When we use images, they are codes for constructing consciousness. When we use the term house, it's a metaphor. Metaphors have *pattern resonance* with the structural frequencies of our consciousness. Living in houses is familiar. We all respond to the instinct to make the house our home. Our houses have rooms and closets, attics and basements. Attics and basements are for storing stuff that has some value because we can't throw it away, becoming forgotten memories or memories of relatives that we might like to forget. Closets are a good place to hide skeletons. In literature, houses are stories about consciousness. There are haunted houses or houses of the Lord and they take on different qualities. Houses get connected to homes, hearts, and families. It's a vibrant image for us, and it's helpful. The vibration of "house" gives us a meaningful context in which to make our home.

We can look at ourselves as a house and as a master of a house. Archetypally a house can represent a whole tribe, like the Biblical House of David or Samuel or something like that if you are familiar with Bible metaphors, or home industries, with masters, guilds, journeymen, and apprentices. Certain families would be producing and living in the same house. Perhaps your house uses the metaphor of a country squire. These images are vibrant inside of us as a way to begin to navigate within ourselves.

Soul, as a vibration, is often used and misused because of our beliefs about Soul. Soul is a nebulous term, but we keep using it until someday we may understand it. Even abusing the term Soul can be helpful. Religiously entitled people talk about saving our Souls or finding lost Souls. The truth is that Soul is the only thing that can't be lost. We can forget it, forget what we did with it, use it for or against ourselves, make up stuff about, or believe our Soul is lost. Soul is the only thing that is not "bad" and is never lost. But in trying to understand it, we keep working with it and exploring. Let me put that a different way. We can gather that Soul has a central prominence from all the different ways we use and abuse this term. All of our misunderstandings point to Soul.

When we are in the Soul frequency, there is a knowing, a sense of peace and love that is in itself...of itself. We find reflexive phrases in scripture like *It of Itself, I Am that I Am*. The Soul refers to itself, that is its nature. It doesn't refer out to other things to know itself. It just is. Yet, Soul adds to itself through experience. We do understand from repeating the word that Soul has a deep core vibration for us. Soul is where we intrinsically know the power of love.

By now we've changed a lot of misunderstandings about ourselves to land where we are willing to respond or be more vulnerable to the essence of ourselves, to essence that transcends our thoughts about ourselves. Perhaps there is an innate goodness, an indwelling spirit or essence of God inside our Soul as its central nature. It's hard to figure out, but once we embrace a resonance of it, we can use that resonance as a measure of love and as a calling, a way to track ourselves. Then we can make a statement like I am Soul and feel the vibration of that statement inside of us. That's very powerful, it is central to our Soul nature. When our centering authority is the axial alignment of the Soul within, we are in a pattern resonance beyond the reflective circumference from which we house our Ego.

The Soul is incarnating into an expression that we are calling a human being with a body. The Soul incarnating into a human being is a natural way, an appropriate way to look at our personality as a housing for the Soul, a place to operate from, a home away from home. Perhaps from the Soul's viewpoint, we could call it a vacation house, a little chalet in the mountains of earth. That's a beautiful way to conceptualize the incarnated Soul: this body we wear always held in the arms of earth.

Construction

We build our house and it has geometry or geography. The first aspect of our house is that it has a center and a circumference. We have been practicing accessing this center, this axial vortex of energy that is our center. We can imagine it. If we practice enough, we can even feel a little shift when we consider our center. A circumference implies there is a boundary that holds the space and also reflects back like a mirror, creating circulation between center and circumference. We live our lives, we move out into our lives, and our lives reflect back to us. There is physics in this reflective relationship and that physics becomes the basis for our house. Once we sense the archetypal reference for a house, we can see how many cultures have a similar view. Artwork displays images reflecting the consciousness of "Soul" and "house" in the houses of many cultures.

On the physical level, we have a body that senses where we live life and where life meets us. When we go deeper, our emotions reflect, and whatever is in our mind reflects, and that creates a dynamic process. The Soul is part of this axial alignment which lines up in the body. We start constructing our house of Soul and begin to have experiences, deciding things, making beliefs, and building from the alignment inside of our space. We populate our house in resonance with our Soul plan or building code.

Our Soul's house can be imagined as a sphere with a centerline. Episodes in our life become rooms in our house, and sometimes those rooms look like the house we lived in at the time of the incident in our memory. We start creating little contexts for each category of experience. We grew up in a family. The values, beliefs and traditions of that family became internalized and now have their place as rooms in our house. Sometimes we absorb our family's codes, and some of those inclusions tie us to other people's authority over us. We build a house, and we may have another little house for our mother-in-law or guest that stayed to long or not long enough. We need to check to see if we have a mother-in-law or guest house inside of us or at least a room. We want our mother-in-law to be well loved and not forgotten in neglect. In the next room over, maybe something happened that was traumatic and shameful, and people helped us forget it and put it away, and that became a room, and we forgot about that room. But now we find these strange things influencing us inside and we might think we have a haunted house, so we have to do something with that once forgotten room. Usually love will clean the room, redecorate and transform negative memories of relationships into caring, positive memories. You get the idea...*Love will have its way.*

Small

We can get stuck in a room of our Soul House and think it is our whole house. A student recounted this when she had an image in a meditation of a baby in her arms and this baby was just beautiful. It reminded her of a memory from before she was born. She saw a lot of people looking down on her and the baby from a high place. There was some connection between this baby and beauty and all these people. For the student, disturbing people is difficult. She doesn't want to disturb people out of a sense of herself as small.

This student remembered something the Dalai Lama said: when we think that we are too small to have an impact, try to sleep when there's a mosquito in your room. It completely changed her point of view about mosquitoes and her perceived smallness. She didn't want to disturb, yet to think that something so small could have such an impact wasn't realistic. She felt her loving was like the mosquito and that a lot of people were irritated by her love. When love irritates, I suggest it is from resistance. The one being loved is resisting.

Love brings vulnerability and that vulnerability brings healing. We need to have compassion and stay present while the irritation gets over itself and adjusts. In a sense, when we believe our loving is inadequate, that will be reflected back to us. Over explaining ourselves won't help. Trusting our loving and allowing loving time to work is more effective. Love will find its way. We need to take a moment and let the love go out to others, the world and universe first. Then when we speak, love will be a carrier wave for our speech. Just add this to the process and then we will find our authentic speech and our authentic speech will have love with it. And our words not only will be more precise, but they will carry a vibration that communicates powerfully and effectively. With love on board irritation will serve as a conduit for love, if it exists at all.

Though we may believe ourselves small, as we realize the authority of our Soul and the power of love and claim that authority as the true executive of our personality, we shed the misunderstanding that small in stature means small in power. By looking through the lens of our personality as a house of Soul, and by affirming that "I Am Soul, Master of My House," we transform our Presence and evict all the internalized forces that make us believe we are small. In our conversation with the student, she shared a dream in which she gained further insight into her essential authority:

In my first image, there are a lot of rooms. It was more like a stairway of windows where I can go through all of these rooms. So I went through all of these rooms and I was on another planet with some people sitting around a fire. The good thing was I felt comfortable. Finally, I found a home. I saw my parents, but I didn't know what to say, and I was just sitting there.

I don't know why. I remembered the question about the room which needs attention, and there was again this picture I had in the meditation of a lot of people looking in from above. This time I went in. I just knew my life as it is and as it was, but the difference is that now I know where I came from. I feel there is a link between talking and reaching in with my love. It's about learning to reach people with my love and with my talking. How to do it or to have the courage to do it? There is a link, but I don't see it. The link could help me to do that or be in service to that.

Loving helps me take my place, like when I have a sense that I came from a place. It gives me more substance, more confidence. It's like a support. Like I am a citizen. It feels real because I am here, but I'm coming from another planet. It's weird. That's probably true for everybody. It doesn't distinguish me from anybody else. It's just like oh, I came from someplace!

I am true to myself. I am on my side. I don't give myself away to other things or some purpose or betray myself or something. I am loyal to myself. Another way to say that is I Am Soul, Master of My House. That's loyalty. And then life can arrange itself to bring me what I need. I get it.

Enough

Everyone has their agendas for us. We may have been taught that we are not masters of our house, however recognizing that we internalized this subversive lesson is helpful. Noticing that it is our house implies perhaps that we should have mastery, or that we get addicted to a drug and that becomes master. Or we swear an oath, take a vow or a pledge, so then that is the master of my house. Some cultures strongly exemplify this view. This can also carry over from another life. It's like we move from one place to another and even though we get a new house, we start populating it with stuff we brought with us from the other house. That's called karmic reincarnation and internal decorating. Perhaps we have special Akashic moving vans that bring the furnishings that decorated our past-life house or buses that bring ancient guests to haunt our new house. Staying clear at home in our own house is a complex project. The more we participate in karmic reincarnation, the more we bring with us the old pattern of forgetting the Soul and substituting an abstract or doctrinaire sense of Soul. There comes a time when we've had enough of our sloppy housekeeping. We want to reclaim our house. We experienced too much confusion, too many aches and pains, too many conflicts, and had too many buttons pushed, and we need to do something! We want to do some remodeling, and it starts with reclaiming our authority. It's not as hard as we think because we have always been using our authority, though often unconsciously or half-heartedly. We have just been using authority against ourselves.

Our House

The affirmation I Am Soul, Master of My House enables us to position ourselves more powerfully in our lives. How we order ourselves in our own house is everything. We have levels of consciousness like our imagination, emotions, mind, and archetypal consciousness. Our house is in a world of duality where realities are oppositional and reflective. Depending on how we use that polarity, it presents two kinds of masters. One has to do with domination and the other has to do with loving. The heart is in the center of our house. This is our house because we are going to be occupying it and the Soul has a way of filling our house. When the Soul is master, polarities in the house will work harmoniously and conflicts are mediated through the love that is present in every room of the house as well as in the house as a whole.

We can compare the house to a computer. Our computer/house has a lot of software in it, designed to be used and activated by our Soul. Our personal field connects with the universal field. The universal field is composed of heaven and earth because this combined force field resonates with our true alignment, constitution and purpose. This alignment is where power comes in and energizes our reality. In this alignment our house of love becomes a gift and a home for our Soul and our Soul's purpose. We use this metaphor of heaven and earth because it resonates with our true alignment, constitution, and purpose. We can power our house with karma or grace. Karma always comes with a utility bill. Grace comes with unlimited free power.

Review

Our Soul/house relationship is a review of our life purpose. We are standing in the consciousness of our house. We may have noticed that our house has gotten cluttered. We try sorting things out and some of them we forget about or discard. They end up in the basement or the attic. Random clutter starts influencing the frequency of our house and the way wholeness flows through it and how we present ourselves in life. Part of our spiritual work is to clear our clutter, to be willing to look into shadowy areas and bring in the light. Even our discards can clear up by bringing in the light. In fact, sometimes in our storage bins, we find something that is precious that we forgot about. These precious finds may be a great idea or a discarded project we had so we bring them back into play.

Transcendental Leadership

I Am Soul, Master of My House is an endeavor that reclaims authority in our house. We invite a guest into our house or they impose themselves into our house, and pretty soon we have been pushed out of our authority. Our beliefs and belief systems factor into our loss or retention of our own authority. For example: to re-arrange the furniture and decide what we want to keep or discard. Anything created can only be changed by a higher authority and we have two levels of authority. Our authority begins with: I Am Soul, Master of My House, then we have another level of authority which we could say is love, or God, or whatever. The love/God authority is master of all. This authority works the way it works. Often, it does not work the way we think that it ought to and we find this out eventually. When we get these two authorities working together we can clean house. When we clean house and bring order within our house, we then bring transformation to the world. "As we transform ourselves into loving, the transformation of the world into loving can take place." (John-Roger) Do not do it the other way around, because if we try to clean up the world first, we will get into duality, into fights and will experience disappointment. We will add to the mess. Our realization of this truth is a turning point. We created our internal mess by internalizing the mess in the world. When we try to change the world first, we just make more of the same mess. We must resolve the conflict within us, we must seek first the "heaven" within us. The tactics of Ghandi and Martin Luther King jr. were based on this principle.

We construct and populate the rooms of our house with our beliefs. We either invent these beliefs or accept them as they are imposed by interests that conspire to use us, to use our energy, and use us to fulfill things they cannot achieve on their own. In this world we have a room in our house for politics. This room requires careful design and vetting as to who we invite in for a visit or what beliefs we incorporate. Political parties and politicians are in the business of organizing and mobilizing human resources. This is not good or bad. We have to sort out and know the people well that we are preparing a place for and asking to complement our leadership role.

Measure

We have a measure of loving. Our center is love, and it is in a dimension that is deeper than any created reality. Whatever level we are operating on or whatever our belief is, we can measure these beliefs to loving and with authority decide to reconstruct those beliefs or keep them. If the belief is not resonant with loving we might choose to change the belief. To the degree that we base our reality on fear, we phase out our access to this measure and we may begin to measure based on external calculation posing as inner criteria. We must tend to our measuring room through vigilance, precision, humility, Presence and loyalty to our Soul and the singularity of love that resides in our core.

We often experience our measure to love as conflict, as relation, as depression, or as disturbance. When this happens, we are merely ill at ease. These sorts of feelings are measures that are divergent from love and reflect our journey. They are not good or bad, they rather offer us guidance. There are things that we have commissioned for our lifetime to do, resolve, accomplish, or complete. Joy, enthusiasm, peace, and freedom are also measures of these commissions. We use the measure of love to bring our resolutions into balance. This is an internal process. We choose what to identify with and what to assign a room to as an ongoing practice within our house. Beliefs are steps on the way, but they are not there because they block us. We made these beliefs and they got us this far. Our beliefs are experiments and temporary measures. When an experiment does not work, we take it apart, re-evaluate, and do another experiment. We can fall in love with our experiments. We often take results personally. For example we might tell ourselves, "That is such a beautiful belief. I do not care if it is screwed up and ugly; it is mine." We measure another belief and decide it is useful and another turns out to be a false identity. We measure it according to loving and it comes up short. When the measure is true, there is a resonance. When it does not measure true, the awareness is flat, or discordant, like in a sour taste or off-key note.

Experiments and Implants

We have rooms assigned to beloved experiments and some work and some don't. When we find such a room in our house, we can ask, what was our purpose for these rooms or for being involved in the creation in that room? What was I trying to accomplish? We then look for what we would like in this room. As we read this, we can reflect on the rooms we have visited or constructed.

Other rooms in our house are the implanted ones. We have either created the implants, promoted them, or allowed the decoration and occupancy. That makes every one of them our responsibility even though they were imposed on us. Taking responsibility is where the power is. This is I Am. Everything else is what I am doing, or trying out, or exploring. As we are evolving, we do not forget ourselves in the midst of what we are doing. Deciding what to choose and what to toss away becomes very easy when we remember our own Presence in the situation.

Imposed ideas have to do with other peoples' agendas. For example, a charismatic leader gets a bunch of folks hypnotized to his agenda, or a parent in their lack about their own lives uses us to compensate for their lack. The other thing that parents do is celebrate our integrity, so we are encouraged to go out and explore for ourselves. Whatever the situation, we are intended to leave our parent's house, metaphorically. Sometimes there is no house and we are living under a bridge. We can look at it metaphorically. We leave the house and go out on our journey so we can sort things out and learn to track ourselves in our success. Our process is set up for us to win. Sometimes we have trouble, and we put our parent's house on top of our house and try to live in both houses. Perhaps we were homeless growing up so now we have a house but we a still homeless.

One of the clues that informs us that we have created split loyalties and competing tenants in our house is that we have trouble sorting out what we want to do to find our way. We need to go back and clean house. If we find imposed ideas, we either invited them or let them in, promoted or allowed them, or we had the same distortion and colluded with the ideas. At any rate, these situations are here to help us wake up aspects of our Soul. When our awakening to Soul progresses and begins to overlight our character, competing thoughts arise and try to stop the awakening by criticizing our interest in awakening. The negative voices may say, "Why would I want a belief like that?" It is a challenge to wake up because the Soul is eternally trying to fulfill itself. At some point conflict is going to become intolerable. In terms of imposed beliefs, we find the replacement by looking for the quality or virtue that is trying to wake up inside of us. When our virtue awakens, we evict the substitute belief.

Alignment

We measure whatever we do, make or find according to the loving. If our reference to loving reveals a distortion, we will know it, especially if we have built up a habit of being honest with ourselves. There will be trust in our Soul house of loving. We keep refining our sense of loving until we can say yes when speech or action resonates with love. Loving has resonance. In my experience, when I speak to someone and it is the truth, even before there is a chance to stop resonance, resonance is there in the center, in our centers, in our axial alignment. When truth resonates in our attuned axial center, we are like strings in the harp of creation sounding from celestial winds. That is an excellent way to know or be sure about our truth-teller inside. Accessing our truth-teller is a matter of building up our skill. Not to worry, we have plenty of opportunities to practice.

An essential part of developing our alignment is building our authority. Practicing a connection with resonance will ultimately build our authority, our most in-depth agenda. As our authority grows, it starts to take over the house, converting all of the rooms and everything in them to resonate with loving. In this instence, I love the biblical phrase: "as for me and my house, we serve the Lord." This is a loving kind of statement, an affirmation. If we find a predatory belief, we can replace it with "in my house, we serve the Lord." We serve the love. In fact, by declaring this truth, we might be surprised at what kind of creatures flee from the basement or the attic storage of our house.

Answers

We have a conscious location and an unconscious location that come together in Presence and organizes on whatever level we are present. With soul-world thinking Presence is total, omnipresent, and everything synchronizes, and we are integral to that Presence within our location. Wholeness thinks as a wholeness. Some of the metaphors people use for this perspective are: scissors can't cut themselves because they are the scissors, or water can't get itself wet, we are in it and of it. *Thou Art That* or *I Am That I Am* or *I Am Soul* are the truths of the embodied Soul, which we call Presence. We are a nexus of heaven and earth. We simultaneously exist until we choose a frequency. Examples of selecting a frequency are: going to the store, contemplating a topic, or incarnating. Once we choose a life, the frequency holds until we die or are reborn. When we are reborn, we change the organization of our house. The room occupants from the world leave and all the rooms are occupied by Soul and Soul friendly qualities and colleagues.

To occupy ourselves as Soul, we try to exclude everything else when we are thinking about a problem. Once we master that skill, we are ready to add higher consciousness. When we can hold to the frequency of our thought, we don't have to exclude. We can include, thus not limiting the range of our intelligence to our mind. We choose a trajectory, a frequency, say we are thinking about how birds fly, then there is a bird flying, and we look at it, and as our curiosity selects deeper questions, we may see the anatomy and design of the bird. We might see a drawing of the bird. We may find ourselves flying and seeing through the bird's eyes. That's thinking, <u>and</u> it's in a different way. Some people are used to visual thinking, but we all do it. We can believe we are more of a linear or rational thinker while we also observe. When we observe, we are also looking back at ourselves from the circumference of Soul eyes and, by doing so, the observer effect chooses love as a response to life throughout the land.

Another way trajectory happens is that we have an interest, and depending on whether we want a general answer or a specific answer, we connect with that interest. Then in our small place, we have to let it take us to a more significant place, that may go out on the other side of the fence, or maybe it goes up, or it just dissolves. The frequency of our focus transfers our consciousness and then we are worked with, in the sense that we are giving our question wings of light. We made our quest into a bird, and that's why it came up. But it's out on its adventure. We give it to the sky.

Everything we create will come back to us, our question comes back to us as well, and if we question with integrity, we will get an answer. If the question wasn't honest, we will get back the hidden agendas embedded in our question, such as being confronted with whatever brings us our bias and control, and, of course, our fear that spawned the control. The answer comes back according to our preconception of an answer. Regardless hidden agendas come back. Our creations don't always come back right away. They can, but it might come back months from now. Despite time, our creations return in some more mature form, usually when we are distracted by something else. Control presupposes what we want the answer to be. When we want the answer to take care of our fear, our desire amplifies fear. When we want support with fear, that is different. Requesting support will amplify the love we need so that we can respond to any fear, fearlessly.

A more graceful approach to support is to allow answers to come according to their way. A question may just occur to us, and oh, there's my answer. Or somebody may say something that triggers an answer. Or we pick up a book and read about our answer. Or we may turn on the radio and somebody tells us about our curiosity. Or our friend comes up and tells us about our subject of interest. We are open to how answers come back. That's the way God "thinks": centering and paying attention to circumference is a reflective, simultaneous process. This kind of process is going on all the time. The way God thinks is like a simultaneous, synchronous, continuous conversation with all creation and all life, the result of which is a fully functioning universe on the macro level, while on the micro level the functioning is up to us to decide whether to collaborate or perpetuate dysfunctional realities.

In our stillness, we're not putting out questions or talking about answers. In the silence, when we're just listening, we begin to become sensitive to the carrier waves of the conversation, and that often feels like a current or a Presence. It could be a sensation or a sound. The way the universe lives is as sound, which we can hear audibly or through synesthesia. We listen or pay attention and we can hear, sense or feel the translation into sound. For example, we might be playing music and feel it in our body. But then when we are not playing music, we have a feeling in our body like we are listening to music. That's what carries the energy. In scriptural metaphors such as "in the beginning when spirit moved upon the face of the deep," we can imagine this as a metaphor for creative thought. When we imagine we move our consciousness in a deep way.

Passkey

There's another way consciousness is exchanged or transferred that's not flowing on a current. It's a way of being in which everything is in the same place. It's one of those things that transfers from one medium to another. Say we feel love for someone, love, not desire as in I need something or I lack or I have to have something. Without condition or expectation, we feel love and stay with awareness of love and then suddenly it expands. If love is related to a person, we can check with them later and say well at four o'clock I felt this love as you, in contrast to love for you. Maybe its interesting to hear their response. When we are entangled in thought about a person, we do not move with such freedom. When we are entangled with them, we know their location. We want to join them. When we have intent along with the passkey of love, we can join them. That's an exciting way to understand gaining access to someone through love. We have a room dedicated to simultaneous communication with anyone, everywhere. We have a room in our house where we can always visit with anyone.

We can also access holographic resonance where we have one molecule of something and it's a holograph of the whole thing. Stated as the Pythagorean axiom: the small part is to the large part as the large part is to the whole. We are similar to a holograph. If it's in our metaphysics or imagery, it's in the symbolism of everything everywhere. When we realize that we are also thinking like this, first it sounds like it's something we need to attain or develop, but then we realize that we are already doing this. We have to notice that we are doing holographic awareness and that it requires dropping off some of the ways that we think about ourselves, for example the judgment that I couldn't possibly think inclusively. Another judgement might be that only special people can think inclusively. These judgements prevent us from knowing that we think with holographic resonance. Our holograph contains all of the resonances of God.

When awareness of integral thinking comes alive in our inner sanctum, we understand that we are nurturing inside as well as being developed in the large part, the wholeness. As an attractor, we draw results to us at the level of our focus. Imagine this as a room of manifestation in our house in which our intent and passkey admit us into a space that brings substance to thought. If we are considering attraction to be on the physical level, it finds its way. Our manifestation starts seeking itself, so it comes into reality. Manifestation is a tricky one because we can't use our wish to manipulate, such as wanting a person to behave a certain way, a tendency we all seem to share to some degree. We think that if they only act our imagined way, we would feel better. Of course, what this intent puts out is our desire for them to keep behaving the same ways so that we can feel awful. By wanting to manipulate their behavior, we inadvertently divide our intent in a way that works against the outcome we want. We can't work divisively to get something to happen through the wholeness. We can't act disingenuously and expect to see the desired behavior manifest through the wholeness.

We can manifest relational change. Let's refer to that change as a room in our house. Intention plus passkey (love) enters a room of mediation. Entry is internal first, molded to the eccentricity of each person. If prerequisite issues to our manifestation need resolving, the manifestation may take a while so be patient. When we set an intention in motion internally, we actually might have to change ourselves or a pattern of thinking to have that intention manifest in our life. We either want to work on a relationship or develop a project. Either way, we work on it inwardly. When our project is not manifesting well, we need to look within to see what we may have to resolve, some inadequacies, or something we acted against once upon a time. A block in our manifestation often reflects patterns that need to be resolved before the manifestation can come about in our life. For example, we open a room in which we are sequestering shame. Shame often obscures the treasure that wants to become a reality in our world. Shame may mean that we are misunderstanding our goodness and that goodness wants to manifest in our life. The remedy is to place love in our shame room.

Action

We move into our creative action internally and then all of our unresolved issues and judgements surface in our life. We wonder what's going on with this? But when issues and judgements come up, we say oh yeah, this must be some reorganization I needed to do with my own psyche to be compatible with my dream coming true. We know that we can be kinder with our self and more grateful for our challenges because these aspects are part of the process, and rightly so. We think that the only reason we do anything is to get something or be something, but it's really to transform ourselves. That's always the inner agenda so we want to embrace change. We must recognize the illusion of going against ourselves and blocking our eventual triumph.

As soon as we have a greater way of thinking, we catch our judgments, coercive strategies, and the ways we disrespect ourselves or others. We realize that we are judging ourselves or holding onto a limiting belief or protecting our shame. We know that these thoughts exist in a medium and a reality that has no permanence. Even so these thoughts are a vehicle for us to change our consciousness. If we want to know how these thoughts are changing our consciousness, we can look at the symbology or information coded in the process. We can further develop awareness of our process by being more aware when we're listening to each other. What was that feeling? What was that fear about? It is about clearing up the fear, not about fixing this or that. Somehow or another the reason for something happening is coded in the metaphor of the event. When we unpack the codes, we know the meaning and the truth. It's like analyzing a dream, we start getting clues about why and how we are involved in the dream, and that accelerates our understanding, unpacks the meaning and often completes our reasons for the experience.

When we affirm that I Am Soul, Master of My House, we're building our house, we're furnishing our house, decorating our house, and populating our house with the many ways we love life. We are in a process within a context of clearing, balancing, and remodeling our house through the authority of our Soul. We look at the cosmology of ourselves and see matters of love, issues of sexuality, matters of support, matters of seeing or reaching, and in this cosmology there's a specific symbology or coding. We code with these various images and know that we're going to have experiences involving our coding. We wrap our experiences in a thought form or a hologram and that becomes a room in our house, giving space for affirming our authority that I Am Soul, Master of My House.

In My House

I often think of people as writers. Writers have a room where they go to write and they can create whole realities in there. And some of them say that their characters come alive and have lives in there. The writers go into their writing room and they write down what they see going on. We all have a writing room by many names, but they're all the same in important ways. Our writing room feels like when we were very young. Maybe we had a playroom and a little box of toys and we would go in there and play or maybe invite friends over and have our magical thoughts and play. We created a context in which we explored realities, much like the holodeck on Star Trek. (The holodeck on Star Trek is a room for computer generated holograms that create tangible realities allowing the participants simulated real experiences of realities that they would like to live. The simulations seem so real that you could go on a fishing vacation, dine with friends or practice martial arts.) We enjoyed magical play when we were young and then we grew up, but the playroom is still there. For most of our childhood play was a pleasant experience. How do you know that? Well, let's find that place where we like to play. We look around maybe inside of ourselves. We find the playroom and open the toy box with intention and with the passkey of love and...there it is, and we go inside, and we are right there in the energy of…way back then, or way back there. We start feeling like we did when we were younger. We can even join a familiar game with ourselves. That's how we go into that place.

Let's explore something more recent. Say we went on vacation someplace and liked that vacation. When we came back that vacation becomes a room inside. If we want to take a little time and go on vacation, then we go into that room. We go inside, and we are in that place again. Say it was on the coast and we imagine that we are walking on the beach and we feel the sand on our bare feet and the warmth of the sand, and we hear waves and the rhythm of the waves. And maybe it's near a harbor and we hear a boat whistle, and birds fly over, and we hear them. See it's not long before we are in that vacation room again and we start feeling the energy of that place. Even though we are in a room inside our consciousness, our physical body starts shifting as if it is actually in our vacation reality. We can feel the air the same way because it's all integrated.

Writing, play and vacation rooms are pleasant. And there are some rooms that we leave the doors shut, perhaps even locked, because the experiences held in those rooms were not pleasant, especially if someone wanted to punish us by telling us to go to our room without our supper. We learned that we could have a room and banish part of ourselves there when we want to punish ourselves, or maybe we don't know that is what we are doing and we unconsciously adopted someone else's agenda for us. Maybe we shut ourselves in one of those rooms and then we forgot about past shame and we are unaware that the punishment continues in secret. We have an internal daily cycle, so just like we have a dining room table and our family meets for dinner, in the internal family aspects of ourselves we mirror the external behavior. That's what we are familiar with because we interact with ourselves in comforting or punishing ways all the time, and that becomes what's immediate. And so the other rooms kind of fade out. They don't disappear, and thus we are already considering, "oh I wonder where my rooms are?" And that thought calls to us, and we wonder if that confusion explains the loneliness we feel. Is it coming from one of those rooms that we forgot? We use that loneliness frequency as an attractor. We move into it and it's like a door that takes us into the room where the lonely person is, and then loneliness starts becoming apparent to us. As loneliness becomes conscious our love moves in that room and our responsiveness to our need wakes up and we can love and care for the lonely person and resolve our loneliness.

When we get into these troubling and uncomfortable frequencies, we're unaccustomed to talking about them and we don't have a language that appropriately expresses our feelings and experience. These frequencies have an experiential style that is intrinsic. We have to translate the frequency and that's not easy. We might say: "I feel like my heart has been beating very fast since we entered the room earlier and this tells me there is something important, but I don't know how to express that. I'll try and say what I felt today. There were moments when I felt very, very connected to the life force that I have, and I felt that connection with a very open heart. That's something I often experience lately. I can live my connection to life force and that's exciting.

There are other rooms in which we accrued a lot of responsibility when we were sucked into the importance of issue x versus y, in which there may not have been a need to make a distinction between one and another, between this and that. In other words the distinction was made out of a divisive agenda. Forced choices are fine for making distinctions or contrast between one thing or another. Often distinctions can imply separation but not conflict, so there may or may not be intended adversity, even though separation often implies adversity. From the transcendental perspective resolution of adversarial forces is key to leadership. Each room has a higher dimension in which seeming opposites unify. When you allow the possibility of unification, opposites are inherently in a unity that initiates mediation. With mediation we can have distinction without separation and resolution becomes intrinsic to the rooms.

Anything from a smaller time inside of us is not separate. It's just inside. Our neglect may make the small place seem separate. When we visit the room we played in when we were little, our playroom is still inside, a small place that is happy and transcends its diminutive status. The happy place is not another small compartment, it's the whole life. We may have a little project that requires attention. The project comes from an orientation that collaborates with a bigger place. When we enter into that bigger project of our life, the smallest project is integral to the whole process of life.

It is Not I

We have looked at many rooms in our house and this activity of observation and Presence claims authority in our house which initiates a transition. A colleague shared a fear with me that illustrates the experience of transformation that occurs as we claim authority in our house. He said,

> *I'm going through a strong transition now as if I am going from a small place to a much bigger place. And as for my heart, I feel good. At the same time, it raises so many fears that sometimes overwhelm me completely. It goes on for a while and then it goes away and then it comes back and so on. Especially the biggest fear is since I work with groups and I teach as well, that I will be rejected because I love. To be rejected because I love is my greatest fear.*

I can relate to his fear in my own experience. I used to have a recurring dream where I would be talking to a group of people and then the people would start leaving until there was only one or two or nobody. It's been a couple of years since I had that dream, but the reoccurrence of the dream lasted a long time. That caused me to pray. I encouraged myself to prepare by asking for divine assistance. I came to realize that what I want to teach, is not just about me or what I know, it's about something more significant, not only in content but in the way I do it. The sense of lack in my message was frightening in a way I did not realize. My compensation in waking life was to judge my teaching based on thinking that I was the knower, that it was about me. The remedy of the dream came through the realization that my message arose from a spiritual source. It was not really about me. It was the Soul that spoke and the Presence of love. Speaking from this Presence facilitated a flow of lifting energy, a carrier wave that was the greater message. My dream was there to help me line up with the Divine.

Sometimes the room that needs healing is in our past. Say, as a baby we wanted to be fed and we were not fed right away, so we are still dealing with that trauma. This may have created a sense of lack. We can time-travel back to our orphaned self and supply the loving that resolves that sense of lack. The result of loving is that the fear of abandonment no longer distorts our teachings. When we trust inspiration, we are using lack as a receptacle to be filled, making the act of teaching a conduit for a higher expression. When we teach, we say "It is not I but the love within that does the work."

As my colleague unpacked the metaphor of being fed (receiving the love he needed), he clarified the nature of his abandonment. His father played a more significant role in this abandonment. When we unpack issues, we do so with the awareness that those involved behaved the way they did in service to the agenda of our Soul to resolve issues or develop skills or consciousness. My colleague shared:

It's my relationship with my father, which is very difficult right now. I don't want to see him. He's too much of a prick and so on. He's too aggressive, not really in love. He's an idiot. He's masterful at controlling his family and controlling his children. That doesn't solve my problem. If I do it by rejecting him, he comes back. I don't care to be around him right now.

My colleague has some clarity in realizing that his assessment and judgment doesn't change anything. When we are mistreated, of course, that hurts and it's traumatic. What we do with that pain is our part. If my colleague still has that kind of anger, he still wants his father to do something which indicates that he has his version of the same thing. Like father like son. What is my colleague going to do with his control issues? What does he want to control? Does he want revenge? He wants his father to change so that he himself can feel better. That's called revenge. In truth, the father is helping him with an essential piece of his life. His father is reflecting how his son maintains his institutionalized rejection. We started with the fear of rejection from others. See? Resolution is up to him. Based on behavior, he seems to want to be like his father, "I get to reject and feel justified." In truth, he wants to love his father. Loving our parents is instinctual. Thus his fear of being rejected is in his teaching because he inherently loves. It is a classic reversal. The set-up is to resolve the distortion. From that perspective, his father is perfectly helping him in his movement to resolve the sharing of his loving. To heal, my colleague has to take care of it inside himself.

Once we use the passkey of love and intention, we enter the room with our magic cleanser Ho'oponopono (resolution through living love). Our external reflection shows us what we haven't resolved inside. The good news is that the ultimate resolution is inside of us because that is also where we find transformative power. I Am Soul, Master of My House centers us inside ourselves in transcendent and relational loving. When an issue is in us, we can reach it inside where we have power. We entered the room and began our Ho'oponopono process. That is good news. We can deal with the issue. If we resolve the issue inside of us and it is ours; we can resolve the issue. And when we do, resolution starts to reflect out and then the issue is changed and we become changed. By attacking the demon in the world before resolving the inner demon may just be wasting a perfectly good, terrible experience. It is not I but the loving within me that does the work.

Sometimes we savor our issue. Our anger is sweet, and our self-righteousness is exhilarating. The room where my colleague keeps his father is crucial to resolving the demon within. Well, he does not need the demon anymore so he might as well have a "come to Jesus" meeting with his self-righteousness, and through resolution of living love erase the information that is informing this reversal. In this case, the application of Ho'oponopono is straightforward. We use the image inside and remain clear that this is not his father; the demon is a judgment about his father; the demon is an image coding a reversal of love. However, the resolution calls forward the person in the world to fill the role as a negative coding. In a sense, there is a resonance between the image within and the external role. In this case, his father's image is accessing the frequencies and code that needs erasing. My colleague places his awareness in the room where he keeps his father and sees his father's image. As he is present with the image he says: "I am so sorry. Please forgive me. I forgive myself for all the times, places, circumstances, and dimensions in which I created, promoted, or allowed, the actions and orientations represented by my father. I take my authority and I forgive myself. And, I forgive myself for all the ancestors involved in sponsoring this expression. I love you. I love you. I love you." (Ho'oponopono) He must repeat this frequently, as the erasing occurs. At some point, he and his father will feel the shift. They then have a choice as to what to do with this shift.

The transformation is to change the information within my colleague. If there is to be a change in his relationship with his father, it will happen. His father is able to change as well because my colleague changes how his father lives in my colleague's house. But as it resolves inwardly, my colleague's and his father's experience will orient to the new information. Love will connect and respond to love shared. As it resolves, his response from others in the network of this relationship will change. In my colleague's house his "father's" room is one of love and compassion. He can now have a relationship with his father in the world based on who his father is in the world, rather than my colleague's internal image of him or my colleague's karmic need for his father to be a certain way. It is not I, but the love within me that does the work.

Method

There is an old adage that admonishes us to put our house in order. The image of house is immediate, powerful and simple. As we review the complexity of our discussion of I Am Soul, Master of My House we intuitively respond to the power of this affirmation. In that resonance a movement of energy begins to organize our perception and create a response in our subconscious and unconscious minds that organizes our personality so that all the information that informs who we are becomes available through the construct of the metaphor of putting our house in order. Our personality is a *house of Soul*. With our inherent authority of Soul we bring our house to our attention and then systematically review each room. By so doing we clearly claim and integrate the love-based rooms and systematically clean and claim rooms that are dysfunctional. In the endeavor of claiming our house we use whatever forms of resolution or healing that we know, such as self-forgiveness, re-framing, awareness, trauma techniques, etc. Though rigorous, the method is simple:

- Be present and align inwardly with your higher power, seeing yourself filled and surrounded with light and love.
- Affirm: I Am Soul, Master of My House.
- Visualize how that looks for you. See your consciousness as a house with an aligned structure that is commanded by you as Soul.

- Ask to see any forgotten or neglected rooms that need your attention. Enter these rooms one at a time with love, healing, resolution and rehabilitation.
- Ask to see any room in which external forces, interests or relatives have claimed authority over you.
- Ask to see the rooms of enculturated patterns that control you in large and small ways.
- Ask to see the rooms of political and religious injuries.
- Ask to see any ancestral or genetic rooms that require acknowledgement or epigenetic love.
- Use your imagination of the metaphor of a house to illuminate any areas of resource or limitation.
- Use your imagination to remodel or add to your house as your consciousness expands.
- Houses have attics, basements, guest houses and workshops, so be creative with the metaphor of your house.
- Behold the entirety of the wholeness of your house and your loving presence occupying each and every room, from the glorious to the so called perverse, your thought angels of loving living with each guest, your radiant self moving from attic to basement from closet to closet, and behold your house of Soul in all its glory and affirm: I am Soul, Master of My House.

Meditation

Just take a deep breath and as you exhale begin to settle into your space.

As you expand your experience of Presence, Presence in your body, and the Presence of your body in you, just regard that with appreciation and loving. And then bring your attention into that flow of light, that vortex, that goes from above to below up into our heart. It becomes the centerline. And then also bring your breathing together with that focus so you are breathing the light in from above and below into your heart out through your body into your space and follow it out until it reflects into your next breath where you breathe it in. You are also breathing in the air and the light of the space you are in along with above and below. In your heart becomes this place in which all of that is mixed and exchanged, and life is purified with Spirit with the blending of love. And the sense of Heaven and Earth begins to blend inside you. As you breathe with even a more profound sense, you find yourself in the awareness of your Sacred Heart.

Now bring your attention into the center of your head, and as you do, the light awakens there and expands. As you continue to breathe, the light of your heart and the light of your head begin to merge. For many in the incarnation of life, the Soul slumbers in the center of the head, but long ago you stirred yourself awake.

As you continue to breathe, feel the sense of your Soul become tangible within this central column and become aware of a beingness. You feel the ancientness in the sense of connection that moves out through you and embraces all that is and extends up into the highest heaven you can imagine and opens that awareness to the spiritual knowing, to the seeing.

Become aware of a vision you had just before you incarnated into what this life would be, what you would explore, what you would resolve, and what you would need to do it, and the skills, the talents, the virtues, and what you would like to have new, to explore further. You had a sense of this collaboration or communion with the intelligence of everything that worked with you to arrange your vision to what would work and how all the trials and tribulations would serve your purpose. And you were presented with a key. Be present and use everything to transform yourself into loving and you will be master of your life. You will be a master of your house.

Bring your energy down through you and anchor it into the earth. With that anchor, you've made possible the manifestation of your vision. Just take another deep breath, and as you breathe in, collect this great vision and bring it down through your body into every cell to remind yourself in every way of the wholeness and purpose of your existence.

Every role and persona that you have lived is within the purpose of the Soul, never forgetting it was by design. So, for now, claim again that I am Soul and to bring that down into your space into your Presence that I am master of this house, my house. And follow along with that energy and see where it takes you for now and appreciate the truth of this. This is not subject to dispute. This is what and who you are, and this incarnation is your house. No debate. This is the authority from which you live. I Am Soul, Master of My House.

*A nation of men [and women]
will for the first time exist,
because each believes himself [herself]
inspired by the Divine Soul
which inspires all men [and women].*

Ralph Waldo Emerson

CHAPTER EIGHT

Politics

...

Most distortions in politics are based on lack. When Transcendental Leadership translates into the world, our lack quotient is an essential foundational element in the way we formulate policy in relationship to present need. The more lack we hold, the more our policies, programs, creativity, and administrative actions will promote and protect our lack, which includes character lack, emotional lack, low self-esteem, the need to dominate and control, spiritual lack, greed, self-righteousness, self-importance and on and on. We will weave our lack in not so obvious ways into everything. Our perceptual lens will be calibrated according to our lack quotient. Our lack quotient falls on a cosmological continuum of fear and love. In our lack we become infested with our material or ethical poverty, our ambitions become predatory either to get from others and the system or to dominate others and build networks of need into the populace through exploitive fear. If we are not careful, we will crystallize a world of haves and have nots. The *haves* and *have nots* are collectively an expression of the politics of lack. Even with great wealth we can live in the poverty of the Soul. Know this, there is a way we can get lack to work for us, to liberate us.

Receptacle

To the degree our cosmology is fear-based, when we look at something we need or want, we believe that we are lacking. When we obtain it, whether it is material gain or status, we fear we will lose it. When we fear we will lose it, even though we have obtained the external emotional or material thing we thought would fill our lack, we are continuing to live from our lack. To the degree our cosmology is love-based, the want or need is a receptacle to receive, an attractor force-field of abundance, an empty cup to be filled. We see the lack already filled with what we are receiving instead of lacking that which we need. That's very delicate. If we take the lack feeling in terms of that which "I want or need is not here," it makes a receptacle. But if we take lack personally by deciding that we are the lack as a condition, then our space becomes a receptacle for more lack. We have to be very clear concerning lack, so that our lack is a receptacle to receive, to be filled with love, bounty...grace. The way in which we have been working with I Am Soul, Master of My House, we've been building up a context in which we transform lack and fear into love and abundance. To find the lack receptacles we must conduct a room by room search. Do we live in a house of abundance or lack? Do we live in a house of the Lord?

Lack is a room in our house, and it's the kind of room that we can go into and use it to create. It is an incubator. When we find an incubator place inside...it will be in a place in consciousness in which anything that we imagine in that place can come to be. That means it's interpenetrated by the incubator of everything. When it's in this little space inside of us, it's also in the whole space. This is going to sound funny. It is already bringing itself to itself. It starts approaching from outside of us in the world, by approaching from inside of us. Try not to think about this too much because it's a different order of reality and thought, a different reality than thinking, like a thought but it's not thinking. We might say thought is a thought of itself. Intelligence transcends thought. Rather than loving to think, thinking is love. We embody thought through the Presence of love. What better master for the mind to serve than the Presence of love?

Instead of a process of thinking, the result is a little more like laying an egg. Have you ever watched a chicken lay an egg? It's really quite something. The chicken goes cackle, cackle, boop and there's the egg. It's quite magical. Before the actual appearance of the egg, there is a gestation period in which the formation of the egg is accepting fertilization and developing. The whole process begins with an empty nest, a nest that lacked an egg (a great metaphor). This is the way we can use the lack room in our house. We are about to lay an egg, so watch out! Looking at this another way, we might as well include the rooster and start the new day by greeting the sun. It is similar to wanting a cup of tea. Does the flame boil the water or does the want of tea boil the water? As well we must have an empty cup that lacks hot water in order to brew the tea that boils the water because we lack tea. Intention plus the passkey gets us into the tea room, or the hen house.

The world is in quite a bit of turmoil, and rife with political entertainment at this time. No matter how entertaining or infuriating, the survival of the planet may be at stake. That is an existential concern and a spiritual one because this planet is a receptacle of our Soul. We are here gestating a vision. We want to hatch our plans. Each of us in our own way becomes concerned with our visioning. Most of the time we can go about our business, but vison incites us in a healthy purpose. There is an urge inside to do something about the condition of the world, nature and the people who live here. As Transcendental Leaders, we find we have a role to play.

Love Nest

The habit of humanity up to this point is to strive for safety. The nature of the Soul is to take a chance. Survival becomes a receptacle for taking a chance. On the practical level, there are genuine practical concerns. On a spiritual level, we are the source of our safety. Our basic instinct is to survive. On the practical level, how do we get what we need? For practical issues, we look outward. For inspirational issues, we look inward. How we coordinate the two depends on our relationship to lack.

It seems like the preferred way of responding to lack is through conflict, through dominating, through being against, and we have games where we practice competition. The main result of this approach is that it promotes fear. Well in some ways it holds the world together because when we enter into conflict, we vote for the fear approach and this funny dance occurs and our adversary challenges us and we meet the challenge, and then whether we win or lose, we are all voting for conflict.

In this cycle, the guys are in charge and then in the next cycle the girls are in charge. And then we get out of sequence. We are always in the nest together, taking turns as the enabler of fear. There is a different way. Love is what we seek the most, and love is the force we lack the most. Having said that, the world with all its various adherents to lack is a love-nest for the Soul. Our Soul is love and love is unconditional, so the empty nest appears as an invitation. By releasing our identification with lack, we fill the nest with Soul and love marinates our body then grace becomes the receptacle of our world.

Virtue

In evolution, there's a higher way to evolve. Each group has higher virtues and lower virtues. Up to this point in time, evolution has been an aspirational quest in which higher ideals guide cultures and nations associated with those cultures toward aspirational ideals which may be attained for a moment and then fall away. The evolutionary process may degenerate because each thing that arises creates its nemesis and that can be disruptive. The higher purpose of any nemesis of an aspirational ideal is to challenge hubris, to test and see if the aspirational action is Soul strong and love strong. By realizing our aspirational ideals, we become more conscious that our higher purpose is to create cultures and establish nations based on the wisdom and love of our Soul. Yet, a force seems to exist in which fear is the energy that strives to preserve the viewpoint that the nest is empty and in lack, thus giving birth to the politics of lack. We are doing this now. This viewpoint is mostly unconscious, so we don't realize what is going on. The status quo seems to be the reality and we play the game of life based on the politics of fear and lack. And we live unconsciously with our minds trapped in a strange arrogance that the way it seems is the way it is. Both the haves and the have nots live in lack. We don't yet realize that even our sleep is a growth phase, that our sleep is like a fertilized egg incubating and waiting to hatch.

I am suggesting that each nation, regardless of their form of government, is based on higher ideals like cooperation, compassion, liberty, creative culture, even ascendency. All nations have their own higher virtues. They think their virtue is a principle on which they made their country. The trouble with this viewpoint is the belief that their virtue is secure. Better to consider that virtue is a vision we strive to attain and securing it each day requires always reaching for a deeper understanding, fostered by our eternal vigilance. For example, *love will find it's way* is actually God's will. By aligning internally with love as the source of our creative ability, our lack of virtue becomes a receptacle for the virtue of love. The lack creates a space that is a receptacle for virtue. We use lack to judge ourselves rather than to see opportunity. When we focus on lack as a deficit, we manifest lack. For example, say we are going to get coffee and we grab a cup. We look at the cup, and say, "I lack coffee." We can decide we are a failure and destined to be an empty cup or consider that the empty cup is a place to receive coffee. And behold it gets filled with coffee. We lack coffee and we want coffee, put those two ideas together. We don't believe the cup was meant to be empty or that it reflects our emptiness and lack. We visualize what we want to fill the cup. Does that make sense? If we can master this over a cup of coffee, can we apply it to *Novus Ordo Seclorum* (motto inscribed on the seal of the United States, New Secular Order). The politics of lack is incongruent with the vision of abundance and promise as portrayed in our national motto.

As an example of lack, consider that a group of people are for peace. They want to create peace, that is their vision. And then another group doesn't want peace. They want war. The peace group protests the war group. The people who want war react to the ones who want peace, and they get in a fight. The people who wanted peace are now at war with the people who wanted war. See? So, we fill the nest of lack with conflict and that is what hatches. The greatest filler for the empty nest is love. Love inseminates itself and gives birth to greater love.

Let's say we have a position that we call Truth. It has a polarity called False. We identify with the truth. That's our process. But then there's the world we live in and the question of practicality comes up. Practicality is an endeavor to take care of things in the world, like voting for peace or going to a meeting to discuss peace, or somebody is doing something dangerous, so we have to stand up and say stop doing that. But the practical thing is that we are just stopping the action whatever it is. We are not invested in it. When we become invested in these things, that's what gives them force. Regarding the peace/war demonstration, if we are taken with an ideology as if our lives depend on it, we are engaging in a way that will create (hatch) more conflict. Conversely, when we treat the difference as a practical issue, we can dialogue, thus hatching a process of dialogue, which gives birth to transformation.

Star Whale

We are exploring the politics of lack. Lack originates in an externalization of our source of power. Politics and government are essentially managing external forces for safety, security, wealth, and well-being. By joining the authority of politics, we inadvertently betray ourselves and our true source of authority. A student became curious about deepening her understanding of the carrier wave, the wave that flows through us and connects with wholeness; specifically sounds. She wanted to deepen her understanding of that knowing. She shared from a meditation in which she remembered an episode of Dr. Who that spoke to her curiosity. (Dr. Who is a BBC series about a time travel. His vehicle appears as a police box that is actually the time travel vehicle called a tardis. Dr. Who arrives in various situations and circumstances throughout time and provides a remedy. In a sense he is a time healer.)

I watched the Dr. Who episode last night and it was an episode about a whole planet of people who had essentially imprisoned an alien beast as a means to propel their planet. The way they were doing it was like actually torturing it. It was very, very, very deep and sweet where I went with this in my meditation today. In the episode of Dr. Who, they came to realize that they were imprisoning and torturing the beast without meaning to. It wasn't really a beast, it was a star whale. This star whale was actually in service to them already. And it came to help this planet of people because they needed it and because it heard the children crying. My understanding was that it had compassion and came to help. The people of the planet were scared of this star whale so they imprisoned and tortured it in order to make it help them. That's how I understood it. This reminds me of how we torture the environment to power our planet, all the while, when the planet by grace is already here to serve all of our energy needs.

Watching the Dr. Who episode, I realized it was a metaphor for what I was doing to myself and how I was using my authority. I thought to win I needed to be aggressive, to dominate and control resources. In my case, the star whale is the loving, infinite supply of life, ready to give and serve freely. All we have to do is be the modulation on the carrier wave. The star whale is my Soul authority. When we have an adversarial relationship to the world, we distort, dominate and torture our soul-power.

Saving the Planet

When we argue, we often get angry and our temperature rises because we are attached to our position as a sacrosanct reality. In the more extreme expression of this we feel entitled and privileged according to our status, race, class or tribal affiliation. When we behave that way, we are voting for conflict, not the content of what we think we are fighting for. Understanding that while arguing for our position, we are voting for conflict and not our belief is challenging for us to understand at first. Consider that we are in a discussion and suggesting a resolution and somebody else wants to go out and fight, and we say to them "no that's not the result we want." And they say, "We are right so we want to go fight." We then get in a fight with them not so much at first over content but style. You see, by then fighting over strategy, we have lost our way and taken up the way of conflict and might and privilege makes right. On the other hand, dialogue embodies a transcendental Presence that carries the discussion to a higher level of resolution. Dialogue holds that kind of sensibility. This approach is not an ideology but a spiritual practice that enables us to create new practices or avenues for using our differences in a constructive way. Conflict is a result of unresolved *lack* within our personality or tribe. We need to be aware of the tiny "lack" space within our point of view. When we harbor lack, no matter how small, we will too easily fall into a posture of fighting for our position. We can add love into any dialogue. If we have to be an activist, our spiritual practice changes how we are an activist. We don't lose ourselves in the activism. We keep our house clean. We don't give part of our house away to contrary tenants. It is our house, not an empty space in which to invite rogue chickens. "Cockadodeldo!" says the rooster to the sunrise. It is not a chicken house. It is a Soul house.

We have to understand how lack plays into aggressive strategies for resolving conflict. Our lack of value, safety, supply and shelter subtly emerges as a core sense of self weaving through our cosmology of fear and is unconscious most of the time. When we engage each other in dialogue we need to get the true flavor of our lack and the consequences of the lack in our society so that we can be more conscious when we engage each other in dialogue. Culturally, we have a faux trust that everybody is following their own trajectory in a proper and wholesome way. There's probably a role for our contrariness, and that becomes the next illumination. How do we challenge each other with respect? We are all on our journeys with our own wants, needs and karmic variations. Our project is to realize we are mutually involved in manifesting nations with higher values which are ultimately intertwined with a vision to save the planet.

We are taking innate, powerful, creative consciousness and using it as a bridge between heaven and earth, as well as, a conduit for certain kinds of communications. In our creativity room, we hold the planet in loving, not with an attitude of what it's supposed to look like, but rather in discovery of the truth. This creates a magnetic Presence that is a conduit for spirit. We are participating in this conduit by providing wholeness and loving into which everything can properly play its role. We are offering an energy to the world that automatically integrates opposites. Instead of eliminating polarization or trying to stop people from polarizing, we are providing a Presence, a consciousness, a vehicle that promotes the mediation of opposites. This process of consciousness is very subversive. Transcendental Leadership provides a mediating Presence to conflict.

Abandonment

There are times in our lives when we felt abandoned, isolated and alone. That's when we believed that those feelings were all that existed. We constellated our identity into the little one, the small feeling of abandonment. The self that had to handle issues while feeling abandoned got caught in a lonely, hurt experience. We are the ones that entered abandonment. The small self thought that abandonment and loneliness were everything. The person that was in that experience of abandonment and loneliness forgot that they were part of the wholeness.

Now we're in a context of wholeness in which we realize that abandonment is another way of viewing our self, all of our selves. Now when we go into the abandonment room, we don't believe abandonment is all there is. We sense there is something bigger within us. Each room is not separate from the entire house. We are in the wholeness of our self, our house. We practice going into the abandonment room, or any room for that matter, and at the same time, we are aware of the whole house. When we are connected with life force and with a feeling of our heart opening, it means we are connected to wholeness. We are not just an isolated room in our house. We are the whole house. Our small part is to our large part as our large part is to the whole. (Pythagoras)

Homeless

In this following example, my friend didn't have a sense of his whole house.

I was touched by this notion of mastering my house, but the statement implies that I must have a house and I have the feeling that I do not have a house.

The metaphor is that he *is* the house. His confusion came when he placed having a house in conflict with his desire to roam. Given that his profession is architecture, he could easily visualize a house if he chose to. As it turns out, he is quite rebellious. His dislike of himself evidently is a barrier to seeing his consciousness as his house. He is stuck in his homeless room as if it were the entire house. Perhaps this viewpoint reflects into the politics of community and being homeless, and reflects a dedicated commitment to lack. Consider that homeless people might be entrapped in their homeless room and can't find the door. In a sense, they carry the politics of lack for the culture. Many years ago in a session with a client, he shared that he felt trapped in a cell. I suggested he see himself in the cell and then open and walk through the door leaving the cell for the greater panorama of his life. He did so and walking through that door totally changed his life. He is a great leader today in the field of spiritual education.

When we don't claim our own space, we are less conscious of who we may be as an inhabitant occupying our space and who might be taking up residence in one form or another in our house. The homeless person is, to some extent, shaped by the community's projection of homelessness. At some level, homelessness is planned into the community. Consequently, we become accustomed to the various frequencies of outside interests and treat them like they are us in our own consciousness of homelessness. For example, trauma caused by a perpetrator, someone who has attacked or molested us physically or psychologically, continues taking up space as a resident inside our boundaries…inside our house. Whatever healing steps we take, at some point we will have to enter the perpetrator room and evict them or enter his/her house and take back the virtue that was stolen. In this eviction, we include all victims as perpetrators and all such acts as action we take toward ourselves. Often the love with which we enter the room transforms the perpetrator by resolving their perverted version of loving. Often we find that the perpetrator is us as we make our self whole. The true damage comes in forgetting who we are.

When I suggested this to my architect friend, he could relate. He felt a response to the reality that perpetrators take up residence in our houses. I suggested that he take his time and call forward his love and tenderness for himself. Of course, that is his issue, so the act of clearing the predator was a vehicle for loving himself and thus a remedy for his self-hatred. It was a slow process for him, but he could feel the emotion, the warming, and sense of an energy leaving his space as a physical and emotional sensation.

This kind of action constitutes a change of identity and can in and of itself be frightening because of the new feelings and the resulting unknown.

Regardless of when the trauma occurred, part of us remains at that age. Then we start to thaw out the trauma and that part of us is still at that age. We are a mature, competent adult, yet part of us still feels like whatever age we were when the trauma happened. Actually, realizing this is a good sign because it starts a maturing process. In his case the maturation was emotional. When emotion begins to mature, it's going to call forward some of the feelings held from childhood that he is inwardly and secretly consoling. Bringing in the light helps. Love helps. Love and light touch our regressed and traumatized places and then we feel the movement of emotion. Emotion reflects this process, so we stick with it and ride the emotions out. We decide not to run away. We stick with the healing process.

The Journey

Our journey into our house can take many forms. The following is a student's dream narration of a journey into her house.

I looked for my Soul plan. I aligned the light in the head and the light in the heart with the intent that they communicate with each other. It flowed rather well, but all of the right side was rather empty. I wanted to find out some more about that Soul's plan, so I started with that sensation of the emptiness in my right side, and I got in touch with a vision. I saw a picture of three hundred and sixty degrees. On the right there was a magnificent very, very ancient tree. I got closer to it. I could see that it was very much alive. There were some birds in it and it had huge fruit, huge red apples. It was really a beautiful place. But I couldn't see it in front of me; it was on the right. All on the left-hand side was to be explored. I went in the direction of the left-hand side and quite soon I could see a field of flowers, very thick ones.

Then a bee came up, and I don't know if that bee is me, but that bee's mission is to pollinate the field. So the bee worked and worked and worked like there is nothing else to do. That's the only thing that it has to do. It's like a duty. Is this my Soul plan? There was an awareness in me of yeah, I know what it's for and right now that's the only thing to do. And then at some point the bee got tired, so it settled at the foot of a flower and then it becomes like a microcosm. The flower itself is huge. It's like a forest of flowers. But the bee continues but this time on foot.

Then a new landscape appears and there are very big trees, Sequoias. The bee transforms into a squirrel. And once more it has to collect the small pinecones to find nourishment to keep going. This time however the squirrel gets to climb, has the possibility to climb and to jump on the big branches. And from above, it can see an almost endless scope of the trees and also something else. It's as if everything is all right. There's also something else. Okay. It climbs back down and at the foot of the Sequoia tree there's the apple. And there the squirrel takes human shape and I am aware of my Presence. A thought comes up as a surprise, and I don't know what to do with it, so I eat the apple and there's no guilt whatsoever.

That apple is really exquisite. It's like magic. It's really exquisite, delicious. It's juicy and I tell myself it's incredible. My thirst is quenched and I even feel satiated which in my own life isn't always easy, so it's quite amazing, quite incredible. So after finishing eating the apple, I collected the seeds. I left the rest for the squirrels and I left. I knew I was going somewhere. I didn't know where, but I knew I was going there. I went through a few challenges, a few obstacles, the weather, some places, but they didn't stop me. And then I got to a clearing where there was what I identified as a garden, and it was for me. And I was also happy to see that it was surrounded by a natural hedge that delineated its edges. So I planted the seeds.

After that, I saw behind me. Behind the garden, there was a sketch or a blueprint of a house. It was 3-D, but it was like revealing itself, like developing a photograph. The door was open and I went in. It was not at all familiar, but there was nobody in the house but me. I was a bit shy. I went upstairs and I found a very small room and I told myself this is perfect. This fits me, fits my size, with a round window. It felt good to have a place with a view out to the sea and a rocking chair. But what should I do here? So I went back down into the garden. The tree was growing and I noticed the frailty instead of noticing the strength which I also could have noticed. And I was becoming aware that the tree stemmed from the other tree that had nourished me and that I could feed upon that tree and that I could share its fruit. I could offer it to others.

My actions will not be made to satisfy but to perfect. And what turned up was that in that house, in that very home, around the hearth the Soul actually told the story to the bee and the squirrel and me.

We enter into rooms in our house with intention and love as the passkey. In this case, the question was, what is my mission in life? The intention to know the mission came out of love for her life. Each house has a mission room. Our politics is an expression of our mission. Judging or hating her life would not have held a passkey. Once we are in our house with love it is a place of satisfaction. Entering the house may be external but the satisfaction is internal, and satisfaction is also a room in our house. When we place satisfaction outside, the room in the house is often one of disappointment and it becomes a room of lack. When our mission of love is reversed by lack, our politics turn sinister, and regardless of how lovely our narrative, maybe the consequences are dark.

Through love she has an opportunity to see what it is like to live from her fullness. Our house becomes the house of our Soul. Our home, meaning all resolution, is in loving and ultimately resides in the "home" room of the Soul. When all rooms are resolved in love, all rooms reside in the Soul. That changes the texture of things. It may not change the particular things she does, like do this work or that work and it doesn't change the way she relates to her family, but it's from a different place inside. She is not doing or being to satisfy anything or anyone. She is sharing her satisfaction, which changes how she works and how she experiences relationships. In a re-write of the Biblical parable positing that by eating the apple she lost her innocence and fell from grace, in her re-write of this parable, she ate the apple with no guilt or shame and fell into grace. She began a path of awakening to the inner Christ. Living in society makes this a political vision.

Stuck

In some rooms we already know the content of the room before we enter. In the following case, a student found a room that he first sensed through an impression and feeling.

I feel like I am stuck in my chair and my body shuts in on itself.

In general we have a way of framing Spirit or higher consciousness through inspirational thought and writing, elevating music and song, prayer and meditation or a solitary walk in the desert. In meditation, we are building a relationship with Spirit and so Spirit takes care of us. Often our relationship with spirit is doing things we don't know about. We may feel like we are *stuck in a chair*, but probably that impression is integral to a greater movement. Our issues are reflected as rooms in our house. The sense that we are stuck and can't move reflects a condition in a room. The condition is typically serving some higher purpose. Judgment is harmful to the process of unpacking information that tells us the condition present in a particular room. In his case, the judgment causes the sensations, impressions and feelings to recede when he feels judged. It's helpful to wonder why but I wouldn't judge your answers as to why. Try not to judge either yourself or the process. Just be curious. Consider how it might be helpful when he gets through this heaviness so he can be lighter again. From the perspective of curiosity, his political world may seem heavy and stuck. If so, that is a vote. His attitude about life already votes for a depressive social order. A depressive social order is an element of the politics of lack.

As the student unpacked the information, he had an experience of tightness, being fed up and tired, with a lot of the heaviness in his life. Perhaps it is time for a vacation, so we consider that this is actually a vacation room rather than a punishment room. The time-stamp on this room seems to be current, so just the politics of the day could produce the symptoms of depression. For example, we may have a viewpoint that the politics in the United States are in retrograde. That is a room in our house, and we ask, "are internal politics a reflection of the external politics, vice versa or both?" Well that's life in a way. But we're sensitive to our politics. Sitting on top of his stuckness, the student is in a profession that is working to help people. And it's the right occupation because he cares about people. Sometimes when people don't care about themselves, it makes their profession hard work. They come for help and the first step is to change their attitude about their life, and when the politics of the culture are not supportive of people, the repressive feelings are amplified. Living in a system based on lack makes resolving our lack more difficult.

There may be a bit of a mirror in that. Given that repression due to lack accumulates and there may be some resistance, when he feels heaviness, that's the light trying to clear the heaviness. That's maintenance. Walking around we generally don't notice but then we sit down to start meditating and we really feel the repressive energy. Sometimes I'll feel pretty good and I sit down, tune in, and a pressure will come over me and I'll experience pain. And then that pain works itself through and I feel pretty good. With his attitude of punishment and unworthiness, his attitude accumulates more heaviness from his clients, and his meditation feeds the heaviness. With a change in attitude, his meditation would be more uplifting and clear the heaviness.

In terms of unpacking, we now have the element of the work the student does as an element of the content in this room. Apparently, this extends out to influence his sense of his house in which he does not take up his full place. He has an authority that he is not standing in. His shame and self-judgment act to limit his authority. His lesson in humility is limited. We can be humble in a way that we receive grace as overlighting love or we can be humble in a distorted way that says we do not deserve grace. Perhaps then there is a karmic context to the room and in that case, enough is enough. He can forgive himself, accept the grace, and let go of the mantle of shame he has been carrying. Then his service can amplify loving rather than compensating for his lack. We can remodel the room now with, "I am a loving, caring person that knows how to recognize my gifts without feeling better or less than other people." Then we are on our way, I Am Soul: Master of My House.

If the room has a habit-lock on it, we might look at it as a habit. For example, some people have to give up smoking, but we have to give up the habit of not taking our place in the world and staying loyal to lack. Smoking is often a habit that is temporarily attempting to fill a lack. We can look at this dilemma as a houseguest that stayed way too long. This is a perspective, or a way to look at it. We say, oh why did I allow that guest to stay too long? And our answer might be, well I just got used to it and I didn't really update my perspective. Then we realize it is time to pay attention. The guest that stayed too long will limit our expression as a distortion of energy, protecting the habit of lack and making claims on our resources. Perhaps the guest would also like to leave and our neglect is holding him or her back. By using our passkey of love and taking authority in the room, we dispel the energy by becoming conscious and choosing the intention of love.

Before the issue of the guest staying too long was off to the side and a little unconscious, and he forgot and tolerated the guest. But now he needs to wake up to the guest and just be grateful, forgive, and send the guest on his or her way. Just say, "thank you for the visit to my house; I'm sending you home." Your action might take a little ritualistic response. What is it called when we want to gently dismiss someone? Every country has a different way of saying it. In England when they fire somebody they call the person *redundant*, meaning we don't need you anymore. See, to them it's not a heavy thing. The hesitancy to reclaim authority can be a carryover from earlier in life or from another lifetime, say from a monastic lifetime from which we are living again the ethic of admonishing ourselves not to take our place, while cultivating the ability to be ashamed of ourselves in the guise of surrender and humility. It was a way to seek salvation by denigrating ourselves that goes in really deep, so deep that it eclipses our awareness of our Soul. You see it has also been about how we see our relationship to God or Spirit or Love. Do we really see living love as something that welcomes us into its orb, into the intimacy of wholeness? Based on our action and choices, perhaps we do not. We are integral to the light, integral to the mission of Spirit. Perhaps we need a political part of love. In the pursuit of our mission, as Transformational Leaders, whatever form our organization takes, its formation begins in the heart-room of our house.

Get Over It

The Emerald Tablet, like the Lord's Prayer, is an ancient document that guides the alchemical process of incarnating, refining, and distilling life. It is a condensed statement of how our expression is perfected. Everything that we go through in our trials and tribulations is a process of perfection. But striving for perfection is inevitable, so we have to be careful of the way we put perfection inside of us. It's best to look at perfection like something we are remembering, "Oh I forgot I was perfect." Perfection is not an attitude of self-importance like saying, "my perfection is superior to others." If we use understanding that we are already perfect as an excuse, that's not the real thing. But if we allow perfection to be a comforter and realize that we live in loving, that is the real thing. Ultimately, we are an expression of divine will, of *love having its way.* The process of our humanity is the perfection.

We are always doing better than we think we are, so relax. I think we start entertaining negative thoughts about ourselves when we lose our sense of being part of the whole. When we start catching ourselves thinking badly of ourselves, it's time to sit down and have a meeting with ourselves and get connected again and push the negative viewpoint away. It's essential. I guess that's why we have a daily spiritual practice because we live in an atmosphere of a negative world. It's easy to lose awareness and forget who we are. When we lose our way, we have to resolve that in ourselves. Gratitude is the key. In gratitude, manipulation and the economy of domination do not work on us. The best politics unfolds from our Soul.

In the Bible church I grew up in, we had what we called a *"come to Jesus meeting."* We would call on Jesus and confront all the foolish thoughts we have like indulging negative attitudes, thinking badly of our self, drinking to addiction, or gossiping about our neighbor. In that fundamentalist context, our list started with drinking too much or smoking too much or carousing too much. That may not seem extreme, but it is still identifying with negative thoughts about ourselves based on the cosmology of lack. The politics of lack is the fulcrum of power. It becomes a metaphor that we regard as truth. We have to challenge ourselves sometimes and to see the good in ourselves as well. Sometimes this takes a *"come to Jesus meeting."*

We have this saying now, "get over yourself." We have a negative self-importance in the form of being impressed with ourselves as special or we are disturbed and think we should get special consideration. We are just as loving as every other loving being in the universe. That's one thing we can't help. Love is our perfection. We can pretend, but we can't help being loving. So, get over the negativity. It's hard to think of it as 'not real' when we are identified with it. We are enculturate with the need to persevere our lack, whether in the role of the haves or the have nots. Each time we work on ourselves is a refinement of the same issue. Pretty soon we won't be able to find that same issue anymore. Then we have to find something else to talk about. In the context of Transcendental Leadership, I Am Soul, Master of My House is a "come to Jesus meeting." Let's do some serious house cleaning and remodeling. We need to primarily look for rooms we assigned to political entitlement. As we enter each room we ask: whom do you serve? If our room does not serve the Lord of Love, that room is redundant.

Apple Sauce

In our world there is a mythology that Eve ate the apple and the world has been going downhill ever since. But that's a terrible distortion. That was the adventure of...game on! Eat the apple and hey, enjoy it. There's no shame in there. This has been translated as shame because of a power trip, a deep archetypal shame that became implanted very early in our culture, in our politics *du jour*.

Eve eating the apple and the power trip of shame is woven in with gender and power distortions. Incarnating as a woman has challenges that go back to a story about power and purpose written by politicians posing as spiritual authorities. The room of authority is in the house. Distorted spiritual authority is going on too, and that's a powerful realization. It's like eating the apple has become a metaphysical conception of something new inside. When we eat the apple, we own the seeds. What's going to come from that? Apple sauce? It's like planting a new seed, and we don't know what kind of tree is going to grow from it. They say it was an apple, but that was made up. We don't really know. That's the way consciousness is. That is the way biblical metaphors and political myths emerge. The myth is that eating the apple was forgetting. Consider instead that the eating the apple was remembering: remembering that we came to bring love and become Transcendental Leaders in a new secular order.

Becoming conscious and waking up invites transformation. This journey is about becoming conscious of ourselves. The nature of our reality is to become more conscious, to wake up. When we embrace, I Am Soul, Master of My House, we embrace and take responsibility for ourselves in a tactile, tangible, real way. We simultaneously embody a somatic as well as a Soul experience. It is a new heaven, and it's a new earth. We know that we are going into the unknown. Our destiny in life is to go into the unknown. That's the point. That is the intention, and the passkey is love. More applesauce, please.

Nations

Each nation has an ideal that was incorporated at the time of its consecration. As such, each nation is purposed with fulfilling and bringing their ideal to the world. Just like our purpose in life has a destiny, nations have a purpose and go through the same process of evolving that an individual does. Nations are operated by those people who have chosen to be incarnated into the consciousness held by their nation of choice. Sometimes the "nation of choice" is prescribed by the individual's karma. Sometimes we are born in one nation and our karma is to go to another nation. We are not obligated to stay a patriot in our country. If we choose to stay in a country, we are going to be challenged as an integral player in the evolution of that country's national ideal.

In the United States, historically and even unto today, immigrants come here from all over the world. Many come from Mexico and South America. Each person brings their culture with them and adds it to the ideal of the "American Dream." One of our purposes is to be a melting pot. It's more like making a stew because each one adds their culture to the national stew. On the East Coast, we began as a Christian, Anglo Saxon country, mostly Protestant and Catholic. Native people were already living here and they accepted the new arrival with a mixture of love, support, curiosity and antipathy, although the people who met Columbus may have a different story. Our Thanksgiving is based on a romanticized version of the New England experience by Anglo story tellers. After the European arrival, things went south. The good Christian founders betrayed the trust of the native people due to fear and lack. We used religion, military might and deceptive agreements to dominate the indigenous Americans. Without lack as an inner reference of self, there is no fear or need to dominate. For those who had the authority, genocide seemed like the way to go. Once we tasted genocide it was hard to let go into love. Addiction to power has become politicians' drug of choice. The cure is addiction to *remembering*, which is addiction to love and truth.

We had the ideal of love from Christianity blended with entitlement. Our sense of entitlement was subtle. People came to America to escape repression and to find a new life but then they established their own entitlement, repressing the native population and soon importing African slaves as a labor class. Despite that, an idealism of freedom and equality for all emerged amid repression, slavery, and genocide. The United States has in its DNA a destiny of soul searching and transformation, a quest to bring a higher vision of a *new secular order* and *freedom and justice for all* into being. We also have a strong work ethic and a love of capitalism. However, the powerful are driven by a character of lack that collaborates with the lack of those ingrained in the ways of poverty. We embrace a capitalism based on lack, resulting in institutionalized greed and poverty, haves and have nots, which overshadows the national ideal of prosperity, abundance, and well-being for all. Europeans did come to America with a higher vision, but when Europeans landed on the American shores they also came with a shadow, and higher ideals were already hijacked by entitlement. A few years on, Emerson admonished the Cambridge students suggesting that their calling was for the first time to build a nation based on the transcendental wisdom of the Soul.

Elements of Emerson's vision existed in the wisdom of the indigenous people of America. The Native Americans preserved their connection to the land, as best they could while they were under siege. Indigenous ideals are now reemerging as values in the current American culture. Resolving the various expressions of lack and fear will eliminate the root causes of greed, entitlement, and the economic divide, as well as tribal hate and anger that breeds in the lack of have nots and the fear of the haves. Now, more than ever, we need mediation and a lifting integration of

Transcendental Leadership as foreseen by the American Transcendentalists such as Emerson and as also expressed, through examples among many indigenous groups such as in the Hopi Prophecy and the Iroquois teaching of the Tree of Peace.

I have not studied what all of the purposes are for all of the nations. This topic began when I was teaching along with my wife Karey in Switzerland with a good portion of students coming to classes from France. We had taught there for several years, so we were very familiar with the Swiss psyche and we felt at home there. Most of the students were from Switzerland or France and mostly French speaking. There were a few students from Germany who spoke English. The translation for the class was English and French. When the topic of nations' purposes came up, we looked at the virtues and ideals of mostly France and Switzerland. In Switzerland, a confederation formed as a nation out of idealism. A group of people came together from different ethnic and linguistic forces (German, French, Italian, indigenous Swiss) and then decided on a nation. The idealism of a need for common good brought them together and inspired them, and it made them strong. Switzerland was set up to preserve the situation there, striving to be a colonial power is not in its DNA. When we start looking to see what is going on in a country, we observe and study the culture and political climate.

Modern France has an idealism that is inspired by liberty, equality, and fraternity. It grew out of a rebellion to an arrogant, entitled monarchy. For a time the republic was co-opted by an emperor fostering an early and distorted version of the European Union. Before that, there was a terrible clash between Protestants and Catholics that sent many Protestants to Switzerland. As in the United States, democracy in France was hard-won by a persistent national evolution driven by a higher vision. As in the United States, we see ancient archetypal clashes reemerge as refugees roam the earth due to forces similar to the forces that almost destroyed Europe over the evolution of nation states ending with the formation of the United Nations, North Atlantic Treaty Organization and the European Union. Ironically a motivator of Napoleon's European conquest was to form and unite Europe; however, his method was military conquest, rather than a collaborative confederacy based on an ideal of the common good. In the modern day European Union, we see that the vision continues but the approach is ostensibly based on a collaboration of shared support rather than a domination of one person's vision no matter how inspired.

Does any country live up to its idealism? Probably not. But it is set up to inspire achieving their ideals. The country we are in has ideals that are archetypes driving the inspirations of the times. But human beings are in residence in their messy houses. Factions within the nation have differing views about what the ideals mean. The differing factions try to promote their agendas in reactive ways that split apart the national ideals, lowering the vibration of the country in a way that affects all the attitudes of every citizen.

When we are working with beliefs about our country, to lift those beliefs, we have to relate to the national ideals the same way we relate to our own ideals. We can get in a fight with the factions as activists in society and that might be a good thing. The society is an out picturing of the inner worlds of its citizens. Imagine the nation as our house. These factions inhabit rooms in our house that compete with the authority of the Soul and the law of love. The fight will not necessarily hurt in the long run, but it is about dealing with the divisiveness of a tribal approach. We have to look to our higher values. We want to promote those higher values, purely, and not attack aggressive factions. The conflict is inside of us. As the old adage goes: "A house divided will fall." We look at the respective values based on our citizenship and promote those values. We need to look at beliefs that interfere with the higher values of our nation, not to judge ourselves but to put our house in order. By so doing, we are participating in the milieu of the nation in small ways that collectively result in a large change in the nation. We could not even imagine how much our little loyalties promote the higher values of the nation. Collectively, as Transformational Leaders, we individually lift the consciousness of the nation.

Simplicity

The house is an excellent metaphor for our space and our person because as an archetype it resonates with the embodiment of I Am Soul.

When we activate this resonance through the metaphor of I Am Soul, Master of My House, we can very rapidly bring social and political elements into focus. We incorporate our national identity and our sense of world citizenship as rooms within our house. As we review our national, environmental, and planetary values, we organize and sort through the content of our house. Some rooms need cleaning, some need reorganizing, and some rooms have guests that are at odds with the higher ideals and values that we want to promote within our house and our communities. Endemic racism is a shadow occupant of many houses in today's America. Forces in the world shape our inner architecture and the converse is also true, as we take authority in our house, we shape our relationship to forces and gain leadership in relationship to those forces.

From the perspective of Transcendental Leadership, our loyalty is to the soul of nations rather than to political forces that control and manipulate the scenarios of the day. By holding to the higher values of our nation, we challenge, by our Presence, the adverse agenda that seeks to control our perception. By asserting mastery in our house we assert a corresponding resonance in our political reality which initiates a corresponding authority in our world. We live in an intelligent, interactive energetic milieu that is susceptible to dominant attitudes of the day and that milieu is also responsive to the higher virtues of the nation. There are different kinds of actions allowed on many realms of consciousness, and there are actions that have to be true for all of the levels of consciousness. Our house has doorways and windows into every dimension of the matrix of consciousness and in all the inner and outer realms and through these doorways we can act on the many dimensions and levels.

Our House is a metaphor that corresponds to the cosmology of spiritual physics that align and give us place in the universe and the many dimensions of that universe. The correspondence of the house metaphor to the macrocosm of our dimensional reality provides a simple way to participate in the various dimensions and levels of consciousness. Our perception of place describes a center and circumference organized from our heart. Through that center, we align transcendentally through our pineal gland (Tisra Til). Our heart sits in the middle. And then in the vertical alignment there is a center that we call the I Am, which is our spiritual authority in the embodied world, so whatever we declare from that authority becomes a law. When we say something like I'm unworthy we inadvertently set up a law inside of us that makes sure that we are unworthy because that's the law of the realm. It becomes a house rule. Our I Am authority is very powerful. We can review all the things that we have declared ourselves to be that we have had to undo. We can undo them with the same authority that we used to make them. Through the I Am, we have the authority of self-forgiveness.

When we declare that I Am Soul, we open that energy and the accompanying frequency that becomes active through every cell of our body and every aspect of our space, and of our house. By declaring, I am Master of My House, we make it clear so that frequency goes out through our body, through our cells, and through our rooms and our realms. Anything that has been allowed, promoted or created in those realms that doesn't align with Soul is resolved or pushed out. Anything that has had its way with us now has to obey our command because of the clear message of I Am Soul and Master of My House. As we line up inside, anything that is contentious has to respond and be obedient to the I Am Soul authority. Some continuous energy just clears, some imbalanced patterns rearrange themselves and some areas of concern are grateful because we finally took charge whereas other areas get a little rebellious and require reminding for a while. A rebellious pattern will go along with us for a while and then come back, so we have to remind the rebellious pattern that cooperation is necessary. We have to remind ourselves that we have a few habits that aren't the best, and we remind ourselves until we become habituated to I Am Soul, Master of My House. This action instills a sense of responsibility and care for ourselves and our realm. When we feel opposition, confusion, or attack, the first thing to do is declare that I Am Soul, Master of My House. This declaration brings us present very quickly and then we are ready to deal with the situation.

Clearly we need to take leadership into our own house, attend to where we place our attention, what we think about, what we focus on, and our attitudes. Our surface, our circumference, is like a skin and this surface is either connected to and resonates with all that exists or it is out of phase and disconnected. External interest in the body politic may try to keep us out of step with our wholeness. We want to stay connected with our wholeness. The fastest way to maintain connection with our alignment with Soul is through gratitude. And the quickest way to resolve any pattern that is out of alignment is by using all situations to transform ourselves into loving. We have the authority of I Am Soul, Master of My House while Spirit puts its hand on our heads and fills us with love and everlasting grace. In the body politic, we first vote internally with the spirit of liberation and then externally in the politics of the land. Through the clarity of Soul authority, we can discern the true from the false.

Meditation

Settle in your space and enter into that perspective within yourself where you open up the inner connection between heaven and earth. As you awaken to that connection, also start tracking your breathing where you breathe in the light from above and below into your heart and then expel that into your space. And as you breathe in from the earth, the oxygen and the prana, as you breathe in the Spirit from above and below, mix that in your heart. And breathe it out through your body into your space. And on the next breath, there will be an element of exhaling where you give up to Spirit and then also exhale into the earth. So in this cycle you're purifying yourself through breathing in and out from the earth, breathing out from above and below. While you're doing that, we're just going to say a prayer.

So just take that lovingness and expand it out to fill your space and feel the circulation of loving through your body, through your cells, and bring your awareness into the center of your head. And as that light opens, bring it out to fill your space.

And now from that awakening place, just make that personal statement that I Am Soul, Master of My House. Just be present with that.

And take this love and use it as the light to begin to explore within you and within your house. As that sensibility opens for you, just ask inside is there a room that needs my attention? Trust where the indication takes you. Just stand before that room, wait a moment, and have a sense of what may be within. Permit the full range of possibilities. And when you feel ready, just step within that space. Allow the loving to go ahead of you. As you step into that space, become accustomed to the frequency of that space and see what unfolds for you and what you need to attend to, awaken to, and follow along with what appears.

It's all occurring within you, so just follow the spontaneity of the dialogue, of the exchange, of the process, and trust the way it proceeds. Trust the way it comes into balance and wholeness. If you find that doubt or fear enters in, just repeat I Am Soul and be present for yourself for whatever is needed.

As you complete this, just ask to be guided to a room where you have incorporated a force from outside of yourself and included it inside of yourself and stand before the entryway to that room. Send your loving ahead of you and then step into that space and allow what is there to reveal itself to you.

As you awaken yourself to this, allow yourself to reveal the response from yourself and cooperate with any actions required. And again if there is any controversy, just repeat to yourself I Am Soul, Master of My House. Be present.

Now allow yourself to move around within your house to any other room that may be inhabited by something that needs your attention at this time. It's a like prayer inside, keeping in mind your destiny for the highest good at this time. Reveal any room that needs attention at this time to balance, to love, to be made whole, to resolve any orphans to welcome home. As that love expands, just follow through. You may be visiting more than one room at once. Allow the process and the incredible capacity and genius of the loving to do all things.

And when that process continues, just come into that vast space, that alignment in the center of your consciousness, and we just now ask for that Soul love, that Soul light, that Soul Presence. And as it resonates with the Soul of all, we gather that light and just let it down through the center of your being to the center of your house and wash through all of the rooms, all the corners, from the attic to the basement. Begin to build within and just fill the house.

And repeat once again I Am Soul, Master of My House, and by so doing you vote to transform the politics of lack in the world.

*I feel safe
in the midst of my enemies,
for the truth is all powerful
and will prevail.*

Sojourner Truth

CHAPTER NINE

Sanctuary
...

The only compass for traversing life that is true is our heart because it can track the loving and love is the only energy that knows for sure where it is going and what it is doing. Everything else thinks it knows where it is going but often diverts the loving or makes love conditional. However, loving always finds its way back even though it may take a while. We may think we are pursuing ordinary goals like: I'm going to make this career, or I'm going to do that job, or go to this place or be this person. We think these actions are a destination or a goal or something we want to achieve, but all of those are just vehicles for loving. Everything we do in life is just to get from one state of consciousness to the next. Sometimes we like the bus we are on so well we don't want to get off at the next station. We even block our awareness that our permanence in a place is an illusion. We may wonder, what's traveling? The one that travels through the experience of our life is the Soul. The true part, the Transcendental Leader part, is just having the experience. The Ego part thinks it is doing something either important or unimportant, accomplishing things or failing. The Ego believes in what is going on, which is also an orientation that erodes our sense of Sanctuary... of security and safety. The Ego wants a place to rest, but all of these things that occur are ways to travel in consciousness. Soul awareness is like riding on a train because we can rest and travel at the same time.

Inshallah (God Willing)

God's will, according to the Bible politics of my youth, promised but did not deliver Sanctuary. What I came to understand was that God's will is simply that *love will have its way.* This gave me a certain orientation for my life compass. Love is a true guide. Some things are direct, and they just happen straight away. We can trust the process while we are discovering love's way in various situations or circumstances, as life will challenge and entice us...worlds without end. The Bible politics were based on evidence that we were doing God's will depending on the church's party line or their interpretation. Love has no politics and love delivers Sanctuary.

If we consider that our lives are guided by love always sneaking around getting its way, we can pay attention to that. We pick out the love frequency, which helps us see the truth in events, and we see how deeper purpose is working. We can see how fear is controlling us. We can see how controlling is not needed. We can see how to act when it helps, truly helps, rather than when our help adds to the conflict. Love provides a very important turning point. Perhaps it is the right-hand and left-hand way. We look to the heavens holding both hands gently palm up: Inshallah. With our embodiment of this gesture, we wonder what is it that is threatened? In this gesture we are entrusting the faith of...God willing: *love will have its way.*

Love that Awakens

Most of the time we don't notice our breathing. All the while the rhythm of our breath and pulsing of our heart weaves love, prana and air into the metabolism of our life. Now we are noticing this miracle that caresses each moment of our life on earth. Breath brings Sanctuary and the intimacy of life that circulates through us. Breath brought life to the universe.

When we pay attention to our breathing, the exchange begins on all levels of consciousness. Breath creates a context that makes it very easy to listen inside. And as we listen inside, our breath begins to balance the discontinuities of our mind and begins to call forward the celestial sound or serenade of life...the internal melodies that create the reality in which we live. As we continue to listen inside, a kind of spiritual vision opens up and sets aside any preconceptions about what that vison is for us. As the vision opens we assume for the moment that we are just fine the way we are.

We begin to sense the internal geography, the geometry of what is present in the space that is us through the symmetry of the center and circumference, as if we have our own internal horizon. In that horizon, the sun rises and sets, the moon passes, day and night, and the stars go by in the circumference of our own person. Our vantage point is the vortex of light that flows through the center of our body, while simultaneously we perceive our internal geography from the horizon. We sense the intractable nature of ourselves that has this capacity and even a role as a bridge between heaven and earth...no theology...just Sanctuary.

As we breathe in, we imagine our life force flowing from below and our Soul force flowing from above. We join the currents of love in our hearts and breathe out as the love flows through the cells of our body into our space. We find ourselves in the exchange between our essence and the essence of the world. We allow these loving currents to flow through our experiences without thinking too much about it. We experience the revelation of meaning through breathing. As we respond to the loving currents of breath, we feel at home with the Presence of Sanctuary.

Soul-Self

Learning to allow the flow of love through our breath helps us to appreciate more of the place we are in, a perfect meditative place. Placing our attention on the center of our head, imagine a light there and as we do we see a light or have a sense of light, which may become our form of seeing. Enjoying this Presence of light and just by paying attention to the light, it begins to expand. It's not a force, but more of a pulsing permutation as it grows larger. Continuing breathing provides a complementary awareness that coordinates our consciousness in a way that eases or eliminates worries. Just below the surface of our awareness, we may even feel a pulsing. The light expands. It grows quite large. We may actually feel the light push out through the periphery of our skull and our skin so that it is larger than our head and incrementally our body. Our sense of adventure invites us to place ourselves within the ball of light. The sensation could be much like stepping into a light vehicle with anticipation of a journey. In this vision, we experience the simultaneity of our heart and brain. We are synchronous with all that is. In this synchronicity, we become the mantle of Sanctuary that surrounds and holds our physical body. We extend our Sanctuary a little bit more until it encompasses roughly an arm's reach around us. In this space, we feel things move around or adjust. Just notice. It's not time to work on any issues. It's just time to be present and absorb Presence.

Now the Soul-Self, the divine self opens within the space held by the mantle of Sanctuary. Our body relaxes into the safety of this space. Now our Soul is a Sanctuary within a Sanctuary. As we become aware of this prism of Sanctuary, on our request, we can receive even greater levels of love. Try it out. Settle into that space. In this context, in your Sanctuary, begin to touch into certain layers and frequencies inside. More precisely bring the light to them because they represent an overlay like a skin that we want to shed because it can create a limitation or a controversy. We are enticed to treat these limiting layers as integral to ourselves. It's just a surface, a skin we wear that looks like it might represent our interior. That surface is not us. We want to create a distinction between the loving Presence that is us and the world settling upon us. We invite our awareness to notice how the world challenges us and just touch those areas inside, not for or against, but just to mark them. This is the way we experience ourselves when we are challenged by the world. And this is the way we experience ourselves being present with our challenges in the world. With as much compassion and kindness as possible, be present with this awareness. Then we just take a deep breath and release our breath and allow ourselves to settle. In this way we embody our Sanctuary.

Specters of Chaos

There are tribal voices that have become aspects of ourselves. We just ask to be as aware as is appropriate for this time about those tribal voices which are our family, our neighborhood, and our cultural group. They are invested in us. These are all nice things to be aware of and important to understand, but the tribal voices are not us. Though once a form of Sanctuary these tribal voices may no longer hold. They are something we took on, not good or bad, but we can now just make this distinction inside. Be present in our loving with those tribal voices and with great respect and appreciation, just take a deep breath and release them. We follow on with this process wherever it moves us or places us. As you become aware of any cultural voices feel free to repeat this process until you feel settled or complete.

There have been times in our lives when we had expectations of something that we hoped would give us love or fulfill a dream or ways to be seen or ways to have intimacy that did not work out and that left us hurt or disappointed. Ask to be aware of those times. Even if we do not connect with or see them all, the intention is sufficient... just trust it. Allow a moment to be present with those times and experiences of lost expectations. Honor them and appreciate them. We can disidentify with them as something that happened. These expectations were tied to looking for something outside of us that is not outside of us at all but is only given by our Soul from within the Sanctuary of the Soul.

The specters of chaos are going on in the world in ways that trigger fears inside of us that appear as threats, as something that would take away our national identity or destroy all the banks, cause mass earth changes that flood everything or collapse the internet. These threats don't have to be logical. Specters of chaos cause irrational fears about calamities in the culture or devastation to the planet. These fears might not go as far as a "zombie" apocalypse, which is a Hollywood fantasy of a dystopian time when we lose our souls to a craven mass mind becoming the walking dead bent on devouring the living. Often in story telling this dystopian outcome begins with a pandemic that is triggered by our human arrogance messing with our human chemistry for some medical breakthrough, advance in human evolution or cross species gene splicing in our laboratories. As a specter of hubris, the metaphor is an apt warning. Perhaps zombie is just a metaphor for our addiction to walking around asleep, giving our power and authority to a charismatic leader who justifies our hate as a sacred privilege to be acted out on others. When our life style is forgetful of

Soul, we sleep walk through life, vulnerable to the mind control of the latest fad, conspiracy theory, evangelical sycophant or gangster politician. Let us settle into that place inside where we can touch our eternity and deep love that is forever and dares to look into those places within our subconscious that may harbor these kinds of fears. We settle into ourselves and our loving and breathe and as we do this we realize that we are love that awakens into eternity.

Being a Person

Consider that "being a person" is in constant conversation with life and with each breath and that reality reorganizes itself based on what's going on inside of us, what we are paying attention to, and our unfinished business based on what we paid attention to in the past, forgot about, or dumped in our unconscious mind. Life is always relating to these conversations whether we are asleep or awake. Love is awake! Life is awake! Love serves us in any way that it can. Love and life work perfectly together. They are not broken. Love is Sanctuary.

If we get too distracted in trying to fix ourselves, find our limitations in terms of what's broken about us, what we have to fix, what we have to do to get better, what life will give us, then we get more things to fix because life offers us that kind of support. Life will give us false Sanctuary when that is our preference. What do we do with that?

There are some things we want to improve, need to resolve, or have unfinished business with. When we shift inside, we realize these things are usually in the form of the many things we haven't completed into the form of loving. There are many things we want to do and resolve and wake up to, but we get to have those aspects of ourselves because we are working just fine. When we change one of the biggest pieces of information (that there is something innately wrong with us that we have to fix in order to be good, to be whole, be successful or get the love we need), then we can be peaceful in ourselves, in our Sanctuary.

There are many choices and forks in the road to be taken. Not choosing is a choice. We can stop at the fork in the road or does it matter?

Are some things always true regardless of the road taken? We just look out the window in the morning and so far so good. We're still breathing. We can still overlay the missed thing with loving and find peace in *I don't know*. Every morning, every day we are just here being a person, and that is enough.

Reflections on the World

We should never buy a house until we check it out with due diligence. We might think, that's a nice house, however, when we incarnate, we only have a look at the plans for the house. We may like what we see, or we may not be sure about the house, but the angelic architect points out the house we need. When we incarnate, we as Soul enter the house of personality and body, and we have a choice. Will the Ego or the Soul be master of this house? When the Ego is master it is a puppet to the world. When we choose Soul as Master of our House, we center in living love and the world reflects the choice of love through grace and our House is a Sanctuary for the Soul. In Buddhism they talk about the Abode as Sanctuary and living in the house as a *skillful means*. It's a safe place, a place held sacred for us, a dwelling of compassion, love and peace. The sanctuary is an abode and a refuge. The implication is that the world is tough. We need a place to rest, a place to reflect and to rejuvenate. A refuge is like a spiritual abode. It has the quality of protection and there's some kind of authority there enforcing the protection. Once we find the place of refuge within, we can amplify it by using it, by going there, and by being there. By doing so, we can establish our Sanctuary.

The drama in the world makes it hard at times to reflect. Each situation and challenge invites a reactive response. We have difficulty relaxing into a place of peace and stillness required for deep reflection. The abode is a place where we can consider things. There are certain actions that take us into the abode, into the Sanctuary: being present with what is, asking for the Presences of the light, the Christ, the Buddha, Allah, or other great teachers or deities, watching our breathing, centering in living love through our willingness to move into a meditative space. These are ways to relax into Sanctuary. We just go in as a movement of intention and humility.

In Sanctuary there is a guideline about being present with what is. To be present release yourself from judgment, so you can be present with what is. More precisely, we are there to be totally free of identifying with judgments. In Presence, we line up all the way through the levels of our consciousness from the physical to the Soul, through the Basic Self, Conscious Self and High Self. We are not being pulled into the past with our regrets. We are not being pulled into the future with our fears and anticipation. We are just present. When we are present, Presence is the Sanctuary.

Once when I was teaching, a loud noise distracted us. At first, in the suddenness of it, we didn't know what it was, so we just stayed present and it worked itself out. We saw what was reflected and what we noticed. There was a wedding in the adjacent facility and finally we knew that the noise came from the wedding. We closed the windows and blessed the wedding. And we also got a blessing from it and a metaphor about the internal process. There was a great balance of the external wedding and the internal wedding. There's no ripple in that. There's no separation or conflict. After awhile we may need more fresh air, then we'll deal with that and re-open the windows when we get to it. In that way our inner peace will flow into the outer celebration.

Responsibility

I spoke earlier about unconditional love. It gives us what we pay attention to. We are building energy internally about a project we are interested in and the first way unconditional love serves us is to teach us about our project, about its essence and how to apply that essence. I think one of the reasons some pharmaceutical drugs have side effects is that the scientists that invented them didn't pay attention to the essence first to understand the purpose of the substance and the drug's relationship to the whole, before they looked at its application. Did the scientist question the relationship between the purpose of the illness and the purpose of the substance that they were concocting to help a patient with the purpose of the illness? One of the ways a drug company works is through finding a formula and then looking around to see what it will fix, then market to that fix. Then they assign the drug to whatever makes money, which is backward. The approach I'm talking about is working from the essence first, then working for the practicality. This approach invites unconditional love into the process from the beginning, as illustrated by the example of George Washington Carver.

We are collaborating with all of life. A lot of times, the first thing we try to do is move on our project, to move on the outside to make it happen instead of moving into cooperation with love and the essence of the project first and then acting. How do we move into cooperation? Well, in our inner Sanctuary exists a deeper dimension of consciousness that is eternal and beyond duality. It's not for or against anything. It hasn't entered into the realm of manifestation yet, so in a sense you give it over to God...the real God wholeness...bypassing the God of projection. Well, it's a good idea to have that kind of collaboration because God is a universal intelligence that is everywhere present and knows everything. God is not a puppeteer. God's Presence is loving us unconditionally while we find the compass in our hearts, while God's love is acting in everything on our behalf according to our preference. God's grace can bypass a lot of obstacles for us because it knows how to bring the realm of manifestation about. We first bring our consciousness into our inner dimension, our Sanctuary, and open our collaborative spirit to God's Presence. And then we start being present with what is and what we notice and we experience an incredible collaboration with the Presence of God. Another way to say that this is what we take responsibility for.

Narcissism

In a way we are never alone in the sense that we are always in relationship to something, relationship to others, relationship to our habits, always trying to relate to what's going on in life, to find our way or establish comfort or take care of ourselves. We may start looking at the common and ordinary things that are clues to divine wisdom. Apparently in our evolution, we must have intended that we often fall asleep. In our activity, we fall asleep to our inner self. All that means is that a great wisdom goes unconscious but does not abandon us. When something goes unconscious for us, it goes out into the collective and becomes part of everybody's unconscious. Then the nature of reflective reality is that everything reflects back. Through reflection everybody is trying to help out and remind us of what we forgot about ourselves and we are reminding them about what they forgot about themselves. But, it seems, most of the time none of us are aware that we are reminding each other.

One of the things we tend to forget is our adequacy. We're trying to help each other out from a basis of inadequacy, so we easily fall into a pattern of trying to teach each other that we're not enough. And since we forget who we are, we are afraid and we operate out of a basis of fear. We build castles, we build armies, and we try to protect ourselves, physically and metaphysically as an attempt to handle our fear. Even our spiritual philosophies take on a duality of war with angels, good and bad, evil and good. This dynamic keeps playing. We keep coaching each other in this reality of fear and it never seems to end unless we wake up and realize that there must be something more. Our habits look outside of ourselves. We're always collaborating based on resonant frequencies. We choose our collaboration based on frequency. Our collaboration has a dark side. We can create a false Sanctuary. We can bond through our syndicated narcissism, our self-importance. We can also create a false-Sanctuary through our poverty and fortification against predatory forces. We think we are important because we believe our lives are in jeopardy. Our remedy is in the acknowledgement that everything fails us until we wake up to our Soul. In our awakened state Soul reaches out through the fabric of our consciousness and provides true Sanctuary.

Conscious Soul collaboration seems like a big project, but in Soul collaboration, we can't escape the truth. If we look at the simple things we do, we can start finding keys to the truth. When I was growing up, people valued a kind of empathy, which had the unintended consequence of shame, or was shame actually intended? We have to think of others, we can't think just of ourselves. From the viewpoint of Ego and the viewpoint of duality, that meant sacrificing ourselves through doing for others. From that perspective, we have to do for others to be adequate, which creates codependence and shame. Collaborating to maintain a false

Sanctuary, creates a pattern and it's split there, pitting one thing against the other. If we take up our own behalf, we become narcissistic which is considered negative unless you are a narcissist, then you think it's great. Narcissists use everything and everybody to take care of themselves at the expense of others. In both cases, thinking of others at the total expense of self or thinking of oneself at the total expense of everyone else, we betray ourselves. Betrayal eventually runs its course too. You can begin to think, or say, "oh, wait we are caught in a world controlled by duality," which doesn't solve the puzzle of who we are and what we are doing here. Narcissism is a false Sanctuary. A false Sanctuary does not endure. When we live in a true Sanctuary, we take care of ourselves and then we are able to take care of others.

We might say, well, it is about us and it's about everybody else also. There's a clue in this statement. Is there a way we can take care of ourselves and make the situation about us and yet also take care of everybody else? We may not have the answer right away, but we have a perspective. One example is when we are flying on an airplane and the cabin loses pressure, the guidance is to put on our oxygen mask first so that we don't lose consciousness while trying to help someone else with their mask. That perspective helps us realize the nature of our Ego and it's beautiful design. It's a steppingstone to giving us a location and a position in this world. In a way, the body, the Ego, is a sacrifice to the Soul. In the Soul what is good for us is good for everybody. The Soul is here promoting our evolution while, ideally, Ego is in service to our evolution. When we are asleep, we take that service into our self or in service to keeping the integrity of who we think we are. Some people say yeah, narcissism is like an imposter in my life and they think that's bad news. I think discovering our narcissism is good news because we realize that there is some truth in looking at life from our perspective. We take our narcissism and say, "well, is there a principle here about the way life really works"? This statement is produced out of fear. We start investigating the foundation of that fear. We keep the "take care of ourselves" piece and put ourselves first part but not from the old way of narcissism, then life reflects a truth inside. When we put the Soul first and Ego second, we dispel both the co-dependent do-gooder and the narcissistic aspects of ourselves. Life is Soul centered.

When we put our Soul first, there's a guideline we can use: When our life is not working out, check inside, check our relationship to God and our relationship to ourselves because when those aspects are intact, the relationship with others comes out of loving. When we put our relationship to the world in a relationship to others first, we separate from God and ourselves and fear comes in, and fear puts things backward. It is necessary that we stop everything and check our priorities. In the Sanctuary of self, we can reorder our priorities.

Loving First

The ability to reorder our priorities is the power of the Sanctuary. We could say, "oh I can do this within myself, I've just taken all my misunderstandings and put them in-service to wisdom and compassion. When I see somebody else, either putting themselves down too much or putting themselves up too much, I can see how the victim hurts this person and how the victimizing makes this person sensitive." That view of others is a reflection to remind us of something, reminding us that we need to work with the victim and victimizer within. Maybe it will work the other way too by rehabilitating a false-self. We can gain an ability to rehabilitate our viewpoints. When we see somebody seeking outer resources for Sanctuary, we can assess their behavior because we've had the experience that they are demonstrating. I can take the grace of the Sanctuary and extend it out into the world but it doesn't justify anything. Our grace throws a blanket of loving from the Sanctuary onto the situation. Sanctuary surrounds them with an environment that has something new in it. If we judge, react, or punish them, then we help sustain the adversity which sustains negativity. When they reach out unconsciously toward us to affirm their reality, looking for a familiar response, they find instead the loving Presence of Sanctuary. Our loving starts to mingle with their conditioned negative perspective and they start to breathe in the loving and then start to mimic the loving and that loving begins to subtly affect the habitual way they justify themselves. Our interaction with them finesses the frequency of their negativity into a loving frequency. The process is not very dramatic, often appearing as a mood change that becomes a game change.

Out of a world filled with fear, we have taken the habits and skills we used for survival. If we inhabit those skills and techniques with loving then we have some practical understanding. For example, when someone is exhibiting negative behavior we might confront them and try to prevent the behavior, but not punish them. Our Presence is just to limit their activity until we assist them in waking up to their goodness. The challenge often shows up in their commitment to continuing to be a victim. Often victimizers are seeking revenge for a time when they alleged that they were the victim. Victim and victimizers are living out a cycle much like an addict attempting to resolve their trauma in their addiction. The victim becomes the victimizer and the victimizer believes they are the victim. There's a technique when dealing with alcoholics, for example, in which we confront them, and it can be quite dramatic. The confrontation causes the addict to wake up and see the cycle they are caught in. We can help each other by confronting our self-centered ways to become Soul-centered ways.

From our loving and our experience, we may as a practical issue stop, limit or enforce something, but never to get even or punish. This approach assures that there isn't any cruelty in our action. We do not need to use cruel methods as weapons like armies that rape, or like armies that take all the goods, or in misogynistic domination. We don't need these methods. We apply balance to our relationships, and that balance still has to do with the practicality of life, of building communities and developing commerce. There are certain guidelines that make life work. In our desire to be a good spiritual person we may adopt behaviors that we think or have been told may be helpful. The Ten Commandments are guidelines for behavior. In Buddhism we have the Yamas and then the Niyamas (the dos and don'ts) that are just like the Ten Commandments. These laws may help hold civilization together, but it's one thing to use these guides for practical purposes and another when we distort them for power, control and domination. For a law to work properly, we need love to give the law wisdom and grace and to know when to make an exception to the rule. Loving makes the world work for everybody. It's not so much out there in the systems that are established, but it's how we approach those systems from within ourselves. An approach from love first always works best.

Robert D. Waterman, EdD

Heaven on Earth

When we begin opening our hearts, we run the risk of disappointment. Out of disappointment we often become a cynic who is always putting a negative spin on everything that creates or promotes good. That is a tough stance because cynics use positive sensitivity for a negative intent and then end up acquiescing to the very thing that troubles her/him in the first place.

A dream of a golden age or a desired heaven on earth is an archetype that humanity keeps striving to obtain. But some people's vision of heaven is another person's hell. We're dealing with a heaven vs. hell situation in the United States today. This fear engenders a perspective of heaven on earth, which in my vision of heaven on earth seems to be destructive. There are different reflections of this fear enactment. It's a force on the planet, a zeitgeist, perhaps like the vision of the Third Reich or any vision of supremacy of one group over another. We thought we were through with that "vision" too, but it keeps coming up again. Just like some people thought we were through with racism in the United States but our underlying systemic racism is increasingly becoming evident. If all of this domination stuff is in the unconscious, how much stuff is there? It just keeps arising resulting in possible dystopian visions. Some people even crave supremacy because then we would be reduced to something they deem essential, perhaps a perverse yearning for a simpler life. Sanctuary provides a simplified life through an appreciation of complexity.

The way I like to approach these dystopian ideations is to look at how deep and how large I become to encompass and permeate our dark tendencies in love? What's the long vision and the depth of self that enables us to make sense of life as it appears? To elaborate, generally we accept that we have all lived before and we are eternal in the sense of Soul. We keep coming into embodiments to gain experiences and if we have been there and done that enough, pretty soon we catch on and the current embodiment seems to be working. But maybe we are on the leading edge and we have a clear focus. However, next to you is somebody who, instead of having one hundred incarnations that were new, they did the same incarnation one hundred times, accruing little or no wisdom but ample karma. They are stuck in a rut spinning their wheels. It could be called wheel-spinning-rut-karma. They are not even making new ruts. We have to allow for this possibility. Everybody's doing the best they can with the experiences they've had, but there is a drive within us that knows things can be better. Look at people and whatever situation they are in…they are usually trying to make it better. Even if they are a drug addict living under a bridge, they try to manage their day the best they can. But because they are so taken over by addiction, they can't follow through with their dreams of breaking out of their addiction. We may look at these people through the hopelessness of it. On one level, it is a product of an attitude of the whole culture about living and life and an attitude of general caring. But while we care and feel powerless, some of that has to do with our ability or willingness to respect that person's karma. For all we know the last thing they have to work out is going through this experience of addiction. So, sanctuary is not always just being safe. Safety can be complacency. Consider then that the value of Sanctuary is to be safe in an unsafe world, in the world and not of it. When that occurs, peace from the inside out can work.

There are some basics to consider regarding inhabiting our Souls. As we start to taste the Soul and really give over to it, Soul is just there for the experience, a reality provided for us to have experience, good and bad. This seems hard to relate to in a way. The Soul is loving, so what is this good or bad experience about? Well in the short view it's hard to understand and in the long view it may be easy to understand because in our loving we have as many chances as we need. We are supported until we wake up fully. Support yourself, just stick with yourself and don't give up. We can find Sanctuary in perseverance, when we persevere to the end.

Many of us have been in situations in other lives in which we reached for a dream, a heaven on earth, and almost made it but the dream fell. In fact, the dream has fallen so many times that there's no trace of it left on earth. We believe that we can go back a few thousand years and it looks like everybody was primitive. But repeating civilizations extend back further than that. We find fewer indications of civilizations that were more ancient because the evidence is not apparent, so we think civilization is relatively recent. Though the history of humanity has been folded and obscured into the many cycles of earth, we have a sense of the greater arc of our development. Do we give way to cynicism because it looks like we are taking our civilization apart faster than we are lifting it up? We can frighten ourselves with our own story if we like, but there is something at the core about our own resilience and how we persevere. Our resilience comes from our Souls. In a sense we are Souls traveling through life, growing and expanding through experience. One view is that we graduate from life, we overcome the earth and go on to other adventures in higher worlds. Does this mean our goal of heaven on earth is a false one? Is our dream of heaven on earth an illusion of investing our salvation in the production of civilization? These two visions intersect in our awareness of Sanctuary, an awareness of being in the world but not of the world. The way becomes clear as we live our lives as the embodiment of love.

The Truth, The Light and the Way

The construct of the Sanctuary is a natural part of us. Some people might call it the Buddha within or the Christ within or Allah the merciful, but it's a state in which we get in touch with our eternal nature. And in that knowing, we will always exist. In Sanctuary other things that are not eternal will fall away. When we commit to this truth, it changes our relationship to life so that all things that are false will get challenged. When the world disturbs us, that is simply what's going on. For one thing, we are being shown an opportunity; we are looking at something that's going to fall away. Do we really get that disturbances are temporary? Conflict only has a reality if we need it, and when we are done with it, something else happens. When we doubt that this is so, we are not really trusting the knowing inside, and we create more anguish from our doubt, and we will actually preserve our dystopian outlook in our pessimism and cynicism. How do we maintain the integrity of our own inner Sanctuary and not give it away to what seems to be an impossible task? Our body is a Sanctuary for our Soul on its journey on earth. As we awaken, the Soul is a Sanctuary for our body on its journey. Then, our Soul transcendence is the Sanctuary of our eternity.

The universal impulse to look for a better life or "heaven on earth" is a projection. Is the archetype really pointing inside? Heaven on earth is internal, and when we are in the internal heaven, heaven is on earth and we each bring heaven to earth. It's an internal promise. When we live in terms of the internal heaven on earth, life will come around to meet us. How do we sustain heaven on earth? We remember that the challenge is an inside job. Each of us brings Sanctuary because we have within us *the truth the light and the way.*

Meditation

Just bring your awareness inside your body, into your heart, your loving, and bring that through your body and into your space. Just begin to breathe all of those elements and dimensions through this heart space as it expands as you awaken through that alignment within you that harmonizes every dimension and every level.

As you breathe out through the world and into your heart into your inner worlds, you also breathe from above and below, and through that center and circumference, you create your reality. You have the reflection, and you have the circulation of the source.

Once again bring your attention to the center of your head. As you do that, light opens. You move your awareness and sense of yourself into that interior place. That is our inner sanctum, the inner sacred place that is our abode, our sanctuary. And as we do, we cloak ourselves in that consciousness and our Presence becomes a sacred space. The only thing that can come against this space truly is what you invent, so take care to promote those habits and perspectives that keep light and life circulating through you in a way that purifies the world instead of adding to the pollution. It's a simple process, but it takes vigilance. You respect that the living of life is all relational, so it is always the love within you negotiating with the love of others to create the best plan in the best action as best you can. You are always negotiating. But what empowers that is the love within you vibrating with love within them. Sometimes trauma is such that it comes out really strange. But be not fooled by that. Your love is intact and working. Your job is not to fix them but to love them while they fix themselves.

We find ourselves in this world, in the cultures of the world, and the life of the planet, it all has a history and a process of resolution that we call karma. We cooperate with karma through appreciation, appreciate the earth, appreciate the level at which we use the earth because the earth itself too is rising and will work with you. So appreciate it's gifts no matter how achieved, and the way that we harvest those gifts will evolve.

And now the generosity of life, all the experiences you need are brought to you whether your need is to resolve, to accomplish, or to fulfill. The key is simple, use everything to transform yourself into loving. The truth will be revealed. The transformation will occur. Be present with what is and see what you notice, because it is the rising of inspiration within your noticing that selects your action in the world.

And above all, be the love as your Soul, the essence of God within that, with all your mind, body, and spirit as a first priority. And then love your neighbors as yourself. We are all one. I did not say judge your neighbor or judge yourself. Love your neighbor as yourself, the self that is the Soul. By doing so, you orient yourself to live in a way that those things that are healing and uplifting can find their way through you and to you. There is a discipline to this, it's not a lazy process. It's not a passive process. It is active. It is activating, waking up to an ancient truth within you. The love of God moves as an expression of your being. You decide.

Let's not be shy. We ask that whatever we can receive to restore ourselves and strengthen ourselves and fortify ourselves within that, this is given to us. In that gift, we commit to using it well.

Be vigilant when you find yourself going against that gift. Call it for what it is and forgive yourself. Allow this energy now to take you where it needs to as it fills you, supports you, and moves out from you into your life into the days to come touching those that you will meet and making the way clear. This is your birthright.

*We say that the faces of coming generations
are looking up from the earth.
So when you put your feet down,
you put them down very carefully-
because there are generations coming one after the other.
If you think in these terms,
then you'll walk a lot more carefully,
be more respectful of this earth.*

Oren Lyons

CHAPTER TEN

Synchronous
...

Sometimes when we start out and there's a fork in the road, we have to choose which path to go down. Along the way we make choices that take us one way and then we may think back and wonder, "what would've happened if I had gone the other way?" For me those questions can really stay with me for a long time, like the other choice is waiting. It's not a terrible regret but it's a strange regret. Regret holds the other choice in waiting. I might think that if I had gone the other way, I would have been so much better, braver, stronger, fulfilled or more successful. We don't realize that choice is synchronous, that both choices are affecting the calculus of our reality in real time, which may or may not be linear. All events in our past play into the present moment. Resolution is not the end of an issue. We move into Synchronous reality when all instances speak love in the moment, even in the so-called future ones. Through our Basic-Self, we stochastically create scenarios of the future, like feelers into the dark of probability and possibility looking for the optimal, most adaptive choice. In a way we are like a blind person tapping our way forward, listening for echoes and familiar textures. As we awaken into the High-Self, we gain a sense of plan, karma and destiny. From the perspective of the High-Self we have perspective and choice as to which scenarios to play out. We take the blinders off and have direction, guidance and access to the highest good.

Calculus

Each choice adjusts the calculus of our soul-driven participation in the time/space of this world. Some choices we make are direct and others are a bank shot. In a game of pool there are corner pockets and side pockets. The process of the game is to use a stick to shoot balls into the pockets. We can shoot the ball directly into a pocket or use a bank shot off the side rail into a pocket. Before we shoot, we choose whether to take a direct shot or a bank shot. Using the metaphor of a game of pool, our so-called mistakes are bank shots. Choices from love are easy whether straight or bank shots. Our choice of fear or hate, takes a few more banks. When we know the game, we can recode the algorithm each time we choose. The most effective way to play the game is to use everything to transform yourself into loving. We change the calculus each time we create, promote or allow transformation of anything into loving. When we conduct our transformative endeavors on the basis of fear, we also change the calculus for which the ultimate correction is destruction or the Phoenix rising from the ashes approach. Respectfully, we have "been there and done that." We cannot destroy the whole because the fabric of the whole is a process of unconditional love. In the present we incubate our future and as our future approaches us from the horizon, we continually renegotiate our existence. Life is a synchronous process of continually renegotiating our existence...spontaneously...moment to moment.

At our birth, we became an agency in a time and context, which is variable in the calculus of our reality. Everything synchronizes in the now and is coordinated simultaneously but is not necessarily occurring simultaneously or instantaneously. This is a function of the multidimensional rubrics cube of perception. Universal love operates through an algorithm of the highest good of all discrete entities and systems. When we travel back on the timeline and resolve a regret, the shift in reality communicates through wholeness, as a corrected frequency through what Bohm called the *holomovement.* Regret is a placeholder, magnetizing a return of a similar choice. Resolving regret releases change into the whole and the information can inform our present and possible future. Some futures want to be so powerfully and our collaboration is as strong as that future, that our present strives to join.

Considering this, we could have chosen another way. It would have taken us down a path or valley in which we could have gotten stuck or distracted or caught in something that was unnecessary. When we think about those options, it was really lucky that we didn't do that. We might wonder if our future spoke to us and advised us to make another choice, even if that meant not existing in our present form. We can be grateful for the path we chose. The only law of synchronous creativity, whether informed from the past, future or infinite dimensions, is that love is having its way. What may appear as chaos is often an action of multidimensional bank shots with pockets everywhere.

Maybe we are living upside down. See, that's just a perspective. In a way we are living upside down because it's a reflective reality. When we look in a mirror, we can find a clue. The image is reversed. In the camera, the image on the film shows up the other way around, and upside down. Our consciousness is a mirror and is contained by a mirror. Perhaps the camera actually turns it right side up. What we see here is upside down and backwards. You can see why we get disoriented when we start going inward or when we see how we record something inside. It's upside down and backwards from out there. It might be right side up in the right way inside. Perhaps we never thought about this before. The reason we feel disoriented is that we are always reorienting. We need a different reference point to do this journey of inward business. We must start getting comfortable in our present orientation. When our sense of self is more present, we can gain context in that sense from an internal reference point, an axial alignment that is timeless or an all-time dimension through which our Soul can ascend and descend freely. Our internal reference point is essential for the journey inward because we can't rely on our bearings from what's reflected back to us. We are Soul arising and descending in the center of our world as our Soul approaches us from the horizon. When Soul touches Soul, we are timeless and spacious everywhere.

Love Pocket

That which is true for the inner journey is also true for the outer journey. When we're looking for truth or facts, we can always be tricked. The only compass I know for traversing life that is true is our heart compass because it can track loving and love is the only energy that knows where it is going. When we are centered in our love, our guidance is synchronous. Anything else only thinks it knows where it is going.

When I think about God's will, I remember when I was growing up how the churches I attended conflated God's will with a dogmatic Bible interpretation that seemed intended to control our thoughts and beliefs. They would say, "Well it says such and such here in the Bible so that is God's will." What was really going on was they were using their interpretation of God's will from the scripture to control others and bolster their own sense of righteousness. We all need to feel safe and secure in what we believe, so I have full compassion. However, you can tell this dogmatic view was something I had to get over because I'm bringing it up again. Maybe I'm still working on it. I guess some of that is because I'm still working on the politics of religion in general and how it is used and misused in the collective world of duality. We can distort the lens and the mirror as a means of control. Making fear the center of our heart will lead to that distortion. This is probably true to some degree for all of us because it runs deep in the human psyche. In the insecurity of life certain people, with a little more insight and power, found out that they could use these fears and distortions and put themselves in the office of spiritual or political authority in order to manipulate the situation. These pseudo authorities can be very dangerous to the public.

On the other hand, there are other people who are awake and can use spiritual authority to guide us, give advice and channel higher energies. When awakened authorities spoke to people and lived with them there was an uplifting. Another measure of this construct is that the left hand authority was fear based and the right hand authority was love based. If we use our heart as a compass, we can follow everything that is love based in the culture, in society, and in our life and avoid fear-based pitfalls. One way to avoid fear-based "authorities" is to just stay away from them. And the other way is to place it to the side or step aside ourselves so the fear-based "authority" loses its power over time. Hopefully that takes just a couple of weeks, but it might take years, especially if we of are part of a family or a clan that is invested in fear as their primary orientation to life.

My viewpoint is that God's will in practice reflects that *love will have its way*, (just in case that wasn't clear to this point). This realization gave me a certain orientation for my heart compass. Some things are direct and they just happen straight away. Love can be direct in that way. However, there is something else going on inside for us to resolve. If it's happening in our society, it's ours to resolve. The important thing to remember is that resolution doesn't end there; it begins there. We can react to issues out of anger or fear, or we can follow how the loving works through those issues. The process is different for each person. Sometimes we must stand up and challenge what is false. Remember, love is synchronous and it creates a magnetic vortex in which all of our choices continue to broadcast like satellites finding a way to re-enter loving. Choices are bank shots that all ultimately aim for the love pocket. The so-called bad shots are just bank shots, but love still finds its way, always. Love is never lost.

Truth Cannot Hide

It is amazing when we wake up to loving in relationship to our karmic identity. When we remember that we are love, the karma is discontinued. In other words, the purpose of any issue or disturbance is to find a way to transform ourselves into loving. When we do that our world changes. We have more grace in our life, more synchronicity. We enjoy ourselves more even though we may be caught up in a bad situation. Through loving, we don't take things so personally. If we consider that life is guided by synchronous love always sneaking around and getting its way, then we are living on a higher plane. With synchronous love, the choice of truth is evident and spontaneous in any event. We can observe the ways that deeper purpose is working. Alternatively, we can see that fear is controlling people and we can choose to avoid being controlled by fear ourselves. We can see to act where it helps, truly helps, rather than acting in a way that adds to the conflict. That is a very important discernment and ultimately a turning point.

When we reach forks in the road and we practice the Presence of synchronous love we build a habit and we always pick the right road because we have so much helpful experience and multidimensional guidance channeling through the lens of the moment. Eventually we have an inner guidance that knows how to track higher causalities in life. Inner guidance leads us through love that is entangled with wisdom everywhere. Inner guidance is synchronous in the now moment of our experience.

Another misunderstanding is that we have a lot of ideas, viewpoints and projections about what God's love should look like and why bad things seem to be allowed, unjustly of course. To clarify, it's sometimes challenging to get past our own prejudices to see the wholeness. Our tendency is to segment and isolate elements of reality in order to exert control, even if that control is to make ourselves less than we are. Encountering the unconditional loving of wholeness can be confounding and confusing. I spoke earlier that we get what we pay attention to. Unconditional loving is unconditional; therefore it supports everything. It is supporting us in everything that we pay attention to and this is also a little confronting for us. To embrace the wholeness of unconditional loving, we must change who we think we are. We need to think of ourselves as integral to wholeness. As a synchronous sentient being, we are connected to all life and in our place, we have agency as a conduit of unconditional love and wholeness, to all that is. What we choose and what we pay attention to is responsive and it doesn't go out of its way because it is every way. I was going to say "go out of its way to help" but it doesn't. Nothing is out of its way. When we seek to gain through the exploiting or dominating of anything, we are diminishing and corrupting ourselves. When we reside in our truth, we are indistinguishable from everything, and everything is a relative in a complex system of relationships.

Whatever Seems

If we get too distracted in trying to fix ourselves, find our limitations in terms of what's broken about us, what we have to fix, or what we have to do to get better, then life will give us more things to fix because that is the kind of support we seem to be asking for. So what do we do with that? Well when we shift to our internal reference and measure to loving, we can ask: what do we want to improve, need to resolve, or have unfinished business around, which is usually answered in the form of many things that haven't been resolved into loving? There are many aspects in our lives that we want to do, resolve or wake up to. We get to have those aspects because we are working just fine. We can change one of the biggest obstacles in our lives by realizing the false reference that there must be something innately wrong with us, that we must fix in order to be good, to be whole or to be successful. One of the ways we use this truth is through taking on challenges—whether they are as simple as repairing a light switch to resolving racism in the world or bringing peace to war zones or sweeping the floor—and realize that they are of interest and not something we must do to be good or more spiritual. That is the spectrum, the continuum of our reference points that reflect our challenges.

Whether we are a perpetrator or a victim, when we start using everything to transform ourselves into loving, and we wake up to loving in order to transform ourselves into loving, we are making a choice that adds to the consciousness of humanity. We are choosing a consciously loving way to live. This way to live is not composed of a list of behaviors or laws or control, but a style...a loving way to live. This path promotes loving that will mesh with any creed, any viewpoint, or any philosophy, and use it for the greater good. As Transcendental Leaders, living through love is what we were created to be and to do. Whatever seems to be going on or whatever else we appear to be doing or being as our role in the symphony of life, as Transcendental Leaders, we are synchronously participating and creating reality through a frequency of love in each moment.

Passport

Consider that we are building an Ego. What good is the Ego if it resides in misunderstanding? Well that's partly what the Ego was designed to do. Throughout our developmental experience we build our Ego so that we can function in this world and fulfill our destinies on earth. Our Ego is a combination of the sense we make out of Soul purposes and world realities. When we get into situations and circumstances in our lives we often make choices in which we are defined by external expectation and demands instead of Soul truth. When our Ego construction strays too far from our center to the point of attenuating the Soul's voice, our soul impulses are reversed in our Ego expression. Reversals approach from the mirror of life acting as adversaries, creating conflicts and often posing as friendly enticements, though these reversals are ultimately subversive encounters. We inadvertently live our reversals *as if* they were our true or Soul self.

The reflection of Ego is amazing. I used to have a repetitive dream in which a person was chasing me and I thought they were going to kill me. It went on for years. And so I started reading a few books about dreams and discovered something about lucid dreaming. In lucid dreams, we are awake in our dreams and have choice. I decided one night when I was dreaming to just stop running. I turned around and faced the one that was chasing me. It was very embarrassing. It turned out to be me. I'd been running away from myself all those years. I was running from my true self as a centered, loving, responsible, powerful being with the essence of God living in me. Ego is like that and when excessively shaped by outer concerns, Ego will often deny the truth of self.

The Ego is designed to be effective in the world and help us learn how to function well at the level of society or culture we are living in. It's very tribal in that sense and usually tied to a location. We can reincarnate enough and embody these different locations inside of ourselves and after a while we start noticing that one location is like the other and there's really not that much difference. We all live in a deep-ecology of the same planet, so we invent things that do similar things, realizing this mutuality is a process of maturing the Ego. Part of spiritual growth is learning not to kill the Ego or do away with it. There have been religious practices that have tried to suppress or kill the Ego but they didn't work. Let's work toward maturing the Ego and incorporating it into something bigger because we *can* do that. Our Ego needs to find its place in the fabric of life. We need to honor the Ego's basic survival purpose, while guiding the higher evolution of the Ego as an emissary of the Soul.

The Ego is like a passport into the world. When we go places, we know that the authorities will let us go there because we're official. At each border or boundary, we are given a stamp in our passport, recording our passage into that country. If we don't have a healthy Ego, we don't have a passport or the stamp, so boundaries become barriers, or walls. A healthy Ego will allow us to go anywhere because we can stand up for ourselves, we can make choices, we can know who we are in relation to other people, or who we are in general or at least hopefully make a distinction. This becomes a practice for us to love our Ego, our personality and our style. All we want to do is to orient our Ego so that it becomes more congruent with the mysterious Soul that we have been inviting into our awareness as our core self. We invite the mysterious Soul, this inner sense of substance that transcends everything, into ourselves. We want to bring this congruency so we can tell when we are resonating with the Soul. We will know because our Ego will relax. In other words, when our Ego resonates with the Soul, it loses its fear. The Ego is generally very fear oriented. Most of that fear comes in because Ego is attached to the body, and we need to survive and live long enough to gain experience without dying. Whether our Ego as our passport is love-based or fear-based it will get us into the country of our travels and, perhaps, one day get us into the "promised land."

We carry beliefs about who we think are, and those beliefs can be very stubborn. If we change our beliefs, our survival instincts often think we will die, so we need a little finesse sometimes to change them. I just love the word finesse. I like the way finesse sounds. It's a quick way to reach an understanding. Finesse implies being subtle and gentle and making a smooth bank shot. You remember bank shot: "mistake" shot off the rail into the love pocket. Let's find our way and see if we can work our lives so that the negatives and the positives can both be utilized to get us to our resolution of the challenge at hand. Finesse is one of those terms that brings in the Soul.

Our passports need to be kept up to date if we are going to travel through countries, social or ethnic groups, or the inner dimensions of consciousness. We must keep our Ego up to date if we want to have a little freedom of movement here on earth, and using the analogy of correspondence, the internal realities of heaven. By "up to date" I mean that when Ego works through fear, it is tied to all the things in the past where we judged ourselves or judged others out of our fear, which makes the Ego superstitious of the future. By updating our Egos, we have to bring all of those fears and judgments forward and become current and transformed into loving. Then, once we bring all of those fears and judgements up to date, we must act as if we did the update. We may reminisce about the past, but it no longer defines us, just like a passport is not our identity. It's a credential that lets us navigate the world. The Ego is just a passport but it is not our Soul. The Soul needs the passport to navigate this world. When our Ego is synchronous, our passport gives us a world level credential for sanctuary...we can travel anywhere. Our passport Ego is time bound, our Soul is eternal.

Synchronous Love

Now that we are masters of our house, we turn to the passkey of simplicity through which all movement and Presence is coordinated: synchronous love. All this work we are doing with Transcendental Leadership is intended to take advantage and cultivate our aptitude for conscious synchronous creativity. And, for me anyway, it has taken getting a lot of ideas that limit the scope of my humanity out of the way.

The guiding principle of creation is that *love will have its way*. The way we coordinate our lives with that principle is by using everything to transform ourselves into loving. As we fully open our hearts to all that is, we enter a synchronous relationship with the heart of everything; with humanity, with nature, with the elements of the earth and sky, with solar systems, universes and galaxies, with the infinitesimal creatures that knit the framework of reality and the immense Being that inhabits the matrix. We are connected through love with all that we love, then in the distinctions of the locality in which we live, we have recreational challenges.

Head Heart Narratives

The first step into the synchronous awareness of love is to dissolve or change all the beliefs and accretions we have built up to protect our hearts. When we were hurt growing up, we built armor around our hearts, we became habituated and normalized into that state. Now we are aware that we have a sacred dimension within our heart and we would like to go to that dimension. When we try to enter the sacred dimension, we encounter beliefs, ideas, protections and superstitions from which we built up ideas about ourselves and what it's like to love or not love. The continuity of our work is through forgiving and resolving beliefs that limit our loving. Even with tender work, residues remain in our energy field that have a pattern of earlier times when we were less acquainted with our loving.

As much as we've done to resolve limiting barriers so that we can go into the sacred place in our heart, there's a filament, a membrane or armoring that has patterns that we put there to protect our heart. This armoring still holds a place in our consciousness. We can ask ourselves "what are the ways those barriers continue to stylize my personality"? What is it about my personal style that is still using those barriers as a template for living and loving that puts a slight distortion on the way I exchange my loving with people, or how I hold my space, or protect myself, open up to people, or experience myself as integral to the unitive love that is the fabric of creation?

When we are with a group that holds a relational center of loving, that continual reflection of love helps to keep us centered. When we are away from that group, we can gradually run down and dissipate our center-holding love and our orphaned places (times in which our self-beliefs did not incorporate love) begin to assert themselves, even organize into tribelets. We can consciously step back into those spaces/times and incorporate loving in those memories and balance the pattern. However, when we touch into these places unconsciously, they start to collaborate with similar elements in our environment and we start collecting allies for our own shadows that we didn't know we had. Those elements reinforce our old patterns. Then we will go into a style of being that's not quite authentic. In learning to rest in loving, we learn that the purpose for looking at these issues is to consider how important it is to stay vigilant and aware, and keep making small adjustments and polishing our loving. These small tune-ups are going to make a big difference while we continue to keep our beloved circle of friends close to us.

Along with the heart, the other basic center is the head center. Loving is circulating through the head as well, and then the part that goes between heaven and earth, the Transcendent Self has the ability to hold in the universal dimensions of loving consciousness. When we started out with soul transcendence, people said "Put your attention on the Tisra Til (pineal) and wake it up." The Tisra Til is a doorway...a passage into the far country of Soul. Maybe the doorway opened twenty years ago when we were first studying ways to awaken to Soul, and now we take holding our will in that frequency for granted. It's another very subtle thing because life's always pulling us here and there.

What we don't account for is that our perception of life, though convincing, isn't quite as it seems. Perhaps it never is or was. We become accustomed to our shared jargon because we've been working so much in the light together. The jargon itself becomes a narrative, and our narrative about the light becomes a distortion of the light. And because of the way our psyche works, our Basic Self, our survival self, takes that distortion as reality. Maybe we need a narrative check. Have we gotten to a place of consciousness where we've created a closed loop with our narrative, a narrative of our heart, a narrative of our head, a narrative of our relationships and our groups, our studying the light, and our narrative about Transcendental Leadership? We get a really good feeling going and then the loop closes so that we're in a universe of our own perception. Any time that happens we're not integrated with the field of everything. We are not living in the synchronous flow of the creative universe. In an odd way we are synchronous with the out-of-sync frequencies in the universe and co-creating with imbalance. If there are forces that do this, perhaps we can join them. When I was in the army and we had a mission, we would synchronize our watches and orient our compasses so that our maneuvers would be synchronous. By analogy, our time piece is our life on earth and we are on a mission, we synchronize our time pieces to Soul so that our heart is our compass.

We Get What We Are

Synchronous creativity fits into the setup and framework we're living in: the head, heart, center, periphery, and circumference. The heart center keeps us in reality, and through the vertical axis spirit is flowing in and out of us into life, incorporating all of our beliefs that code the frequencies of our life-field. In this way our reality reflects to us our internal programing. That's the setup.

We can always count on reality being exactly like we are. That's good news, and kind of scary. Life is just going to show us ourselves and when we really grasp this, we can look at reality on two levels. One is the Soul level where we are consciousness as a lens of the light, where circulation of the "all" love is going through us, a condition in which our axial alignment is in pattern resonance with our breathing in and out of creation. When we're embodied in this Soul place, synchronous frequency is coming through. It comes through and is present all the time, but I'm talking about being conscious of it. We are usually conscious on the Ego level. The Ego is embedded in the synchronous matrix regardless of our awareness. On the Ego level we identify with whatever patterns that are in our personal field. These are Ego patterns that we invented, borrowed, implanted, enculturated or inherited. We are a distinction between the personality and the Soul, or the Ego and the Soul, not as an oppositional distinction because Ego and Soul live as an integral expression, but because they're looking in different frequencies of the mirror. One of our basic challenges is finding out how we stay in the light. To stay in the light, we need to be present with what is and see what we notice, and then we respond. It can be that simple. Everything else will take care of itself because we meet ourselves in the Presence of the light. The synchronous dialogue of past, present, future, above and below forms the narrative of our life for good or ill. The invitation to Transcendental Leadership occurs when our loyalty is to love and love is the measure of life. In that way we become conscious of the synchronous relationship of our consciousness with the flow of everything.

When we're in a consciousness of acceptance, we are accepting everything our perception is showing us. That's different than agreement or viewpoint or having other ideas about our perception. Our attitude is in acceptance. Then there's the consciousness behind acceptance, the Soul. When the Soul looks out, or when we look out as Soul, then we have awareness of synchronous creativity.

Synchronous Soul

We think of creativity as having an idea, planning our idea, and putting it into action. But really, creativity just is. The invention or innovation we are seeking is seeking us. Synchronous creativity is co-dependent or collaborative depending on the frequency pattern of our own identity. Whatever the setup is that we are, we're making our reality all the time. We are collaborating, and "God knows" what else is collaborating with us. That's a true statement, "God knows." By tapping into that idea, we move into a very different relationship to our creativity. We may have our Ego making plans talking to people, and loving the fame, but the Soul is present in a different alignment. The Soul is in collaboration with everything, whereas the Ego tends to be co-dependent, colluding with its reflection from life and who it believes it is. The Soul is inherently in collaboration with everything and is conscious of the truth that creation is synchronous, whereas the Ego does not understand that with each moment, as the Buddha is alleged to say, "each moment we are building up or tearing down our reality."

From the Soul's viewpoint, we see all of reflections of life that the Ego sees. But we also see the Soul on the other side of the mirror looking back at itself. When the Soul looks at something, it simultaneously sees an inside/outside perception. When the Soul looks through the inside/outside perception, the Soul is also looking back through creation from outside of creation. It's not just like looking in the mirror in the morning and combing our hair. Soul is *looking* in through the obverse side of the mirror *combing our face*. It's like that, as well as, it's a bunch of fractals revealing where every belief, every texture, and everything going on in creation has a little refractive participation. The mirror is everything, everywhere.

The home of the Soul is the other side of the mirror looking back through the mirror. When Soul is looking back at us, it's also looking back through everything. You're looking out from the Soul and every other Soul is looking back at you throughout everything else. Souls can be in the same place at the same time. I know we are kind of fond of having an individual Soul, but it's just individually conscious while it's connected with everybody else. Soul is individual, but it's also not individual.

The Soul is tracking in a very different way. Soul is present with synchronicity, the synchronous everything. The mind can't keep up with that. In Soul Presence, there is a spontaneous collaboration going on, and we only know what that collaboration is doing if we are intimate with it. This is another way to look at bilocation; we are in our Soul and we are also in our personality. Our Soul is always sitting behind our personality, informing our personality.

The only way I know to stay in synchronous Soul is to be so loyal to loving that love will hold us in the place of synchronous Soul. There's a place in the heart that holds incarnational love, and there's a place in the head that holds the transcendent love. We hold incarnational and transcendental love in the same place and we allow love to hold us in that space. We can probably touch this continuance of love in spiritual exercises, in that inner silent place. It's kind of eerie sometimes, because when you get into that place everything else seems unreal, but then you must act like it's real because everything is watching, and besides it is the joy of living on earth.

Total Responsibility

For many years, I've heard the statement, *the blessings already are*. I have discovered that we are the blessing that already is and the blessings we are to receive already exist. The blessings function as a synchronous flow of love through the matrix of reality. This statement reminds us that in the synchronous nature of Soul exists a simultaneous time dimension in which everything also exists. So how does our reality come about? How does the Soul play a part in bringing things about? The Soul is bringing everything into Presence for us and at the same time, as we are doing our due diligence in the world, the Soul is active, negotiating all that will come to be with all that is and has been. All Souls reside in the synchronous depths of all that is. Souls are out of the *Word*, the Sound current of creation, and Word made flesh and the one dwelling in the world. As Soul we have an implicit responsibility to exist and be present in whatever world we find ourselves.

Can we live in chaos and peace at the same time? Living in harmony with duality is a measure of synchronous creativity. How do we practice synchronous creativity? Well, let's turn on the news and then practice staying in peace while we watch the news. It's a good exercise. When watching the news we are aware of our synchronous collaboration with complexity. Practice staying in that synchronous place. It's not just a calm place, it is also a noisy place. When we get conscious of these dimensions, it turns into a space. That space has its own breathing and anatomy. While we are watching and being present, we also watch ourselves watching and being present.

Synchronous consciousness is our total responsibility. Whenever feelings come in, just treat them as information. Be present with the information. As soon as we do that the feeling starts telling on itself, whether feeling is coming from outside or inside, or feeling may be leading us to something new. Even if something creates a bad feeling it might be the light trying to bring us something. But if we can't tell where the light is coming from, or if it is present at all, we are still identifying with our feelings. Try watching that one place where a feeling comes in and don't identify with it. One way we can know is when somebody offends us, we want to punch them. That's identifying with a feeling, right? You are sad, so you identify with the sadness. And maybe you don't think you are identified with sadness, and then somebody tries to talk you out of being sad and you start arguing with them. You have identified with the feeling of sadness. "No, that's me, and I have to protect it." To gain strength in our Soul we practice watching out for identifying with our feelings.

Part of staying with seeing our feelings as purely information and not identity is that ability to hold our identity in loving. Not the "in love with" idea but loving. A loyalty to loving is the only identity necessary. It's like learning how we function and using it differently. Ask yourself, what do you choose to identify with? In the consciousness of asking this question, we start building up a quality that is soul-identified. That soul quality will discern self from the information that is coming in or up as feelings, and then we move our attention to seeing feelings as information and start accessing or unpacking what the information is about, how we can learn from it or choose an appropriate response.

Research

Researching how our synchronous creativity works, begins with studying the ways it is working, how it keeps us navigating through life and keeps our life intact, and how our Soul qualities and personality traits collaborate with our synchronous creativity. Learning how our collaboration helps us realize that our synchronous creativity is functioning perfectly. Once we catch on to how it's working perfectly, then we can take responsibility and change the information we choose to feed into our synchronous creativity. We can change the code, we can decide which codes to change, and we can choose out of one code and into another code. Since changing the code is synchronous the wholeness is changing the code with us. That relationship is the essence of our knowledge and skill. We are like a simultaneous sorcerer's apprentice to the universe.

Researching in the light is always quite simple. The light is where loving exists in and of itself, where loving is. And that's the ideal state of loving and light. How is this state of loving and light embodied practically in life? It could look like everything. In my prayer, I say "Thy will be done." What I have discovered for myself is that God's will is easy to understand. It's just an affirmation that *love will have its way*. We are always living in this insight, understanding or knowing. *Love will have its way* is not just a trust, but a knowing that everything we see going on in the world is some version of *love having its way*, so our detective work, despite all appearances, is discovering how *love having its way* is going on...how we are *loving having its way*. We each need to develop our own hermeneutics by which we can discern and interpret the frequency of *love having its way*, so that eventually we have a developed perceptual lens that has perfect discernment.

Coding

While we are still identified with the way things are, or the way things have been, or the way we would like them to be in the future, we can't change anything because our conditioned-self (Basic-Self) will sense change as the equivalent of suicide. The instinct of the body is to survive and that instinct incorporates belief systems that underpin our identity. We can try to dominate the conditioned-self with an assertion of will, but all that does is vote for the dominator model and a fear-based reality as an internal policy. We need a passkey to change the code. That passkey is *intention plus loving*. Self-forgiveness is an example of a passkey that changes the code. Having said that, until we can manage grace, we have the fallback of the law of cause and effect (Karma) or human laws that allegedly enable civilization to function. Living by the law of cause and effect is an ancient practice that works when that is our level of ability, but in the long run it's not enough. The karmic law changes texture when it is held in grace. Somebody always finds a way to control and dominate through the law. Law without love is ultimately an adverse spirit.

Once we learn to align in living love, it's easier to identify with the truth of ourselves and use that as the reference point for evaluating actions by us and toward us in the world. The measure of all thoughts, beliefs, actions, results, rules and mysterious events and apparitions of light is always love. Whether an action is destructive or constructive, it's all referenced to loving. Whether the frequency goes this way or the frequency goes that way, it's just a matter of a strategic reversal. But frequency comes out of loving and to that end it will ultimately return. Our coding makes or creates the distortion and the remedy.

Privilege

We have a transformational habit of doing a therapeutic dance with our shadow as if it were the dark side in a polarity. This dance is not much different than a cosmology of battles between good and evil, wars of conquest like those in the *Bhagavad Gita*, monsters surfacing from the deep in Revelations, or the clash of civilizations. When we have a conflict or issues arise for us, we call for the light. Do we do this as a rescue or bridge, or to disperse or to activate the vortex of our consciousness called synchronous creativity? We have always been transformers acting through the whole and reflexively creating wholeness. We just have been unconscious of our capacities as transformers. Up until now we have needed to filter our unconscious realm so we will not get inundated with too much content. Transcendental Leadership invites a perspective in which we awaken in a realm larger than the unconscious, thus enabling synchronous transformation.

Transcendental Leadership

Our transformational habits may well be transformational arrogance in that we strive to obtain spiritual skill or power. Maybe we get overambitious and say, "I just want the light to bring everything up that is unresolved," and when it does, we are often overwhelmed and our life seems to go haywire, and we wonder what happened. Well the light is helping us according to our request. The learning flow, or karmic flow (life-learning and resolution curriculum) has a grace and each challenge comes in due course when we trust our life. Wanting to speed our lessons out of our spiritual ambition may not be in our best interest. The request to do so is often Ego centered and has the intention of gaining a spiritual power of advantage. When we become aware that we have fallen into a pattern of ambition, we can ask for the drama to step back a bit and cool off and just allow what we can handle. Our request to accelerate our learning can come from a kind of arrogance that thinks we know what it is to be spiritual, how we want to be known as a leader, or an idea of something we want to become. Wanting secret knowledge or siddhas (spiritual powers) is a kind of a deception. In our narrative about the light there may be goals, objectives and ideal states that are really fantasies or outright decoys about what the higher light or what synchronous creativity is.

Just because we have a title, an office, or power, holding the mantle does not mean that we have privilege. Privilege is determined by how we treat others when being in a role of authority or direction. Privilege assumes loving when some other voice is speaking. Negativity can ride in on our speech as tone, inflection, emphasis and even domination. In our righteousness we can deviate from or reject acceptance and make others wrong, or wrong for speaking against our agenda, when they challenge what we are doing. Beware that a false "God" may have co-opted our loving intention through our illusion of privilege.

In the World, Not of It

A woman in our classes in Switzerland had a very beautiful and clear process with I Am Soul, Master of My House. It was a perfect metaphor for her. She had been a professional clown when we first met her and as time went on, she married and had two children and took a break from our classes. Recently, she was back in our classes with her full force. For me she demonstrated an awareness of her life that illustrates a degree of synchronous awareness, synchronous creativity and Transformational Leadership. Her sharing from class follows:

I would like to share a beautiful image I had. I don't remember when during the meditation. I really cleaned up. I did a lot of cleaning in many, many rooms in my house. After a cleaning session, a she-wolf and an eagle appeared. They were very beautiful. I welcomed them and realized that I was both simultaneously. With regard to the she-wolf, I'm really the she-wolf that takes care of herself. I take care myself. I protect my children. Very concretely I feed them since I'm still breast-feeding the last one. So that's very strong. So that image of the she-wolf, I know her. And what was new was realizing that I was also that eagle and that eagle can see very far away, and it can dive.

I heard a shrieking cry from the eagle and the sound of the wind. I could easily fly as the eagle and see great vistas. I see myself very, very small flying and sitting across from it, whereas before I used to feel I was it. It may be that the bird, the eagle itself, is taking up more space. It has grown. I saw that very strongly. And last night in my house cleaning in those rooms I opened the door and in my door there was my brother-in-law. I closed the door again saying all of that will be for tomorrow.

Now it's tomorrow. This morning very early around five o'clock I went on with the cleaning and I told myself no, I'll do it in the group. It will be nice. And in the group meditation, I was really able to welcome him and ever since then I've had a big pain here. So I embrace it. I did a lot of self-forgivenesses for all of those times when I'm dishonored and when I am sticky or not clear. In terms of my brother-in-law, there isn't anything that is especially difficult for me. I hardly ever see him. But I'm realizing right now that as I think about it, what is difficult for me is that my sister is with him. I think that the problem is that when I tell myself that she chooses that, she chooses him and she chooses to live with him.

She is older. It's like some kind of childhood pact was forgotten. So there is a loss of that or a violation of that. I feel now there is a part of me now that is so sad for her actually. She may not be suffering, but there may not be the joy there either. I need to honor that place inside that we share. It's like another room in my house. I can go in there with her and renew our vows.

Lately I have really felt my clown coming back into my life. The wish to be a clown again is coming back. And part of me says when will I have time to work as a clown again? I am already there with my kids, but more official clowning. I feel like I'm letting it blossom. I already have a few ideas. I have a clown room where all the history advises me.

Maybe I am renewing our vows with myself as well as my sister. I think with regard to my maternities which are over, our latest baby is nine months old, I feel like that is the reason the eagle showed up now. Now there are both. That's why I feel the wish and the availability to again be a clown as well. Life is good and great. When I consider that everything has its season, what comes up is the closeness that I had with my daughter the other day. It was so full of love and while it was happening at the same time, I felt nostalgia for it. I was in it, and while I was having it, I was telling myself that this moment is going to pass. I was saying tomorrow she's going to be an adult and the day after tomorrow I will be very old. It was new to me saying that to myself. And I could feel that for the teens I really need to be present to be in the moment. That's the she-wolf and the eagle together.

One way to understand the metaphor of the *she-wolf and the eagle together* is as an ability to hold in our *intent* and *observation*. Our mastery is in our ability to be self-aligned in our location. This alignment can apply to physical location, but here I am speaking of embodied spiritual location, which is how we anchor in our synchronous creativity. The vectors of this location are intent and observation. In our synchronous evolution, we are continually trained in precise intention and observation. When our intent is lock-focused into loving our observation perceives the multitude of elements in our field re-arranged to reflect loving. Loving is the synchronous process and context for meeting life. We meet life in the moment which is the content of our experience. In this sense we are a reality node, an intersection of realities unique to our Presence. We take responsibility for our node while the whole-system takes care of everything else.

To manage our synchronous reality, we continually refine our sense of locality. Synchronous reality is multidimensional and present everywhere and exists in a continual collaborative conversation that relationally and spontaneously informs reality. We are all participating in this consciousness in some degree of synchronous and asynchronous participation. We contribute to and are a recipient of the resulting creation and the efficiency and effectiveness of that system. When we are in an asynchronous participation, we are unaware that we are out of phase with, but not exempt from, synchronous participation. In other words, our state of consciousness has immediate consequences, but we are not aware of that.

As our evolution carries us into a greater consciousness of our place (nodal location), we experience a refined sensitivity to our place and the total field. When we become distracted from the nucleus of our soul, our nodal location, we lose our creative positioning. We are lost and do not know it. We always believe what we appear to be. In this way the one creative love appears as the whole and arises as the individual within each of us. In this way, our reality matches the level of our ability in which we function or the level that appears to us. Our limitation is an illusion, yet without limitation we would go crazy. Thus the necessity to trust our incremental awakening becomes clear. The key to synchronous mastery is practicing being present with what is and observe what we notice, then love will handle the rest.

We Are the Blessing

Synchronous Creativity is the transcendent form of I Am Soul: Master of My House. As we choose the frequencies in our house, we are choosing the world in which we live. We are the agency of a "new day and new dawn," as formulated in our consciousness with each breath. We are the prophesized one we have been waiting for. We are the blessing.

The fabric of the universe works together. "Mycelium" love is the connective tissue of life. We participate in that connectivity according to the varied lens of our perception. We follow the song of our Soul into the high country. In the realm of the soul beyond the reflections of life, we sort out the true from the false. The passkey into the Soul realm is love, all of it. From the transcendent perspective of Synchronous Creativity, we see that when we choose, we choose for everyone, which is a big responsibility and encourages us to bless each breath, thought and act, not out of a concern of shame and doing harm, but out of a desire to be love to all at all times as an evolutionary imperative and purpose to our lives.

Synchronous Creativity is the matrix through which the Transcendental Leader operates. In that resonance the Transcendental Leader joins the power of the collective Soul. When we join in the collective power of the Soul, we become a powerful force of change, healing and support for each other, regardless of where we live or the condition of the world. Much of the world reacts to pandemics, and economic and political challenges through the smallness of their fear and lack, which may be an important perspective for survival. From the perspective of the Soul, events in the world are all opportunities to transform ourselves and the world into loving. In our study of Transcendental Leadership, we have explored ways to align in the consciousness of Soul, center in living love, explore ways to join in the Presence of the collective soul, and ways to evaluate events in the world as opportunities rather than limitations. From the collective power of Soul, we look at the current challenges in the world as a process of giving birth to a new way for humanity.

The way of the Transcendental Leader is always simple. It is the ability to walk on planet earth as a Presence of living love. It's just where loving exists in and of itself, where loving is, and that's the ideal state. How does this loving Presence look in the embodied practically of life? It could look like everything depending on where we are on the fear/love continuum. It is not just a trust, it *is* trust, and a knowing that whatever we see going on in the world is some version of *love having its way*. Our one intention, then, is "to use everything to transform ourselves into loving, then the transformation of the world into loving can take place." (J-R)

In gratitude we speak truth to power while letting love lead. Our detective work, and essential intention, is in discovering how we are *letting love lead* and how we might more fully participate in the mystery of *love having its way.* Perhaps there are no adversaries, only forgotten or unknown parts of ourselves, though obverse, trying to help us remember that we are love trying to find our way home to our embodied Soul on earth, retrieve our refugee selves from the adverse provinces in which we have believed we must reside, and remember our transcendent home in the far country of the heart of all that is our origin. As Transcendental Leaders we must awaken to our origins and take up the cause of building a life on earth that reflects, nourishes, and actualizes the life of our Soul for ourselves, our communities, all human kind, the natural world and all of its inhabitants and embrace our stewardship even as we journey into the stars. We make a difference in life by first remembering that we are the difference.

Meditation

Once again bring your awareness into your space touching into your heart. As you follow your breathing just begin to follow the flow of that energy through you, breathing in the loving from the world and from above and below into your heart and out through your body through every cell into your space. As you do that, just be aware that you're changing what you have done with your loving. You are exhaling misunderstood loving and the experience it carries and inhaling loving that's new and that has in it the flow of the divine frequencies.

As you experience the exchange open into your Sacred Heart.

Bring into focus of your attention to the center of your head. As you place your attention there, light opens up and begins to fill the inside of your head, fill your body, merge with the heart, and expand out to fill your space so that it's above you, below you, behind you, in front of you, on each side of you, and through you.

And once again we'll just organize your Presence with the statement, I Am Soul, Master of My House.

In that Presence just touch more deeply into the silence. And with that intention move into that sacred space inside, this inner space in which you create, and just relax into that space, into its silence, into its loving, and into its vastness. With great gratitude you embrace your Presence into this space.

There is this space that you share with God, the creator, and as it is given to you, you give it to life.

Just bring into your awareness something that you would like to have in your life or have more of, perhaps a simple project or practice. It could be more of a certain kind of attitude. But in whatever way you image that to yourself, bring it into your awareness in the Presence of that deep place, begin to dwell with it and fill out the sense of it and the details and the textures and any way you can bring it alive for yourself. And just weave your loving through every fabric, every filament of it. And soon, as you give it form, it begins to pulse with life.

There's a special place where you place your project because you know you need to tend to this over several days, or let's say three days, so we say I'll bring it back out and bring life to it, detail it, make it more tangible. Then on the third day, I'll release it into the wholeness in whatever way I do that. So now put it in its special place.

Now bring forward inside of you what represents to you the feeling of the country in which you are citizens, not to debate about that, just as a simple thing. If you don't know what country you belong to, just look at your passport and acknowledge the trials and tribulations of being human in a human organization striving to achieve human ideals, just acknowledging that and appreciating the journey.

Now, within that higher sense of nation, select how you understand the higher purpose, the higher ideal for which your nation strives to fulfill and understand and give to the world. We're not interested in giving the country a grade on how well it's doing, we're interested in the special project lifting the ideal. So make that ideal central to your Presence. Bring it into your heart. Familiarize yourself with the textures and any other quality that might go with this. Is there a song that goes with this, an anthem? And in your own way of imaging, what images represent this to you? Just formulate those together and hold it in your loving. Honor it. At some point you will feel it begin to pulse. As you do it, it may inform you of aspects about it that you may not have fully realized or appreciated. It may even explain parts of its history that you may misunderstand just to get clear with you.

And again this will be a three-day project, so place it in its special place so it can incubate and return to it tomorrow. Then on the third day release it into the light.

Now let's bring our attention to the planet we live on and as we do this we go into a world healing frequency that expands our room a bit and fills it with light. And in the background is the starry universe. Allow this transition *to occur within you so there is this great space and start feeling the light stream through it. Coming into focus in the center of the space is the image of the planet, a globe with all the features and rotating, and allow it to come into focus. Either see it or sense it so. To begin with, just appreciate it and honor it.*

As you regard it, this beautiful world, the light from the center of your head and the light from your heart begin to move out as a stream of energy and join together and begin to circle the planet finding areas of imbalance, flowing into those places and finding areas of strife, flowing into the hearts and minds of those people. There is a sensitivity to this stream of energy coming from you and it begins to search out where it is needed traveling around the globe.

Now bring the flow of energy into the center of the planet. Light and love begin to coagulate there and expand filling the deep strata of the earth and healing any traumatic fractures. The light soon reaches the surface and begins to coat the whole surface with light and love and expand out. And then at some point it just ignites into a radiant beacon that shines out into the universe. Be present with this while it completes itself.

For now just step upon the planet, feel the flow through the center of you from the earth up into the highest heaven you can connect with. Be aware of the house around you and from the high place of authority that you have, again repeat I Am Soul, Master of My House. Just let that flow. Live in the synchronous house of the Lord.

*When they go low,
we go high.*

Michelle Obama

CHAPTER ELEVEN

As we incarnate into the human condition, the most essential and most forgotten element of life for each of us is that who we are is the one that *brings love*. In our first breath, we encounter an overwhelming challenge to identify with the world in which we find ourselves and forget the world of love from whence we came. From our first breath on, we are negotiating our identity. In order to center into and hold our Presence as Transcendental Leaders, remembering who we are in truth (the one that *brings love*) is essential.

Birth

Birth is like entering a room. How we are received, met, contained, seen, held, or loved forms our sense of self as personality. Perhaps our mother felt unsupported by her family or the space in which we found ourselves at birth felt like we were alone and abandoned or we felt the circumstances of our conception were unwanted and invested with shame. That is the room we enter. We are the one that *brings love,* yet when we are not received with love, we first experience the contrast and perhaps feel disoriented. In our innocence, we must respond to this discrepancy. Later in life we will have reflective choice, but at the alter of birth, we only have reflexive choice. As we enter abandonment and non-support, the experience comes around us like a garment and in that instant, we identify with the feeling of abandonment and non-support. We then believe that who we are is the one who is *abandoned, non-supported* or *the one who brings shame* and we forget that, in truth, we are the one that *brings love*. By choosing, the one that brings non-support, abandonment or shame becomes the seed identity upon which we grow our life and harvest the fruits of the seed. We begin life as a false self, embarking on a journey to remember ourselves, while life colludes to reflect and reinforce our acquired false identity. As the abandoned one, our Basic-Self proceeds to protect that belief.

Our Basic-Self, our body-oriented self, incorporates our choice into our identity and Ego structure. The role of the Basic-Self is survival and continuity. The Basic-Self then, in direct and subtle ways, will protect and preserve who we have decided we are. Whatever we think we are doing on a visionary, spiritual, vocational or relationship level, the Basic-Self is protecting the seed self we planted at birth, breathing ourselves into this world encoding our abandonment, lack, or shame as a way of being. We may wonder then why, no matter what we say or do, abandonment, lack of support or shame finds its way into the equation. (Of course these are not the only false-self or choices made available to us as elements of our karmic welcome, nor, as we will see, is our first encounter void of true-self choices.) Consequently, we are operating with one set of conscious intentions and a different set of unconscious intentions. While we seek to prosper and form positive relationships on the conscious level, on the unconscious level we seek to be abandoned, alone or shamed. We do not notice that we incorporate both intentions, even though we may notice our self-sabotage as we pursue our creative goals.

Life looks at us and cooperates with how we present ourselves and what we pay attention to. Life brings us what we desire or request. How we identify ourselves and what life brings us is what we ask for. Unconditional love supports us in whatever we want to do or be, so if we are getting an adverse response from life, we may be motivated by an adverse desire or request, whether we realize it or not. The seed of identity that we planted upon entering life is having its way, which is oppositional to God's will which is *love will have its way*. The remedy is remembering who we are...*I bring love*.

As Transcendental Leaders, *we bring love*. When we remember who we are, that *I am the one who brings love*, whether we are washing our car, talking to a friend, working in our garden, ministering to a client, painting a picture, administering an organization, building a bridge, leading a march, or voting, each action is a conduit that brings love. Even though we present a false-self intention, life will also see our unconscious purpose to bring love and conspire to bring us opportunities that support us to actualize both. Manifesting a life of abandonment, shame, blame and <u>love</u> simultaneously can be very confusing.

Forgetting

I have experienced some wonderful moments with clients in which we traveled in consciousness to the moment when early on in their lives they were met with challenging circumstances in which they identified with how they were met and forgot who they truly were. In the therapeutic process when we (the client and I) entered the regenerative moment of remembrance, their false self-identity faded as they remembered their true identity: *I bring love*. In that moment they were filled with the awareness that who they truly were is the *one who brings love*. Consequently, the true impulse of love as the seed of their life awoke within them, synchronously converting their patterns of false identity into love.

I met with another client who told me that no matter what she tried or how hard she committed, she could not change her obsession with shame. She had great love which was easily experienced by others, yet she could not let go of her habit of shaming herself or promoting being shamed by others, even in small ways. Shame was like a ghost haunting her house of self. As we talked, I ask her about key times in her life in which shame was an acute experience. She relayed a few instances and then I asked her about her birth and the shame her mother carried. She said her mother was seventeen when she became pregnant with her and was in a very unsupportive relationship with the father. She was given up for adoption immediately at birth. As I guided her to feel into her birth and her mother's consciousness at the time, she could feel the deep shame of her mother and became aware of how she absorbed and identified with that shame.

For my client the sequence of incarnation went something like this: she came to bring love (her true identity), she identified with her mother's shame (I am the one who brings shame.), she created the seed identity (false self) becoming *I am shame and bring shame*, she forgot her true nature as the one that *brings love*, her Basic-Self adopted and defended her identity as shame, life saw her as shame and organized her life accordingly, and the harvest of the seed was a life of being haunted by shame.

As she became conscious of her feelings and identity as shame at birth, I ask her to also become aware of her true self, the one that *brings love* and *is love*. Proceeding slowly and with great care, daring to feel deeply, she was able then to hold both the awareness of *love-self* and *shame-self* simultaneously. My role was to be present with her and hold as a supportive witness while she engaged these two contrasting identities. As she proceeded the shame-self began to fade and the love-self grew in strength as she remembered that she is the one who *brings love*. She forgave herself for believing that she is the one who brings shame.

Changing the seed-self synchronously changed the branches and fruits as the formation of her life. As we sat silently, she experienced the movement of energy as the internal changes proceeded. She said it felt like a death and rebirth. After our session the recalibration and reorganization of her psyche continued for some time. As time went on, the habits of her false-self continued to fade, translating into wisdom and understanding.

In that moment of remembrance, she became a parent to herself, meeting love with love, reparenting herself as she walked through the portal of her first breath making a new seed-self that remembered that her identity was *I bring love*. Often, we make it through the first breath with love and on our way in the next few days or months when the seed-self of *I bring love* is still new and delicate then later the passage slams shut in some form of contextual violence or neglect. Perhaps our crying brought hurt or neglect instead of love making our choice overwhelming and forgetting easy. Being met with love makes us resilient and able to pass through the many challenges of choice. When we have resilience, the seed-self of love survives and grows, though somewhat damaged, yet holds the implicit promise of transformation, healing and remembrance.

Lifestyle

The complex karma of our hopes, dreams, unfinished business and consequences are woven into the frequencies of the archetypal, mental, emotional, imaginal and physical constructs of our conception and birth milieu. We blend those frequencies into our unique personality. The essence of karma is how we meet ourselves in each moment. The resolution and fulfillment of karma comes when we resolve each challenge with love. Regardless of the political, social or moral acceptability of our lifestyle, the test is whether our expression follows in a seamless conduit of the *love we bring* or follows in an agency of our forgotten self, our false-self.

Issues are steppingstones or roadblocks depending on the locus of our identity. (Our use of the term *false-self* is not pejorative but descriptive of our orientation to our karmic process, which is essentially our road to freedom.) As Transcendental Leaders, before we try to fix or mediate our dysfunctional issues, resolve our shadow, or mitigate external hostility we must remember that we *bring love*, then the challenges become practical concerns as required by the nature of living on earth. As Transcendental Leaders, our lifestyle is not the issue. The issue is whether our lifestyle is a seamless conduit of Soul, *I am love, love will have its way*, or an attempt to compensate for our lack, fear, greed, shame or abuse, etc.

The Long View

In remembering our true self, our love-self, as Transcendental Leaders the transformation of the world exists in our ability to be a parent to ourselves and each child born whether literally or metaphorically. Creative love is insatiable and as a consequence many children will be conceived and birthed into this world. The ways we greet them, meet them, hold them, teach them and walk with them with love is essential. As actors in the collective of humanity, when we forget that we bring love the consequence is shared and multiplied within the psyche of humanity. As in the experience of my client, we can remember...we can be born again. Each moment of our lives can be the first breath. We can meet ourselves and each other as parent, as the ones that are reborn and the ones that bring love.

For too long we have recycled through millennia of endemic patterns of forgetfulness, perpetuating the karma from reincarnation to reincarnation, preparing a context for birth that welcomes successive distorted iterations of ourselves by enfolding and compressing love into misogyny, colonizing, entitlement, racism, domination, pride and wealth-divide. (Wealth-divide is not against wealth but for the circulation of abundance and opportunity for all, and the resolution of poverty producing creativity and crippling policies endemic in our culture.) For this to occur we need to realize that each intention and act is a birth which is imbued with Soul (love) or imbued by a forgetting of Soul.

When we create, we imbue our creation with Soul. Buddhists have a saying that with each breath we are either building up or tearing down. In our forgetting of Soul, a different spirit animates our creations whether it is to make a thing, build a business or establish a government. Depending on the nature of our forgetting, we imbue our creation with the false-self (Soul imposter) energy of fear, lust, greed, hate or the cold absence of love that is materiality. We lose our ability to see and converse with love, life and intelligence that radiates from all creation. We lose awareness of our Soul connection with all creation and the genius that comes from that relationship.

Not to despair...awareness is freedom. Our successive incarnations also imbue each lifetime with our evolving power of love, with the impetus to strive for freedom, awakening, transformation and return to home. Home is the Soul within seeking to return home within the heart of God. Implied in our forgetfulness is our evolutionary imperative in which we have tried to replicate paradise on earth. At our core is an incessant drive to actualize the will of God which is that *love will have its way*. Over lifetimes we build resilience and push through any specter of negativity at birth, which enables us to enter the world relatively unscathed by the temptation from false choice and forgetfulness, and some births receive us as the one who brings love with love...with truth and wisdom enabling us to meet the challenges of life in this world.

When we walk in nature, we remember we came to *bring love*...we easily become aware that there is an animating spirit. In this way we are more like the All Parent and made in the "image and likeness of the All Parent." The All Parent is the Gnostic concept of the Father/Mother God. The Gnostic Lord's Prayer references the All Parent in lieu of the "Our Father...." Transcendental Leaders embody the love of the All Parent and pays it forward into the progeny of each breath, touch, thing made, art expressed, relationship embraced, organization formed...life caressed.

Challenge

Transformation through remembering our true identity (that we came to *bring love*) may not be so easy at first. For some of us this approach is so counterintuitive that releasing our minds sufficiently so we can walk through the forgotten door to our true self, the self that *brings love*, may at first be a bridge too far. The process is most effective when we are vulnerable and in touch with our feelings. Opening our connections between our physical and subtle bodies enables us to feel subtle energy movements as sensations in our body. For the most part, with some coaching, we are ready for our version of my client's experience, finding the moment of our choice by imagining ourselves there fully in the choice point encounter between false-self and love-self.

As we incarnated, the love-self entered the environment of our karmic vibration. Depending on the resilience of our love-self, we identified to varying degrees with the challenging identities in the karmic environment into which we were born. The Soul incarnating process continues over our lifetime. During our developmental years with each cycle of life, our developing physical body can accommodate a greater voltage from the incarnating Soul. Rudolph Steiner had a theory that trauma in a developmental cycle could distort our energetic relationship with life in a negative way and cause an exaggerated flow of negativity to and from our environment. Throughout our lifespan, on the physical, imaginal, emotional and archetypal dimensions of our personality, we develop greater receptivity to Soul or to a distorted perspective of forgetfulness and false identification. The impact of this internal dance is evident in the world today.

The incarnating Soul is timeless, adapting to embodiment, personality and the contextual resonance of life's circumstances. Remember creativity is synchronous. As we awaken to Soul (*I bring love*) the harvest changes and in the *blinking of an eye...there is a new day and a new dawn*. Remembrance is never too late. The *I bring love* identity continues to seek incarnation throughout our lifespan. There may be numerous instances throughout the lifespan in which we are met with love or met with adversity in which we identify with the adversity and forget Soul. We adapt our sense and belief of self to the claims of life and the authority of a reflected external reality, continually trading our center for the safety, security, nurture, esteem and power as promised by the politics of external authority, resulting in submission to opportunistic identities and the abdication of love. Our belief in spirituality may become enshrined in icons, statues, objects, edifices and dogma as our Soul-light dims and slumbers within. In each instance of forgetting we can return to the moment of choosing false identity and forgetting Soul. In that moment of forgetting, we can remember that we are the ones that *bring love*, thereby reawakening to love, transforming our beliefs and circumstances. As Soul we take the long view...we are reborn.

The love that we bring is whole and unconditional yet meets life in active and assertive ways. The love we bring meets negative and positive challenges as opportunities to bring love, to transform our selves, situations, and circumstances into loving. In this way, we enable the transformation of the planet into loving to take place. Our love responds with delicate sensitivity and with firm response to challenges. Love uses yes and no to formulate ethics, character, good works and service. In this way the Transcendental Leader is a spiritual warrior that brings compassion to human need and speaks truth to power...brings the power of love to mediate the power of againstsness and forgetfulness.

Remembrance

When we identify with the false self, our ability of *remembrance* goes to the false self. We assign our ability of remembrance to our false self. Remembrance is the ability to remember. In the need to remember that we bring love and the challenge provided by the magnetism of the false self, we are developing the ability of remembrance, sometime against all odds. We use our will and feelings to take back our remembrance from the false self and remember that *we bring love*.

The nature of life on earth is such that it sponsors loyalty to our false self and behaves like a coalition of temptations that aid us to believe that identity and purpose are an external proposition. A coalition and collaboration of false selves evolves into a zeitgeist taking over hearts, minds and nations. The zeitgeist has authority based on our forgetfulness, which is a hypnotic frequency that masks our authority of remembrance in a cloud of illusion telling us that we only exist as our false self. The one who can capture and personify the hypnosis can promote the lie as truth to the nation and become the purveyor of false remembrance. Even though it appears that we have no power or authority over remembrance, sub rosa we retain the authority to take back remembrance.

The sign of the times (zeitgeist) that appeared as the Covid 19 pandemic shook many of the reference points we used to know ourselves, have a place in the world and find our way. This is disorienting at first because these reference points are the underpinnings of our false self. As a teacher once said, whatever can be shaken within you is not you. A measure I used to evaluate the pandemic was the dance between two ancient Greek archetypes (Gods) of *nemesis* and *hubris*. The pandemic was *nemesis* seeking out and shaking any element that was false *(hubris)*, that reflected our arrogance (arrogance being our forgetting and basing our importance of false identity) saying that this was *a time of remembrance*, that the true zeitgeist was remembrance. Our choice is in how we respond to the disillusionment of the structures that sponsor and reinforce the false self. As the illusory grip of the false self on remembrance loosened, we, as Transcendental Leaders, seized the moment and took back our remembrance that who we are is...the one who came to *bring love*.

We Are the Promise

As Transcendental Leaders, we speak truth to ourselves. We translate the ancient wisdom of our Souls' Journey through metaphoric stories. Our "fall from paradise" and the "journey of the prodigal daughter" are such metaphors that tell us that through our participation in life, we are intended to learn the creative power of Soul by embarking on a journey of serial forgetfulness and remembrance as a means of doing so. All wars, injustice, psychological issues, entitlement, domination, privilege and poverty, etc., originate in forgetfulness. Therefore the solution, and the charge of the Transcendental Leader is to remember...to create, promote and allow activities of remembrance that who we are, each of us, is *I bring Love*. As Transcendental Leaders we bring love to fear, abandonment, shame, lust, greed, hate or the cold absence of love that is materiality.

The firmament upon which we stand is Soul and the measuring criteria for evaluating all things is written in our hearts. As well, integral to our sacred heart resides the compass that gives us direction and orientation. As said in the prophecy of old, *we are the promise*. As we remember our true self, our lives transform as if we had not forgotten, with the added benefit of the wisdom gained through the forgetting. As Soul, our creativity is synchronous: by changing the seed, we change the harvest. Remember that we are the ones that came to *bring love*. Let us join hearts and hands and remember that we are the ones who *bring love*.

Meditation

So once again bring your awareness into your space touching into your heart. As you follow your breathing just begin to follow the flow of that energy through you, breathing in the loving from the world and from above and below into your heart and out through your body through every cell into your space. As you do that, just be aware that you're changing what you have believed and done with your loving. You are exhaling misunderstood loving and inhaling loving that's new and that has in it the flow of the divine frequencies.

As you experience the exchange open into your Sacred Heart.

Bring the focus of your attention to the center of your head. As you place your attention there, light opens up and begins to fill the inside of your head, fills your body. Merge with your heart, and expand out to fill your space so that light is above you, below you, behind you, in front of you, each side of you, and through you.

Now remember a time when you felt abandoned, alone or unseen, or shame. If one of these patterns does not resonate for you, substitute another following the same protocol. Be relaxed in that...not to hurry. Allow your feelings to be present and move with those feelings to a deeper place within them. When those feelings are strong, ask yourself: when have I felt this before? When is the first time I can remember when I felt this deep sense of abandonment, being unseen, alone or deep shame? Take your time and move with these feelings and the images that emerge.

Whatever time or place the process of your feelings takes you, pause in that place. Allow yourself to be aware of the feeling in your body and how your sense of self is defined by these feelings and your judgements and beliefs about those feelings and the event they are tied to. Become aware of your identification as the one that is abandoned, unloved, unseen or shame.... Say to yourself, "This is who I believe myself to be."

Be present with this awareness...there is nothing to fix. You need to open now to another awareness that is also present with you and that you are currently unaware of: I am the one that brings the love that I am.

We all came into life as the one that, as love, came to bring love. That is our true self. So, while holding in one hand the energy of false self, allow yourself to remember the true self, the one who came into life to bring love. Touch the energy of true self with your other hand.

At first the sense of your Soul-self, your true self, may be subtle...keep opening to that invitation through the feelings and textures of love energy. Ask to remember the purpose for which you came to life. Notice how that feels in your body and in your awareness. A memory may come to you of the circumstances in which you made this choice. Just be aware of the memory and how you felt and the circumstances of your parents. Let that awareness be the context and bring your attention to the contrast between the one who came to bring love and the one who came to be abandoned, alone or shamed. Now choose again...choose to be the one who came to bring love, let go and allow the conversion between the frequencies of you as love-self and you as false-self to resolve into a new, born again, seed self of love. As the new seed self of love forms...accept that the harvest is here also.

Now review your life and with each regret, trauma, judgment, shame, blame, defeat, mistake...pause for a moment and say: I am the one who came to bring love...I am the one who came to bring love...I am the one who came to bring love.

With each success, spouse, child, lover, business, carrier, building, farm, flight, adventure, art, service, philanthropy, healing, invention, experiment, discovery...pause for a moment and say: I am the one who came to bring love...I am the one who came to bring love...I am the one who came to bring love

GLOSSARY

Ahriman: In Rudolph Steiner's description of the evolution of the Christ in human history through the resolution of the forces of Lucifer and Ahriman; Lucifer was full of too much indulgence and Ahriman was full of too much control and regimentation.

Akashic field: The Akashic field is an energy that permeates the universe and carries memory of human activity, as such it is also formative of reality; it is similar to Bohm's theory of the implicate order and resembles other postulations of subtle energy and dark matter and energy.

American Transcendentalist: The American Transcendentalists flourished in the middle of the 1800s responding to a spiritual impulse; Ralph Waldo Emerson, Phineas P. Quimby, Henry Thoreau, Louisa May Alcott, Walt Whitman, Emily Dickenson and others all had their ways of reaching higher levels within themselves and pulling back the veil of perceptions revealing the role of transcendental consciousness in human affairs.

Archetype: Original Informational constructs, forces and patterns from which all things of the same kind are copied or manifested; in Jungian psychology a collectively inherited unconscious idea, patterns of thought, or image that are formative forces in the human psyche.

Asuras: Transcendent spirits of deception that pose as high beings of light; Rudolf Steiner refers to the spirits of asuras as radiant imposters of light that fool us at a high level of our Ego.

Avatar: The material appearance of a deity incarnating in human form to bring a teaching.

Carl Jung: Swiss founder of Jungian Psychology which had profound impact on the Soul-based approach to psychology in the West.

Chakras: Dynamic energy centers of the body that link our physical and subtle dimensions.

Cosmic Mirror: The universal reflective dimension that holds the created world by reflecting reality; the frontier between the manifest form and unmanifest formless reality.

Dakanawida: Native American peacemaker whose vision inspired the Iroquois Confederation.

Divine Matrix: The spiritual fabric of the universe.

Double split experiment: Photon appearing as wave or particle depending on how it is observed; observer effect.

Doppelganger: A double of an individual in a parallel dimension.

Dragon: A mythological being representing the basic energy of life.

El Shaddai: A name for the ultimate spirit of God carrying the connotation of the living spirit from formlessness into form, from age to age.

Engram: A unit of cognitive information inside the brain, theorized to be the means by which memories are stored as biophysical or biochemical changes in the brain (and other neural tissue) in response to external stimuli.

Enneagram: A system of numbers representing the nine types of human personalities.

Eyes made of soul: our ability to see through the lens of the Soul. Also, *Eyes Made of Soul: Theory and Practice of Noetic Therapy* by Robert Waterman.

Fishes and loaves: A biblical story of Jesus multiplying a fish and a loaf to a number that fed a gathering of many.

Fractals: First named by mathematician Benoit Mandelbrot in 1975. Special mathematical sets of iterative numbers that display similarity through the full range of scale.

Great Tree: An indigenous construct from South America that enables shamans to metaphysically travel to all parts of creation.

Golden ratio or Golden mean: A universal mathematical proportion that appears as the proportional measure of the body, plants, architecture, the orbital path of planets and proportions throughout creation. A metaphysical geometric relationship of the micro and macrocosm as the small part is to the large part as the large part is to the whole.

Hermeneutics: The unpacking or translating of meaning from sacred scripture.

Hiawatha: A colleague of Dakanawida who brought the teachings of the *great tree of peace* to the five tribes of the Iroquois confederation.

Holodeck: A functional energy matrix on the Star Ship Enterprise which projects holographic life-like realities with great realism that is used for recreation and training by the participants.

Holomovement: A term coined by physicist David Bohm for the movement of the whole.

Ho'oponopono: A Hawaiian teaching for the resolution of conflict through living love.

I Am: A spiritual center of authority in the human constitution.

Iroquois Confederation: five indigenous tribes of the North Eastern United States: the **Mohawks**, who call themselves **Kanienkehaka**, or "people of the flint country," the **Onondaga**, "people of the hills," the

Cayuga, "where they land the boats," the **Oneida**, "people of the standing stone," and the **Seneca**, "the people of the big hill."

John-Roger: Spiritual Teacher of Soul Transcendence.

Karma: Law of cause and effect or action; that which you sow you reap.

Kekulé: Chemist who discovered the structure of carbon and benzene through dreams and revelations.

Living Earth: The concept of Gaia (the earth is alive).

Living Love: Love is a universal living, sentient being.

Lucifer: Fallen angel that promotes the importance of ego and evolution through karma or the Law.

Marianne Williamson: Spiritual teacher focusing on love is the answer.

Mycelium: A fungal spore that networks living organisms.

Mystery School: Various modern and ancient schools, physical and transcendental, that teach the spirituality of humanity and the application of spiritual understanding to practical issues in life.

Narcissus: An archetype in Greek mythology that fell in love with his own image and makes life all about himself.

Numinous: Subtle or spiritual realities that relate to and interact with physical reality in corresponding and causal ways.

Overlighting: A numinous, spiritual energy or Holy Spirit descends upon an individual as a form of consciousness or spiritual being connecting the individual in an integrated way to a higher dimension of reality, wisdom and resources.

Psi-energy: Psychic energy.

Pattern matching: Vibrational correspondence of the frequency of one pattern to another with the application that when we attune to one pattern a resonance with a like pattern occurs synchronizing our focus with like patterns; a practice intended to enable us to access, communicate with, channel or transport our consciousness to specified realities, information, energy or locations.

Peace Prayer: St. Francis, "make me an instrument of thy peace."

Pythagoras: Ancient Greek teacher of spiritual geometry.

Ralph Waldo Emerson: American Transcendentalist.

Rudolf Steiner: Austrian spiritual teacher.

Samadhi: A high state of spiritual ecstasy attained through meditation.

Science of Correspondence: A term coined by Emanuel Swedenborg; the reflexive relationship of inner and outer realities stating that for every occurrence in the outer world there is a corresponding occurrence in the inner worlds which we understand through the hermeneutics of analogy, symbol and metaphor; the implication is that whatever exists has an aspect on every dimension and level of consciousness; in literature we see this as the eloquent way in which deep mysteries of consciousness can be illustrated in common life parables; David Bohm stated this relationship in terms of physics as the enfolding and unfolding relationship of the implicate and explicate order occurring within the holomovement of all reality.

Shabda Yoga: Spiritual practice of attaining soul travel through attending to the sound current through meditative practice.

Seventh generation: A policy attributed to native Americans which considers the consequence of choices we make in the present on each generation following until the seventh generation.

Siddhas: Spiritual powers.

Sound Current: Audible life stream that emanates and returns to the Source of God which manifests creation and is a vehicle for Soul Transcendence.

Spiritual by-pass: Using spiritual teachings to rationalize or avoid dealing with one's personal issues or conflict.

Stochastic: A statistical technique of modeling the probability progressions or outcomes over time.

Sub-rosa: Happening or done in secret.

Synchronous creativity: Creativity in which the cause and effect are simultaneous throughout time and dimension.

Tipping point: When one more instance of an occurrence changes everything.

This Little Light of Mine: Song made popular in the civil rights movement.

Transcendental Leadership: Sourcing knowledge, wisdom and authority from a higher power; a Soul awakened leader.

Zero sum: When somebody wins, someone must lose; contrasted to a win-win situation (non-zero sum game) in which everyone wins.

Zeitgeist: Sign of the times; the defining spirit or mood of a particular period of history as shown by the ideas and beliefs of the time.

BIBLIOGRAPHY

Alexander, E. and K. Newell. *Living In A Mindful Universe.* New York: Rodale, 2017.

Alexander, E. and K. Newell. *Proof of Heaven.* New York: Simon and Schuster, 2012.

Alexander, E. *The Map of Heaven.* New York: Simon and Schuster, 2014.

Assagioli, R. *Psychosynthesis.* New York: Viking Press, 1974.

Bartlett, R. *The Physics of Miracles.* Oregon: Atria Books, 2009.

Beichler, J. *A Physics of Consciousness: The only path to understanding consciousness.* Academia.edu, 2017.

Beichler, J. *The Consciousness Revolution in Science.* ASCSI/SFF Conference Presentation. Academia.edu, 2018.

Brennan, B A. *Hands of Light: A Guide to Healing Through the Human Energy Field.* New York: Bantam Books, 1988.

Cayce, E. *Auras.* Virginia Beach, VA: ARE Press, 1943.

Clark, G. *The Man Who Talks With the Flowers: The Intimate Life Story of Dr. George Washington Carver.* Minneapolis, MI: Macalester Park Pub Co, 1976.

Kazanis, D. *The Reintegration of Science and Spirituality: Subtle, Dark Matter and Energy.* Tampa, FA: Styra: 2013.

Laszlo, E. *What is Reality? The New Map of Cosmos, Consciousness, and Existence.* New York: Select Books, 2016.

Milarepa. *The Life of Milarepa.* Translated by L P Lhulungpa. New York: Penguin Books, 1979.

Nichol, L. *The Essential David Bohm.* New York: Routledge, 2003.

Emerson, R.W. *The American Scholar.* Phi Beta Kappa Society of Harvard College in Cambridge, Massachusetts, August 31, 1837.

Hamilton, R. *How Mushrooms And The Mycelium Network Are Healing the World*, UK issue 33, Garden Culture Magazine, June 15, 2020.

Hinkins, J. *Timeless Wisdom One.* Los Angeles: Mandeville Press, 2008.

Hinkins, J. *Timeless Wisdom Two.* Los Angeles: Mandeville Press, 2009.

Hinkins, J. Passage into Spirit. Los Angeles: Mandeville Press, 1984.

Holy Bible, New International Version, Grand Rapids, Michigan: Zondervan Bible Publisher, 1988.

Johnson, J. *Path of the Masters: The Science of Surat Shabd Yoga: The Yoga of the Audible Life Stream, 17th ed.* Punjab, India: Radha Soami Satsang Beas, 1997.

Khan, H. I. *Spiritual Dimensions of Psychology.* New Lebanon, NY: Omega Press, 1981.

Leadbeater, C. W. *Man Visible and Invisible.* Wheaton, IL: Theosophical Publishing House, 1969.

Merlin S. *Entangled Life: How Fungi Make Our Worlds, Change our Minds & Shape our Futures.* New York: Pengiun Random House, 2020.

Myss, C. *Anatomy of the Spirit: The Seven Stages of Power and Healing.* New York: Harmony Books, 1996.

Powers, E. *Auric Mirror.* Alamogordo, NM: Quimby Metaphysical Libraries, 1973.

Quimby, P. P. *The Quimby Manuscripts.* Edited by H W Dresser. Secaucus, NJ: The Citadel Press, 1969.

Rosenblum, B. and F. Kutner. *Quantum Enigma.* Oxford: Oxford University Press, 2011.

Sheldrake, R. *Morphic Resonance: The Nature of Formative Causation.* Rochester: Park Street, 2009.

Sorokin, P. *The Ways and Power of Love: Types, Factors, and Techniques of Moral Transformation.* Radnor, PA: Templeton Foundation Press, 2002.

Stamets, P. *Mycelium Running: How Mushrooms Can Help Save the World.* Random House, New York. 2005.

Steiner, R. *Knowledge of the Higher Worlds and Its Attainment.* Anthroposophic Press. 1947.

Stibal, V. *Theta Healing.* Idaho Falls: Roling Thunder Publishing, 2007.

Waterman, R. and K. Thorne. *Power of Love: The Ways and Means.* Indianapolis: Dog Ear, 2019.

Waterman, R. *Eyes Made of Soul: The Theory and Practice of Noetic Balancing.* Bloomington, ID: Xlibris, 2010.

Waterman, R. Mandala of the Soul: A Spiritual Approach to the Art of Archetypal Psychology. Santa Fe: Southwestern College, 2011.

Waterman, R. D. *Foot Prints of Eternity: Ancient Wisdom Applied to Modern Psychology.* Conshohoken, PA: Infinity Books, 1999, 2006.

Made in the USA
Coppell, TX
27 May 2021